The Badly Behaved Bible

Also by Nick Page

A Nearly Infallible History of the Reformation

A Nearly Infallible History of Christianity

Revelation Road

Kingdom of Fools

The Wrong Messiah

The Longest Week

The Dark Night of the Shed

The Badly Behaved Bible

Thinking again about the story
of Scripture

Nick Page

HODDER

First published in Great Britain in 2020 by Hodder & Stoughton
An Hachette UK company

This paperback edition first published in 2020

1

Copyright © Nick Page, 2019

The right of Nick Page to be identified as the Author of the Work has been
asserted by him in accordance with the Copyright, Designs and Patents Act 1988.

Unless indicated otherwise, Scripture quotations are taken from the
New Revised Standard Version of the Bible, Anglicised Edition, copyright © 1989
by the Division of Christian Education of the National Council of the Churches
of Christ in the USA. Used by permission. All rights reserved.

Scripture quotations marked ESV are from The Holy Bible,
English Standard Version® (ESV®), copyright © 2001 by Crossway Bibles,
a publishing ministry of Good News Publishers. Used by permission. All rights reserved.

Scripture quotations marked CEV are from the Contemporary English
Version Copyright © 1991, 1992, 1995 by American Bible Society. Used by Permission.

A CIP catalogue record for this title is available from the British Library

Paperback ISBN 978 1 473 68621 2
eBook ISBN 978 1 473 68620 5

Typeset in Sabon MT by Palimpsest Book Production Ltd, Falkirk, Stirlingshire

Printed and bound in Great Britain by Clays Ltd, Elcograf S.p.A.

Hodder & Stoughton policy is to use papers that are natural, renewable and recyclable
products and made from wood grown in sustainable forests. The logging and manufacturing
processes are expected to conform to the environmental regulations of the country of origin.

Hodder & Stoughton Ltd
Carmelite House
50 Victoria Embankment
London EC4Y 0DZ

www.hodderfaith.com

For my friend, drinking buddy, personal analyst and fellow book-club member, Steve. In a way, this is all your fault.

Both read the Bible day and night,
But thou read'st black, where I read white.
                                    – William Blake

Contents

Introduction: Holy ground

I meet them when I give talks or lead retreats. Some are cheerful, but confused; some are subdued and quietly thoughtful; some wear the pained expression of people who have suddenly realised that the underwear they have on has shrunk two sizes in the wash. Others look genuinely shocked and distressed, as if they have discovered that their sweet, little, eighty-year-old grandmother has secretly been selling crystal meth down at the day centre.

All of them say the same thing to me: 'I have this question about the Bible . . .'

It might be to do with the brutality and the bloodshed, the difference between the God of the Old Testament and the God of the New. Or a ridiculously obscure passage that they simply can't understand. Maybe it's a law or command which seems unfair, discriminatory, misogynistic or otherwise at odds with just, you know, ordinary decent behaviour. Quite often they simply can't believe a word of what they are reading – that a fish can swallow a man, that a boat can contain all known species, that God placed responsibility for the entire fate of humankind on two people and their behaviour around a fruit tree.

For many – too many – the anxiety and doubt has become so chronic that they are on the verge of chucking it all out and walking away. But more often it's just a nagging pain, a kind of spiritual ulcer. They've tried all the treatments. They've read the commentaries, talked to their leaders, looked it up on Google, but their questions are not getting answered. In fact, their questions are being dismissed: people just tell them to have more faith, or to pray about it. Or, having summoned up the courage to talk to a fellow believer, they are met with a pained look and an urgent, whispered enquiry: 'You're not *backsliding* are you?'

Yes, I meet a lot of these people. One of them I see in the mirror every day.

'I have this problem with the Bible . . .'

You and me both, pal.

The cognitive dissonance of Scripture

The Church is full of people who know what they *should* think about the Bible, but who actually think something quite different.

We're told that the Bible is the inspired Word of God; then we read bits that are violent, disgusting or utterly baffling. Or all three at once.

We're told that reading the Bible is a Life-giving and Good Thing which Every Proper Christian Should Do with Joy in Our Hearts. And yet, instead, significant chunks of it are overwhelmingly verbose, completely irrelevant, incomprehensible or so mind-numbingly dull that we begin to lose the will to live.

We are told that the Bible is inerrant, infallible and without contradiction, and then discover that there are two different creation stories and two versions of the Ten Commandments and the Lord's Prayer, and that the New Testament writers misquote the Old Testament. Not only that, the Bible thinks the world is flat, with a big domed canopy above it to hold the water out.

We are told that the Bible gives 'rules for life' and that we just have to do what it says. Then we find that some of the rules involve not wearing mixed fibres and stoning anyone who works on the sabbath. Or we open it to Song of Songs to read, 'Your two breasts are like two fawns, twins of a gazelle, that feed among the lilies' (S. of S. 4:5). Even if I could work out how to 'do' that, I'd probably get arrested.

We are told that the Bible is a gift to us from a loving God, and then read bits that make God sound like a grumpy old man having a hissy fit sometime in the Bronze Age. Or, worse, where this loving God apparently instructs his people to lovingly massacre men, women and children.

The result of all these mixed messages is a kind of cognitive dissonance.* We are caught between two conflicting sets of beliefs: what we have been told to believe about the Bible and what we actually read for ourselves.

This kind of thing is hard to deal with. When caught in this trap, the first thing we think is that the problem is with us. It's *our* fault for being stupid. Or for doubting. Or there is something obvious that we haven't spotted. So we feel guilty. And the second mistake we often make is to believe that we are the only ones who feel this way. So the questions and the doubts leave us isolated. But the fact is that we *all* have questions about the Bible. And if you don't have questions, then, frankly, you haven't read it properly.

If we think it's just us, then the temptation is towards denial. So we repress the doubts and questions. We grit our teeth, stiffen our upper lip, clench our buttocks and remind ourselves that 'You've got to have faith' (to quote St George Michael) and that it is sinful to question God. Or as individuals and as churches we don't so much deny the questions as avoid thinking about them completely. Cordon off the doubts. Create a quarantine zone. If there's anything troubling or bizarre in the sermon, well, just move on quickly and we'll all agree never to speak of this

---

* In the field of psychology, cognitive dissonance is the mental discomfort or psychological stress experienced by a person who simultaneously holds two or more contradictory beliefs, ideas or values. This often happens with those who follow gurus or teachers. They are told that the guru is enlightened and holy, only to find out that he drives a Jag and gets up to some very unenlightened activities with a number of his disciples.

thing again. Or file the anxiety away in the 'Things Too Mysterious For Human Beings To Contemplate' folder. The problem here is that *the questions don't go away*. Worse still, every time we open the Bible more questions arise (and sometimes it's the people in the Bible itself who are raising the questions). A thing not looked at is still there. Like those Gothic novels with the mad relative locked up in the attic, we can hear them howling at night. And anyway, some of these problems are too big to avoid: how do you hide away Noah's Ark?

Another response is to redouble our efforts. Go all out to find the solutions. Buy one of those books called *Bible Difficulties Explained* or *The Bible: Your Suspiciously Heretical Questions Answered* or *Bible Contradictions Magicked Away With Long Words* (Subtitle: 'Don't Panic, It Will All Be All Right'). There must be a cure for this, right? A way to massage away the difficulties, leaving only a flawless text, free from contradiction or difficulty. The problem here is that these solutions have a strange way of not actually solving anything. Either they end up forcing us to believe in six impossible things before church, or they simply create more problems.

The thing is, we shouldn't need any of these strategies.

Because the problem is not with you. And the problem is not with the Bible.

The *real* problem is that we've been misinformed.

Welcome to Casablanca

In the film *Casablanca*, Humphrey Bogart is asked why he came to Casablanca.

'My health,' he replies. 'I came to Casablanca for the waters.'

'What waters?' asks his interrogator. 'We're in the desert.'

Humphrey thinks for a moment. 'I was misinformed,' he says.

Apart from the fact that it's always a good thing to put a quote from *Casablanca* in a book, this exemplifies the problems so many of us have with the Bible. We are simply told the wrong things about it.

We have been told, or encouraged to believe, things about the Bible that the Bible never claims for itself. The idea that it is without error or contradiction, the impression we're given that God wrote it all and that humans were barely involved, the idea that there's a correct way to read it, or that it's wrong to question what the Bible says – these are all things that humans say about the Bible. The Bible never says that kind of stuff about itself. Like Humphrey, we have been misinformed.

And exactly the same thing happens to those who would criticise the Bible from the other direction. Critics of the Bible complain that it is not scientifically accurate, or a properly sourced historical document, but these draw on categories that are alien to the Bible itself.

Both sides end up complaining because the Bible is failing at something that it never actually tries to be.

It's not the Bible's fault if people keep saying the wrong things about it.

I once took my wife out on a nice, romantic 'date night'. We hired a babysitter and took off to a local independent cinema to see a film. It sounded perfect: *Pan's Labyrinth* – a foreign-language fantasy drama about a bookish young girl who escapes into a mythical fantasy world. I think it was about ten minutes in, when a man was stabbed in the head with broken bottle, that I began to feel I might have chosen the wrong film. Turns out that *Pan's Labyrinth*, though undoubtedly brilliant, was a lot darker and more violent than I was expecting. My wife spent much of the film with her eyes closed.

But that's not the fault of *Pan's Labyrinth*, nor Guillermo del Toro, its visionary director (although maybe a less whimsical title might have helped). The point is simply that I'd been told – or had assumed – the wrong things about the film. I turned up

5

expecting 'light and charming' and instead got 'dark, eerie, and with disturbingly graphic scenes'.*

Which pretty much sums up a lot of our experience with the Bible. We are told that it's *Bambi*, but when the lights go down we discover it's *Pan's Labyrinth*.

It's like I said: the fault is not with us, and the fault is not with the Bible. The problem is that we've been misinformed.

And here's the thing: all those efforts to explain the problems away, to pretend that the difficulties aren't there, or to demand that readers should not question the Scriptures? Well, they are really just attempts to get the Bible to behave in the way that *we* want it to. But the Bible is not a well-behaved book. It refuses to be controlled by our expectations, to fit into our categories or to conform to our rules. We expect the Bible to fit into our mould – but the Bible wants to break this mould, to shape us to be more like Christ.

The Bible exists to invite us into life, life in all its fullness. I happen to believe that reading the Bible is one of the most important, rewarding, transformational experiences that any human can do. If I didn't believe that I wouldn't have bothered writing this book, or all the other books I've written on the Bible. I'd go away and do something more profitable with my time.

In this book I am going to explore some of the myths we have about the Bible and the ways in which it has been wrongly described. But I'm not doing this because I want to undermine the Bible, or to diminish its importance. I'm doing it because I want everyone to read the Bible, to engage with it in whatever way they can.

I believe we have to think again about the Bible. We have to

---

* To be fair to the director, his style was not out of place for a 'fairy tale', the original versions of which are a lot more dark and violent than the sanitised versions we tell our kids. The Brothers Grimm were remarkably well named.

rethink our beliefs about this ancient, powerful text and the language we use to describe it.

And the first thing we can do is stop studying it.

How to give up Bible study

Here's a fact: most people in history never read the Bible.

I just mention this, because to hear some people talk you'd think that the common practice of all Christians throughout history was to start every day having a 'quiet time' with the Bible open, a mug of filter coffee, a set of daily Bible notes and a journal with a fish on the cover. But this concept is very recent. For most of history, most Christians didn't read the Bible at all on the grounds that (a) hardly anyone could read and (b) even those who could read were unlikely to own a Bible. It was only after the Reformation that Bible study became something that Christians were allowed, let alone expected, to do. And even then, Bible ownership only really started to rise in the eighteenth and nineteenth centuries with the rise of literacy and the spread of modern, cheaper books.

The Bible has been listened to much more often than it has been read. For the early church fathers, reading the Bible did not mean mutely scanning the pages and musing in silent contemplation; it meant speaking out the Scriptures in a way that would allow their power to break in upon people's lives. They believed that *hearing* the Word of God changed people.

Sometimes the life-changing words just sprung out at the reader. Anthony the Great, the founder of monasticism, went into a church one day and heard the line, 'If you wish to be perfect, go, sell your possessions, and give the money to the poor, and you will have treasure in heaven; then come, follow me' (Matt. 19:21). So he did.

Many of the saints whose Christlike lives changed their world were illiterate. For them, the right way to read the Bible was simply to listen to the stories, to learn the texts and to live it out.

I'm not sure when it happened, but increasingly we have turned reading the Bible into a much more academic activity. If you go to Bible college or seminary or university to study theology, you will soon hear the word *exegesis*. It's a Greek word which means 'to lead out of'. Biblical exegesis has been defined as 'the careful, systematic study of Scripture to discover the original, intended meaning'.[1] The task involves trying as far as possible to find out what the passage meant and how the original audience would have understood it. Only then can we correctly interpret the passage for today. Often this approach majors heavily on thorough analyses of the grammar and the meaning of words, trying to get back to the heart of what the writer was actually saying.

This is a good and responsible approach: it stops us from misrepresenting the writer, from finding things in the text that aren't there. It helps us to identify what kind of text we are dealing with, and whether, for example, a writer is speaking literally or using a metaphor. It often identifies crucial cultural or historical readings which really open up the text in a new way. I have spent a lot of time in my life engaged in this sort of work, or attempting to teach the principles to others. But after many years I've come to recognise that there are a few significant problems with majoring so much on this way of studying the Bible.

The first is that it's a very professional approach. The tools we use for exegesis are typically academic: commentaries and lexicons, dictionaries and large, learned tomes. It's a tool for pastors and preachers, certainly. But how much can we expect ordinary people to have the time, the resources, the expertise and the desire to do this? Even the name – *exegesis* – is off-putting. It's fundamentally an elitist pursuit.

The second big problem is that, frankly, it tends to suck the life out of the text. I believe it was the writer E.B. White who said, 'Analysing humour is like dissecting a frog. You can do it, but along the way the frog dies.'[2] I have read a lot of books, listened to a lot of sermons and attended a lot of Bible studies where we started out reading a Bible passage and ended up staring at a dead frog. It is death by exegesis. We dissect the text, slice into the grammar and the etymology, peel back the layers of history and theology, and we end up discovering everything about the text except how it is actually going to change us here and now. Rebecca Solnit wrote that 'museums love artists the way that taxidermists love deer'.[3] I think a lot of Bible teachers operate in the same way. They embalm the Bible, stuff it and mount it, and then we all stand back, gazing at the once live animal as it stares down from the wall with cold, lifeless, glassy eyes.

I've come to this conclusion: I hate the phrase 'Bible study'. And I want to ban it.

I'm not engaged in a *study*, as if the Bible was some kind of specimen laid out on the table. Heaven knows I have spent enough time in my life poring through commentaries and books of history and even wrestling with all those foreign words. I have spent significant chunks of what I laughingly call my 'career' using these tools to learn and teach stuff. And that's not a bad thing. As a Christian I am called to be a disciple – an apprentice – of Jesus. I am called, in fact, to become more Christlike. And it's difficult to be Christlike if we don't know what Christ was like. So reading about him – in the Gospels and in the writings of his first followers – is pretty important.

But reading the Bible is – or should be – about more than accumulating knowledge or understanding doctrine, or any of the other operations that are implied by that deadening phrase 'Bible study'. Reading the Bible is also about questioning the text, exploring both what it says and what it doesn't say. It's about using our imagination and our creativity. It's not just about reading the text; it's about listening to it as well.

One of my favourite stories about the Bible tells of a woman

9

in an African village who was always carrying her Bible. Everywhere she went she took it. And the other women in the village said to her, 'You are always reading that book. Why don't you read other books?'

'Yes,' she replied, 'I could read other books. But this is the book that reads me.'

This, I believe, is at the heart of why the Bible is unique. The Bible is a place of encounter.

It is, in fact, a place where we can meet with God.

Holy ground

In the desert we see a man leading his sheep.

He is a man who has lost everything. He killed a slave-driver in a fit of rage and had to flee his privileged life in Egypt. Now he's wandering in the wilderness.

And then he sees something. A tree. No, a bush. No, a *fire*.

> **Read it yourself:** Exodus 3–4 tells the story of Moses encountering the burning bush, finding out God's name and trying to get out of the task of leading the Israelites out of slavery.

In the biblical account Moses does what, on the face of it, appears to be a really stupid thing. He goes *towards* the flames. Generally, if you have a lot of sheep in the desert and you see a fire, you head very fast in the opposite direction. Otherwise, instant kebab. Instead, Moses goes towards the sight and he finds something bizarre, unreal, extraordinary: a bush that crackles with flame but is not consumed. A talking bush, at that.

> God called to him out of the bush, 'Moses, Moses!' And he said,
> 'Here I am.' Then he said, 'Come no closer! Remove the sandals
> from your feet, for the place on which you are standing is holy
> ground.' He said further, 'I am the God of your father, the God
> of Abraham, the God of Isaac, and the God of Jacob.' And Moses
> hid his face, for he was afraid to look at God.   (Exodus 3:4–6)

It's a key moment in the story: the moment when Yahweh reveals
his name to Moses, when he commissions Moses to go and rescue
his people. Moses thinks he is going to see a natural wonder, and
he meets a supernatural power. He finds that he is part of a
bigger story, that this story involves a deep, personal, life-changing
relationship with a God who simply is. Whose name is I AM.

This, I believe, is what happens – or what can happen – when
we come to the Scriptures. If we are prepared to come humbly,
to take off our shoes and to listen to the voice among the flames,
we will find things that surprise us, that change us, that offer us
a new relationship and a place in a big, big story.

Too often we come to the Bible as a text to be dissected or
mastered or interpreted correctly. The Bible is a book that burns
with the presence of God and is not consumed. What the Bible
really is, is Holy Ground.[4]

Thinking again about the Bible

In 1916 the German theologian Karl Barth cleared his throat,
adjusted his lederhosen and gave what was to become a hugely
influential talk. It began like this:

> We are to attempt to find an answer to the question, What is
> there within the Bible? What sort of house is it to which the Bible
> is the door? What sort of country is spread before our eyes when
> we throw the Bible open?

Good question, Karl. The talk was later reprinted as *The Strange New World Within the Bible*, and it's worth reading, even though Barth is one of those theologians who has managed to achieve influence without ever attempting comprehensibility.[5] But what I like about the image is that it takes us away from the idea of study and catapults us into the language of exploration and encounter. We start to see the Bible not as a book, but as a land, a location.

As we travel into this land together we will have to put aside some of the familiar ideas that we have about the Bible, and that can be difficult. I want to say a few things about this as we start.

First, I don't think there is a lot in this book that would come as a surprise to your Vicar/Minister/Chiefly Anointed Leader – or, indeed, anyone who has attended theological college. We're going to look at the textual history of the Bible, at some of the contradictions and difficulties within the text and at things like whether some of the events actually happened. All of this is the kind of stuff you find in the average biblical studies course at college. (Or, indeed, in the footnotes of many study Bibles.)

Second – and more importantly – I want to say that we're not engaged in an act of destruction but an act of rediscovery. The reason I'm interested in exploring these fissures is that they might lead somewhere interesting. I hope that it will lead you to read the Bible with fresh eyes and with an increased expectation of encountering God.

Third, I really think Bible reading should actually be enjoyable. I've already talked about the deadening effect of the phrase 'Bible study'. And many of you will, no doubt, have painful memories of getting bogged down in some obscure part of the Bible. Not long ago my wife decided to read through the Bible in a year. About mid-February I asked her how she was doing. 'I've got Levitical exhaustion,' she said. I don't think she made it much beyond March. I'm not a massive fan of those 'through the Bible in one year' programmes. It's not a bad thing to read it all, and it's certainly good to go off-piste and visit some of the less-visited parts of this land, but these kind of programmes tend to turn Bible reading into a kind of endurance sport. Reading the Bible should not be like eating our organic greens.* So try to go in with the idea that actually this might be enjoyable. Something might happen. I might, actually, get to experience something new. To help you in this, I've included a few 'Read it yourself' boxes as we go through so that you can read the Bible passage I'm talking about. You're welcome.

The final thing to say is that, for all that I've just said – all that stuff about enjoying yourself – reading the Bible is not without risk.

The Bible is not safe. The Bible is a book which transforms us, empowers us, liberates us. But in order for it to do that we have to stop trying to control it, to tame it, domesticate it, make it support what we want it to say. That might shock us, or challenge us. It might transform our lives. We might go to the Bible expecting a hug and receive a slap in the face. (Or the other way round.) To open the Bible is to risk our theology, our presuppositions, our deepest-held beliefs.

The fact is, you see, the Bible is a very badly behaved book.

---

* Unless you love eating your greens. In which case (a) well done and (b) what kind of weirdo *are* you?

1 The God-breathed book

Imagine you had a bound volume in front of you called *Britain*, which claims to be a one-volume history of the story of our glorious Britannic Nation and how we grew to live together in perfect harmony.

Eagerly you open it and look at the contents. And there is something weird going on. It seems like someone has just bound together a load of different books. They include:

- A collection of ancient myths about the people who built Stonehenge, focusing on one particular family;
- An early telephone directory;
- A book of famous British quotations;
- A series of short biographies of very minor characters from the period just after the Romans left;
- A history of the Norman Conquest written by a man who lived about four centuries later;
- Some songs and poetry from the time of Shakespeare, but without any music;
- A collection of law, which mixes up the Magna Carta and the latest Health and Safety regulations;
- A dream about the future written by a Polish church leader with English as his second language;
- A history of the kings and queens of England and Scotland from the fifteenth century onwards;
- The *same* history of the kings and queens, only this time ignoring Scotland and cutting out all the bad bits.

You would have a problem with the idea that this was 'one book'. It's all so very different.

But that is what the Bible is like: it's not just one book, but the work of many different authors and editors writing at different times, in different places, in different kinds of writing – poetry, history, laws, prophecy, proverbs, stories, letters and many more.

It's all very . . . different.

'The word of the Lord'

SCENE: A CHURCH. INTERIOR.

Someone gets up and goes to the front, standing behind the lectern on which there is a book the size of a small building. She clears her throat and announces:

READER: Now a reading from Psalm 137.

There is a shuffling of pages, while everyone gets hold of a pew Bible and tries to remember where the Psalms are.

READER: 'By the rivers of Babylon – there we sat down and there we wept when we remembered Zion.'

CONGREGATION: *(Thinks)* Right. Already a tad confusing. 'Babylon' I vaguely remember. 'Zion', though, I'm fairly sure was a planet in an episode of *Doctor Who*.

READER: 'On the willows there we hung up our harps. For there our captors asked us for songs, and our tormentors asked for mirth, saying, "Sing us one of the songs of Zion!" How can we sing the LORD's song in a foreign land?'

CONGREGATION: *(Thinks)* OK. That's odd. I get that they don't want to sing. Not sure about hanging the harps on a tree though. Presumably we're talking about a culture which has not yet invented the guitar stand.

READER: 'If I forget you, O Jerusalem, let my right hand wither! Let my tongue cling to the roof of my mouth, if I do not remember you, if I do not set Jerusalem above my highest joy.'

CONGREGATION: *(Thinks)* So these people have been kicked out of Jerusalem. And they have very dry mouths.

READER: 'Remember, O LORD, against the Edomites the day of Jerusalem's fall, how they said, "Tear it down! Tear it down! Down to its foundations!"'

CONGREGATION: *(Thinks)* Oh. This has taken a bit of a dark turn.

READER: 'O daughter Babylon, you devastator! Happy shall they be who pay you back what you have done to us. Happy shall they be who take your little ones and dash them against the rock!'

CONGREGATION: *(Thinks)* Wait . . . What?

The reader pauses.

READER: This is the word of the Lord.

CONGREGATION: *(Not meaning a word of it)* Thanks be to God.

Wait – which 'word' are we talking about?

'The word of God'. That's what we sign up to. That's what we're told about the Bible: 'This is the word of God'. But then there's Jesus. He's the Word as well. But a different word. He's the Word, not the word. And then, sometimes the vicar/pastor/person-who-was-available brings a word about the word. Or even the Word. Not to mention all the times when people have a word for you.

It's all very confusing. Not to say wordy.

In this chapter I want to talk about two phrases that are particularly applied to the Bible: 'Scripture is the word of God' and 'all Scripture is inspired'.

We'll come to the idea of inspiration in a moment. First, though, I need to break it to you that the Bible never really calls itself the word of God.

I mean, the phrase is in there. There are nearly 400 references to the word of God in the Old Testament, with the phrase, 'word of the Lord,' appearing more than 240 times. Where it uses the phrase, it refers to things that God might have said, commands he gave, 'words' that came to the prophets. So, Samuel promises to Saul to 'make known to you the word of God' (1 Sam. 9:27); 'the word of the LORD came to Abram' (Gen. 15:1); 'hear the word of the LORD, you scoffers', says Isaiah (Isa. 28:14).

Significantly, the word of the Lord is a creative act. God spoke and things came to life. 'By the word of the LORD the heavens were made, and all their host by the breath of his mouth' (Ps. 33:6). The most important Hebrew word for the 'word of God' is *dābār*. But that doesn't necessarily mean spoken word; it also has the sense of thing, or action or event.*

In the New Testament the phrase refers to the teaching of Jesus, or, indeed, the teaching of Jesus' followers. 'The word of God' comes to John the Baptist in the wilderness (Luke 3:2); crowds come to Jesus, 'pressing in on him to hear the word of God' (Luke 5:1). Jesus talks about those who 'hear the word of God and do it' (Luke 8:21; see also Luke 11:28); he condemns the Pharisees who make 'void the word of God through your tradition that you have handed on' (Mark 7:13). None of those are talking about Scripture in its entirety, or even the whole of the Old Testament. They are talking about specific commands or instructions.

Similarly, for the early church, the phrase 'the word of God' means either Jesus himself (as it's used in John) or the message the early church is proclaiming: the good news.†

There are two passages in the New Testament that often muddle up the New Testament concept of the word of God with our

---

* In fact, in the words of *The Anchor Bible Dictionary*, 'no conclusions can be drawn regarding its meaning on the basis of etymology, concerning which there is no fundamental agreement.' So that's helpful. (*The Anchor Bible Dictionary* (New York: Doubleday, 1999)), 6:961.

† See Acts 4:31; 6:2, 7; 8:14; 11:1; 12:24; 13:5, 7, 46; 17:13; 18:11. Don't say I'm not thorough.

identification of it as the Bible. The first is the famous 'armour' passage in Ephesians:

> Therefore take up the whole armour of God, so that you may be able to withstand on that evil day, and having done everything, to stand firm. Stand therefore, and fasten the belt of truth around your waist, and put on the breastplate of righteousness. As shoes for your feet put on whatever will make you ready to proclaim the gospel of peace. With all of these, take the shield of faith, with which you will be able to quench all the flaming arrows of the evil one. Take the helmet of salvation, and the sword of the Spirit, which is the word of God. (Ephesians 6:13–17)

Based on this, when I was young we used to do a thing in Sunday School called 'sword practice'. We would tuck our Bibles under our left arms and then the leader would shout out a Bible reference. We then 'drew' our Bible as fast as we could and hunted down the reference. The first one to find it won the competition and was clearly one of the elect. I was very good at sword practice, because it involved (a) looking things up in a book, and (b) winning. And those were two of my favourite things.

Because we're so used to the idea of Scripture as 'the word of God', the moment we see that phrase we think that's what it means. But Paul is not talking about the Bible here. He's using the phrase in the same way the early church did – as referring to the message that they have to pass on.* Elsewhere in the New Testament letters and Acts, the 'word' of God is the *spoken* truth, the Spirit-filled good news which is being spread throughout the world.

It's in this sense that the word of God is a sword. And that's how it's used in the second passage which is commonly thought to refer to the Bible, in Hebrews 4:

---

* Romans 9:6; 1 Corinthians 14:36; Colossians 1:25; 1 Thessalonians 2:13; 2 Timothy 2:9; Titus 2:5.

> Indeed, the word of God is living and active, sharper than any
> two-edged sword, piercing until it divides soul from spirit, joints
> from marrow; it is able to judge the thoughts and intentions of
> the heart.   (Hebrews 4:12)

But the image here is not of the Scriptures as a book, but of
the words uttered with devastating power. It's the same picture
as we find in more graphic form in Revelation, where it depicts
Jesus as a man with a great big sword coming out of his mouth.*
And in Hebrews, the writer uses the phrase at other points where
he means the proclamation of the good news (Heb. 6:5; 13:7),
or where he's describing how 'worlds were prepared by the word
of God' (Heb. 11:3).† Paul calls 'the word of truth, the gospel
of your salvation' (Eph. 1:13) or 'the gospel of peace' (Eph.
6:15).

So for the early church the 'word of God' was not the written
text, but the spoken gospel: it refers to words *said*, not words
read.

Now there's an obvious reason why this might be the case:
hardly anybody in the ancient world could read. Even those
few who could read would have had little access to any form
of written Scripture. So things were remembered, stored and
spoken.

As far as I can find out, the first person to use the phrase
'the word of God' specifically to refer to Scriptures was Origen,
writing about AD 250 where he says, 'let us show from the holy
Scriptures that the word of God also encourages us to the practice of dialectics: Solomon, e.g., declaring in one passage, that

---

* Revelation 1:16; 2:12, 16; 19:13, 15. It also might relate to Isaiah, where
the Greek translation says that the Messiah 'shall smite the earth with the
word of his mouth, and with the breath of his lips shall he destroy the
ungodly' (Isa. 11:4). OK. That's probably enough thoroughness for now.
† The writer of 2 Peter also uses it this way (2 Pet. 3:5).

"instruction unquestioned goes astray"'.* (Although, as we shall see, even then what constituted Scripture was undecided.)

Obviously there is a relationship between the sword-sharp gospel message and the Bible, because it's within the pages of the Bible that we find the information we need to proclaim 'the word of truth'. It's the Bible that tells us how the life, teaching and example of Jesus are good news for everyone. So calling the Bible the 'word of God' is not wrong, in a way, and it certainly reflects church teaching going back a long way. But it's not quite what the Bible says about itself.

Maybe the issue is not so much the phrase 'the Bible is the word of God' so much as the way it is used. I can't help feeling that when some preachers hold up the Bible and say, 'This is the word of God,' they do not mean, 'This is the basis for the gospel of peace which I'm about to share with you.' They tend to mean, 'God wrote this and you'd better do what he says in it otherwise there will be smiting.' It's a way of elevating the Bible – and, more importantly, their interpretation of it – above discussion, contradiction or debate.

More than this, though, it reinforces the impression that the Bible literally contains the words of God – that he wrote it, or at least dictated it, and that everything within it was spoken by him and hence given a divine stamp of approval.

The Bible isn't God-dictated, or God-written. It is God-breathed. Or, as we say, 'inspired'.

God-breathed not God-written

The idea that the Bible is 'inspired' comes from a verse in one of the books of the New Testament – 2 Timothy – which is a

---

* Origen, *Contra Celsus* 6.7 The quote is from Proverbs 10:17 in the LXX. In the Hebrew version it reads: 'Whoever heeds instruction is on the path to life, but one who rejects a rebuke goes astray' (Prov. 10:17).

letter, apparently written from Paul to his protégé Timothy. It says:

> All scripture is inspired by God and is useful for teaching, for reproof, for correction, and for training in righteousness, so that everyone who belongs to God may be proficient, equipped for every good work. (2 Timothy 3:16–17)

Read it yourself: 2 Timothy 3 is a short chapter, but it's certainly had a big influence. It shows how Paul was convinced that he was living in the end times – that conviction is always a background to his writing.

The Greek word translated 'scripture' in this passage is *graphē*, which means 'writing'. It was the common way for Jews of Paul's time to refer to their Scriptures. But the first thing we should note is that, whatever else Paul is talking about, he isn't talking about our 'modern' Bibles, with two Testaments, loads of footnotes and a big black cover. At the time he was writing, the New Testament – the Christian Scriptures – didn't exist. Paul was still writing them, unawares. So the most he was talking about was the Jewish Scriptures.

However, even that isn't as straightforward as it seems, because, as we shall explore more in a moment, what constitutes the Jewish Scriptures hadn't even been fully decided at the time he was writing. Indeed, a few lines earlier in the chapter, Paul cites a story about two people called Jannes and Jambres who opposed Moses. But Jannes and Jambres aren't mentioned in the Hebrew Bible. As far as we know, the legendary exploits were collected in an apocryphal book called *The Book of Jannes and Jambres*. So what Paul is talking about when he talks about Scripture may not be what we think.

And the same is true of the word 'inspired'. Like all the rest of Paul's letters, this one was written in Greek, and the word he uses for 'inspired' here is *theopneustos* – which means 'God-breathed'.*

Theopneustos. God-breathed. So what does that mean?

Well, for a start, it does *not* mean that God wrote the text. If Paul had meant that he would have written *theographos* – 'God-written'. Neither here in Paul nor anywhere else in Scripture does it say that God wrote the Bible. (There are moments when God engraves things. When he gives the Law to Moses at Sinai the text describes how it was written using 'the finger of God' (Exod. 31:18). But this is clearly metaphorical, unless you believe that God has fingers like the old dude on the roof of the Sistine Chapel.)

Of course, there are lots of times when people claim to be reporting what God has said to them, whether giving prophecies or laying down the law, and there are times when God is depicted as speaking, but he never does the actual writing. Other people do that.

As to how they do that, well, there are different examples in Scripture. Sometimes, it is true, the writing down is a result of moments of ecstatic vision. There are certainly passages in the Bible that give the impression of having been composed by someone in the grip of something way beyond them – think of Paul's magnificent passage about love in 1 Corinthians. I always imagine him dictating that to Silas and then pausing afterwards and saying, 'Wow – where did *that* come from?'

And when prophets like Amos and Ezekiel and Jeremiah stood in front of the people and declared, 'Thus says the Lord . . .' Well, God certainly inspired something in them.

But there are just as many – actually probably far more – Bible passages where it's obvious that God is not dictating them. Some

---

* Paul's use of this word is what is known as a *hapax legomenon* – a word that only occurs once either in the written record of a language or in the works of a particular author. *Hapax legomenon* means 'said once'. This may be useful for you at a pub quiz someday. Although I doubt it. Anyway, this is the only instance of the word in the Bible, and there doesn't appear to be any evidence that it was used in common Greek before Paul used it here, so he probably invented it. He was clearly inspired.

of the passages in Numbers, for example, are really just lists of names and tribes – the Bronze Age equivalent of the telephone directory. And in other places the writers tell us that they got information from other books and records.

We can even see this at work. At the beginning of his Gospel, for example, Luke gives a much more prosaic description of his task:

> Since many have undertaken to set down an orderly account of the events that have been fulfilled among us, just as they were handed on to us by those who from the beginning were eyewitnesses and servants of the word, I too decided, after investigating everything carefully from the very first, to write an orderly account for you, most excellent Theophilus, so that you may know the truth concerning the things about which you have been instructed. (Luke 1:1–4)

What is obvious here is that Luke has a major role in the selection of material. There's actually no hint in his prologue that the process was supernatural. He's not closing his eyes and letting God do the cutting and pasting. It's not like that automatic writing so beloved of psychics. What we see here is a skilled historian using his own judgement. Similarly, in John's Gospel, the writer had to make a selection because, he reports, 'there are also many other things that Jesus did; if every one of them were written down, I suppose that the world itself could not contain the books that would be written' (John 21:25). Their language is quite ordinary: the impression is of craftsmen at work.

This does not, of course, rule out God's involvement in the process. We believe in a God who is at work in the world and active in people's lives. It's entirely consistent with God's way of working in the world that the Holy Spirit should help Luke and John select which stories to tell, which bits to put in and which to leave out. But we have to acknowledge that this idea is something that we are reading into the text: it's not something that

Luke himself claims. At no point does he say, 'The Spirit told me what to write.' In the opening to the second part of his history – the book we call Acts – he writes:

> In the first book, Theophilus, I wrote about all that Jesus did and taught from the beginning until the day when he was taken up to heaven, after giving instructions through the Holy Spirit to the apostles whom he had chosen. (Acts 1:1–2)

The point, I think, is not that God *wasn't* involved, but that he wasn't involved in the controlling way that we often think. God didn't write the Bible. And he didn't dictate it, either. The process is much more collaborative than that. And that's why, even in those passages where God tells people to 'write this down', they tend to do so in their own language. Everything in the Bible comes to us through people living at a certain time, in a certain place; the visions and messages given by God are poured through the filter of their culture. It's in their language – whether Hebrew, Greek or Aramaic. It draws on images from their world. The prophets are not like ventriloquist's dummies, their mouths being worked by some divine force. All of them have unique voices. They are passing on messages from God, but very much in their own words.

Another point worth remembering is that, at the time, nobody involved thought that they were writing 'the Bible'. If you had told the prophet Ezekiel that people would be studying his utterances some 2,700 years after he wrote them he would have looked at you as though you were mad. (And if Ezekiel thinks you're mad you really have got problems.) He was talking to a group of exiles in Babylon. Similarly, Paul had no idea he was writing The Letter to Timothy. Let alone The Second Letter to Timothy. He just thought he was writing to his protégé and friend.

But if *theopneustos* – 'God-breathed' – doesn't mean 'written by' or 'dictated', then what does it mean? The Greek root *pneu* – from which *pneustos* derives – 'denotes dynamic movement of the air'.[1] Words derived from it are used to describe things like the blowing of the wind or the blowing of a musical instrument. Or you have *ekpneō*, which means to breathe out, or even to stop breathing (i.e. to die), and *empneō*, which means to breathe in, or to be alive. And, of course, you also get the word *pneuma*, which means 'spirit'. But at its root it's about life: the air that we all breathe.

When the Bible came to be translated into Latin, the translators preserved this kind of meaning. In Latin, Paul's word *theopneustos* was translated as *inspirata* – literally 'in-breathing'. (The Latin for 'to breathe' is *spirare*.) And it's from there that we get our word 'inspired'. We still preserve some of the Greek in words like pneumatic, which means inflated, and even pneumonia, which is an inflammation of the lungs. And the Latin word gives us words like perspiration, respiration and even conspiracy – all of which have to do with air or breathing.

Anyway, the point is that in both Greek and Latin the idea behind the word is 'breath' or 'air'.

Now, when Paul says Scripture is God-breathed, he doesn't really unpack it in any way – an oversight which a lot of translations try to put right. The King James Version, for example, says 'All scripture is *given* by inspiration of God' (2 Tim. 3:16, KJV) which would be OK if the word 'given' was actually anywhere in the Greek text. Which it isn't. Likewise the ESV has 'All Scripture is breathed out by God' (2 Tim. 3:16, ESV), but the Greek text actually says nothing about the direction of the breath. The CEV has, 'Everything in the Scriptures is God's Word' (2 Tim. 3:16, CEV) which is absolutely *not* what the text says. It seems to me that all these interpretations are reading their own view of Scripture back into Paul's words.

I think it's helpful to remember that Paul is a Jew, and as such is steeped in their stories. So when he coins the phrase 'God-breathed', it seems to me that he is alluding to other occasions when God's breath has been at work. Immediately we are thrown back to Genesis, where 'the LORD God formed man from the dust of the ground, and breathed into his nostrils the breath of life;

and the man became a living being' (Gen. 2:7). Or we might think of Ezekiel's vision of the valley of dry bones, where God clothes the skeletons with flesh, and then breathes life back into them: 'Thus says the Lord GOD to these bones: I will cause breath to enter you, and you shall live' (Ezek. 37:5).

Or perhaps he's thinking of Scripture as wise. In one of the books of the Apocrypha, the Book of Wisdom, Wisdom herself (wisely, Wisdom is always female in these works) is described as 'a breath of the power of God' (Wisd. 7:25).

The thing is, looked at in the light of Scripture itself, the image is of God giving life to something, animating it, making it so much more than dry dust, or a collection of bones and sinews, or even words on a page. And that's the point of *theopneustos*. There is *life* in this book – the breath of God inflates its lungs. And as it breathes with God's life, we can listen to what it whispers to us. The breath of God blows on the flames that crackle in the leaves of the tree. The breath of God ruffles the pages, reanimates us, brings us alive.

We are not supposed to just read the Bible. We're supposed to inhale it. We're supposed to take it deep down into our lungs, breathe in the atmosphere, suck in great gulps of the life-giving breath of God.

When it feels like we are drowning, the Bible fills our lungs with the saving breath of God.

When we are panicking and scared, the Bible calms us with deep breaths of the presence of God.

When all the breath has been knocked out of us by the events of our lives, when our tears and sobs mean that we cannot catch our breath, the Bible brings us the oxygen of hope and comfort.

When we are becalmed, the Bible blows wind into our sails to get us going.

When we are light-headed and dizzy, when it feels as though we are scaling new heights, the Bible resupplies us with oxygen so that we can climb even further.

We can argue all we like about the process of how books came together (and we will). We can argue about meanings and theologies and interpretations until, appropriately, we are blue in the face, but all that is missing the point of the Bible. The point is to let the Bible breathe God's life into us.

This offers us a way forward. Because if we believe that God inspired the Bible in the sense of creating it from scratch, writing it, editing it, cutting and pasting all those bits of scroll together, then we do have some problems. For one thing, why did he bother doing it over such a period of time? Why not say all he had to say right at the beginning and leave it at that? Why put in all those extra bits that really don't add much – the lists of names, the tribal directories?

And if God breathed it out, *created* it, as it were, then why use different voices and genres? And why are there contradictions and differences? Why are there mistakes? Why are there bits that no one understands? Surely, if God were the author, then that wouldn't occur.

But that's not what happened. The Bible was written and compiled by humans, but God filled it with his presence. Which is, in fact, a thoroughly biblical thing to do.

The case of the unnecessary Temple

In one of the books of the Bible – the book of Chronicles – there's an account of the building of the Temple in Jerusalem.

> **Read it yourself:** The full account is in 2 Chronicles 2:1–7:11. It's quite detailed and there are a lot of measurements in it. But for anyone who likes ancient building regulations it's entertaining reading. And if you read between the lines it's even more fascinating . . .

This is a 'peak' moment for the Israelites. Everything that they have been through as a people – slavery in Egypt, escape under Moses, forty years wandering in the desert, the entry into the Promised Land, the blood and the butchery of the conquest of Canaan and the reign of the judges, the eventual emergence of David as king, and now the reign of his son, Solomon – everything has led them to this point, this building.

Finally, it's opening night. There is rejoicing and celebration. Large, ancient wind instruments are blown. Incense is burned in industrial-sized quantities. And there is the slaughter of 22,000 oxen and 120,000 sheep. The Ark of the Covenant is brought in to a special room, a choir starts to sing and then – wonderfully – the presence of God fills the building: 'the house, the house of the LORD, was filled with a cloud, so that the priests could not stand to minister because of the cloud; for the glory of the LORD filled the house of God' (2 Chr. 5:13–14). Thankfully, no one had installed smoke detectors.

It's a triumphant opening night. Unless you're an ox or a sheep. Or anyone with asthma.

But if we look a little more closely, a more shadowy story starts to emerge.

Solomon's father, the great king David, was banned by God from building the Temple, because he had too much blood on his hands. Solomon himself is not exactly Snow White. The original, alternative account of his accession shows that he had his stepbrother killed along with others who opposed his rise to the throne.* And Solomon was later to go on and worship other false gods.

Then there's the size of the Temple. While the book of Chronicles describes the building in lavish detail, it's not actually particularly big. Solomon's palace complex – also built at enormous cost – was much bigger. One room in the palace, the House of the Forest of Lebanon, alone was six times the size of the

* 1 Kings 2:24–25.

Temple. Talking of which, the famous cedars of Lebanon used for the Temple and other buildings were supplied by King Hiram of Tyre. Solomon paid for that by giving Hiram twenty cities. But when Hiram finally got to see the cities he didn't think they were good enough. So Solomon basically underpaid his supplier.

Hiram wasn't the only unhappy one. The Bible itself tells us that, far from creating a bunch of happy workers, the project only served to widen some pretty deep divisions in the kingdom. Solomon's building projects were financed by heavy taxation, and delivered using a system of conscripted labour. For a nation that had been rescued from slavery, this cannot have been a popular move.* It was made even less popular by the fact that Solomon taxed and treated the ten northern tribes of Israel much more harshly – basically because they had never supported the claims of his father David. And those cities that were used to (under) pay Hiram were all in the north. So the northern tribes were treated like slaves, heavily taxed and their territory was given away in payment. They didn't forget this: when Solomon died they broke away and formed an entirely different kingdom. It's one of the biggest ironies of the Bible: the Temple was actually responsible for breaking up the very kingdom it was supposed to unite.

At the opening, Solomon gives a long dedication speech, which contains the rather surprising admission that God doesn't actually *need* a house: 'But will God indeed reside with mortals on earth? Even heaven and the highest heaven cannot contain you, how much less this house that I have built!' (2 Chr. 6:18). The Lord, Solomon admits, 'resides in thick darkness'.

So this is a very human building with a very chequered history. It was designed, constructed and inaugurated by flawed individuals

---

* The system was called the *missîm*. This forced citizens to give the government one month's free work every year. There is evidence that the writers of the Bible really hated this: in the book of Exodus, the Egyptian slave masters are called 'officers of the *missîm*' (Exod. 1:11).

with mixed motives and dubious building practices. Its construction led to conflict and warfare. And the architect-in-chief admits that God doesn't actually need a house anyway, thus rendering the entire building a little pointless.

Yet, despite all the flaws, despite the very human background of this place, God's presence fills this building.

Throughout history, men have made many things to contain God: churches, temples, denominations, ceremonies. All of these have mixed motives and chequered histories. God doesn't 'need' any of these things, but it is in humanity's nature to keep building houses, and it is in God's nature to keep turning up.

And of all the houses that humanity has built for God, there is none so great – and none in which the presence of God is so strong – as the Bible. The Bible was written by humans, edited by humans, compiled by humans, translated by humans. But it is God who brings it to life.

Thinking again about inspiration

What does it mean for God to inhabit this book, and how should that change our approach to Scripture?

This isn't just the Bible. This is God's strange new world. This is the burning bush, the Temple. This is a place of encounter. Take off your shoes. You are on holy ground.

So the first thing to do whenever we open the Bible is to approach with prayer. Invite God to be present and to speak to you through the text. The theologian and philosopher (and rather eccentric Frenchwoman) Simone Weil talked about prayer as paying attention: 'It is the orientation of all the attention of which the soul is capable toward God.'[2]

A prayerful reading of the Bible means, above all, to attend to the voice of God within the text. I'm sure that reading and thinking about the story of the Temple raises many questions. That's not a bad thing. But, for the moment, put them aside and attend to God. Is there anything he is saying to you through this story? Is there anything you have constructed in which you can sense his presence? Or anything that you wish him to bring to life?

We should expect to hear from God when we read the Scriptures. But that could come in any manner of ways. So try not to come with a fixed agenda. I know this isn't easy: most of us have some kind of reason for coming to the Bible. We read it because we are preparing something, or because we are seeking answers about something, or because we stupidly thought we might like to write a book about it. Or sometimes we are desperate for guidance, so we do that thing where we mutter a quick prayer, open the Bible at random and stick a finger in. Usually you end up with something like Job 19:17: 'My breath is repulsive to my wife; I am loathsome to my own family.'

I suppose that might be true. It *might* be a message from God. And I'm cetainly not saying the Bible never acts in this way. One morning a few months ago I woke and listened to the news. Some mornings there is so much to be scared of and this was one of those moments. I found myself plunged into a sea of fear and rumour. Everywhere there were people peddling their latest conspiracy theories.

Anyway, I opened my Bible, and this is what I read:

> For the LORD spoke thus to me while his hand was strong upon me, and warned me not to walk in the way of this people, saying: Do not call conspiracy all that this people calls conspiracy, and do not fear what it fears, or be in dread. (Isaiah 8:11–12)

Now I know that this verse is not about the internet. It's not about today's news media. It's about impending Assyrian attacks on Israel. It's Isaiah justifying his own confidence and his prophetic role. I know all that. Yet to me it seemed exactly what I needed to hear.

Sometimes the words of the Bible leap out at us: they confirm or challenge something in our life. The flames roar from the text and we know that we have received words of guidance, or wisdom, comfort, or strength. All that can and will happen. But we should be wary of treating the Bible like an oracle or a fortune cookie. The Bible is not a vending machine: we don't just put a coin in, twist the handle and pick up our candy bar of choice. I think when we put aside our desires, our agendas, our expectations and listen for God he will say some surprising things. We should be thankful when that happens, but we should also remember that it will not happen to order.

A lot of people find it helpful to keep a journal to accompany their reading of the Bible. I think that's a good idea, but I am the world's biggest stationery nerd, so anything that requires pens, pencils or the purchase of a new notebook is bound to get a big thumbs up from me. I do genuinely think it helps to write stuff down. The very act makes us more reflective, more attentive to the text and our responses. I'd just say two things: first, it is entirely up to you what that journal is. It can be a daily piece of prose or a list of bullet points. It could be one verse or thought that sprang out at you, something for which you are thankful or even something you didn't much like. It might just be a doodle. There are no rules.

Second, it's not a command. If it helps to journal, fine. If not, don't do it. This is Bible reading we're talking about, not Bible study. You won't get detention for not doing your homework.

One final thing for this bit: this level of prayerful attention requires detachment. We can't listen properly to the text if there is a lot of background noise. So I think it's always helpful to put away all the distractions, to spend time with just you, God and the Bible.

This is one of the reasons why I advocate the use of a proper old-fashioned paper version of the Bible. There are a number of reasons why I prefer 'proper' books over e-readers or tablets or phones. The first is that I AM NOT A TEENAGER thank you. Ahem. The second is that a book's only purpose is to present you with the text. As the splendidly named Verlyn Klinkenborg says:

> A paper book aids my concentration by offering to do nothing else but lie open in front of me, mute until I rest my eyes upon it. It won't search for a flight or balance my check book or play an episode of the Larry Sanders Show or catch up on Google Reader. It won't define a word, unless the book happens to be a lexicon or have a glossary.[3]

Tablets and computers have a lot of uses, and I couldn't have written this book without the many tools for biblical studies that are on my devices. But listening to God's voice in the Bible requires us to focus. The problem with electronic devices is that they are always calling us away. The device on which we are reading the Bible also wants to interrupt our reading. And the result is that in a world where we are connected to everything, we pay attention to very little.

The Bible calls us away from all that and onto holy ground. Tread prayerfully.

2 The men who wrote the word

A September morning, 458 BC. We are in Jerusalem, in a large, open space in the Kidron Valley, just to the east of the city and near the Water Gate. There's a mix of people here. Some have only just returned from exile in Babylon. Others belong to families who returned decades ago. For those who have arrived recently, the state of the city is a bit of a shock: compared to the might of Babylon this place looks a bit of a dump. The city is in ruins, the walls a mass of crumbling, badly repaired masonry. The first lot of exiles came back almost a century ago. But Jerusalem is still looking rubbish.

> **Read it yourself:** The event is described in Nehemiah 8. Strangely it's not mentioned in the book of Ezra.

But we're not here to work. We're here to listen. A scribe called Ezra has summoned everyone to assemble. He's returned from Babylon and he's going to read to us. There he is, in the distance. He climbs up onto a raised wooden platform and unrolls the first scroll. It rolls up again. That's what scrolls do. Sooner or later someone is going to have to invent a better technology than this.

Anyway, he gets it unrolled again and he starts to read.

He's reading in Hebrew, but who speaks Hebrew any more? We all speak Aramaic, like everyone else did in Babylon. But there are translators nearby, listening and explaining to us what it is we're hearing.

'Who is this bloke?' someone asks next to me.

'He's a scribe,' I say. 'Skilled in the Law of Moses.'

And that's what today is all about. Ezra is reading the book of the Law of Moses. He's telling us our stories, where we came from.

Some of this stuff is familiar. But some of it . . . well, this is the first time we've ever heard it.

Odd, that. Where's it come from? And what else has Ezra brought back with him from Babylon?

What the Jews didn't do

In the history of the ancient Jewish people there are two defining moments. The first is the exodus – the story of how Yahweh rescued his people from slavery, gave them a home and called them to be his people. God made a covenant with Israel – a solemn agreement that they would be his people and he would be their God.

But the second key event of their lives – just as important, although at the other end of the emotional scale – was the destruction of the country and the exile of the people to Babylon.

Exodus and exile. Liberation and loss. These two experiences shaped the theology of the Israelites like nothing else.

Ancient Israel was destroyed in instalments.

It began with a self-inflicted wound when, after the reign of Solomon, a civil war broke the country into two. The two king- doms – Israel in the north and Judah in the south – were minnows, politically and militarily, minor players in the Ancient Near East. From that time forth they were very low down the food chain. The world was dominated by the big predators: Egypt, Assyria, Babylon.

The northern kingdom of Israel was destroyed in 721 BC by the Assyrians. Its people were scattered and its capital destroyed, and that was that. Apart from the refugees who escaped into Judah, or the émigrés who made new lives in other parts of the world, the ten northern tribes more or less disappeared.

But Judah survived the Assyrian invasion and staggered on for another 150 years. Then it faced a new enemy: the Babylonians, who had succeeded the Assyrians as Number One Most Powerful Evil Empire. Finally, Judah, too, was crushed. In 587 BC the Babylonians entered Jerusalem, tore down the Temple and took all the Judeans into exile in Babylon.

The decline and fall of Israel and Judah was a shattering blow to the Israelites. During the centuries leading up to the collapse of the kingdom they faced defeat after defeat, humiliation heaped upon humiliation. But these setbacks didn't just damage their country; they also damaged their theology. Hadn't God promised to protect them? Hadn't he made a series of covenants with them? Wasn't he the greatest of all the gods? Their God – the interventionist God with the plagues and hailstones and all that – seemed to be nothing more than a distant memory. The Bible records their anguish in many places.

It was the prophets who came up with the solution. They argued that God's covenant with Israel was not a guaranteed get-out-of-jail free card. It was not going to remain in place whatever people did and however they acted. There was more to this covenant business than just obeying all the rituals and slaughtering lots of mammals. The prophets argued that Israel and Judah were being punished for their disobedience, but, unlike the old tales, this time there would be no cataclysmic flood, no earthquake, brimstone and fire. This time the punishment would come in the form of enemy soldiers. God would use the shock and awe of the Egyptians, Assyrians and Babylonians to punish his disobedient people.

When the end finally came and the Judeans were marched into Babylon, the truth must have been very hard to take. Babylon was an enormous city, with huge walls tiled with glazed blue bricks, and containing temples and buildings which made Solomon's Temple back in Jerusalem look like a garden shed.

The truth could not be avoided: they were a small nation who had lost everything.

> **Read it yourself:** The final, troubled years of Judea are depicted in 2 Kings 23:31–25:30, among many other places. Ezekiel 17 retells the same story in allegorical form. You might like to check out some Psalms as well: Psalms 74 and 79 lament the sack of the Temple, Psalm 109 gives a kind of potted history of Israel, and Psalm 137 gives graphic expression to the grief, loss and bitter anger that the Jews were feeling.

The feeling of bewilderment and loss is summed up in Psalm 137, written in exile. 'By the rivers of Babylon,' records the psalmist, 'there we sat down and there we wept when we remembered Zion . . . How could we sing the LORD's song in a foreign land?' (Ps. 137:1, 4) How were they to worship God with no Temple? As they said to the prophet Ezekiel in exile, 'How then can we live?' (Ezek. 33:10). What were they going to do?

Well, actually, it's what they *didn't* do that changed history.

When a tribe, nation or people group was defeated in ancient times, it wasn't just that the people – their rulers, armies, etc. – had been defeated; it also meant that their *gods* had been defeated. What generally happened when a group was defeated was that their gods were either forgotten or absorbed into the victor's religion. Your god had been relegated, so you transferred your support to the winning team. But the Hebrews didn't do that. They were stubborn, these people. They carried on worshipping Yahweh. And they went even further: they denied that the opposition gods – the 'winning' gods – even existed.

The Babylonians must have been completely bemused. The Judeans simply refused to lose in the right way.

Instead, they clung to their identity, and to their sense that Yahweh had chosen them. And they found that identity in their stories. Stories are essential to survival. The stories we tell ourselves define our identity as a people. Stories of heroes and villains, history and myth. Stories that sum up the way we are supposed to behave and what we are like. For the Jews in exile it was no different. The first task was to preserve their stories, their writings, to gather their core accounts of where they had come from, to preserve the memory of who they were and what made them different.

The stories gave them some kind of anchor in a world in which everything else no longer made sense. But which stories were they to preserve?

Some editing was needed.

I say 'El', you say 'Yahweh'

In 1883 a German scholar called Julius Wellhausen published a book with the snappy title *A Prolegomena to the History of Israel*. The book argued that the Pentateuch or Torah (the first five books of the Old Testament) was not written by Moses, but was the work of four different authors or editors. It became the basis for what has been called the Documentary Hypothesis, which argues that four different 'documents' form the Torah, and not that it was made as a documentary.

Actually, Wellhausen wasn't the first to spot this. The idea that Moses could not have written the so-called 'books of Moses' had been around for a long time. There were a few clues – little things like, oh, I don't know, the fact that Moses appears to describe his own death. Or that he talks about himself in the third person, and calls himself 'the humblest man who ever lived'. Seems to undermine his case a little, if Moses himself is writing it.* But the evidence is deeper than that. Very early on in the history of Bible reading, rabbinic scholars noticed something unusual about Genesis: it used two different words for God.

Some of the material refers to God as Yahweh – or, to be more precise, using the letters YHWH.† Another set of material refers to God as Elohim. The difference can be seen most obviously at the very beginning of the Bible in the story of creation.

The very first line of the Bible begins, 'In the beginning when Elohim created the heavens and the earth . . .' (Gen. 1:1). And this is the classic 'six days' account. But a little later there's a second account, and this uses the name 'Yahweh'. This begins in Genesis 2:4: 'In the day that Yahweh made the earth and the heavens . . .'‡

> **Read it yourself:** Genesis 1–3 contains the two tradi-
> tions about the creation of the cosmos. As you read it
> you might like to think about what it says about who
> God is, and about the status of men and women. Not
> to mention snakes.

* In the eleventh century, for example, a Jewish scholar called Isaac ibn Yashush pointed out that Genesis 36 included a list of Edomite kings who all lived long after Moses' death. In gratitude, his peers gave him the title 'Isaac the blunderer'.

† This is also called the Tetragrammaton, which sounds like something from a *Transformers* movie but actually means 'four letters', in this case the four letters that were thought to represent God's real name.

‡ Most Bibles use the phrase 'the LORD God' instead of 'Yahweh'. And simply 'God' to indicate Elohim. So whenever you see in your Bible 'the LORD God' with the capitalisation stuff, it's Yahweh that is being mentioned. For ease of use in this section I've replaced the LORD or the LORD God with 'Yahweh' and God with 'Elohim'.

So each account of creation uses a different name for God. One uses 'El' or 'Elohim'; the other uses 'Yahweh'. But it's not just that there are two different names used. The actual accounts themselves are different. The first one – the Elohim version – is the classic six-days edition. Here's a rough outline:

1. God separates light from darkness.
2. God separates the sea from the sky.
3. God separates dry land from the sea, and fills the earth with plants and trees.
4. God commands lights to hang in the sky – the sun, moon and stars.
5. God creates sea creatures and birds.
6. God creates animals – 'cattle and creeping things and wild animals of the earth of every kind' (Gen. 1:24) – and, finally, humans. God creates men and women at the same time: 'So Elohim created humankind in his image, in the image of Elohim he created them; male and female he created them.' (Gen. 1:27).

The second account is very different:

In the day that Yahweh made the earth and the heavens, when no plant of the field was yet in the earth and no herb of the field had yet sprung up – for Yahweh had not caused it to rain upon the earth, and there was no one to till the ground; but a stream would rise from the earth, and water the whole face of the ground – then Yahweh formed man from the dust of the ground, and breathed into his nostrils the breath of life; and the man became a living being. And Yahweh planted a garden in Eden, in the east; and there he put the man whom he had formed. Out of the ground Yahweh made to grow every tree that is pleasant to the sight and good for food, the tree of life also in the midst of the garden, and the tree of the knowledge of good and evil.

(Genesis 2:4–9)

In the Elohim version, plants arrive on day three and humans on day six; in the Yahweh version, there are no days mentioned at all, and humans are formed before there was any vegetation, when 'no plant of the field was yet in the earth and no herb of the field had yet sprung up'. In the Elohim version men and women are created at the same time; in the Yahweh version man is formed from dust, and only later is woman formed, taken from the rib of man. She is the original order of spare ribs.

Two different names; two different accounts. And it's not just in this bit of Genesis, either. Different 'Yahweh' and 'Elohim' material occurs throughout the Torah.

How to explain this? Well, although some Christians and Jews have spent many hours trying to reconcile them, the obvious answer is that the material clearly comes from different traditions. In one of these traditions God is called Yahweh; in the other he is called Elohim. And someone has edited it together to form a much bigger document.

Since the nineteenth century, most scholars accept that the version of the Torah we have today has been edited together from various texts; not just these two but other sources as well. The most widespread version of this theory identifies four main sources, each with different perspectives, emphases and interests. They give these sources the names J, E, P and D. Here's a quick rundown:

J or the Yahwist. This source calls God 'Yahweh', focuses on the history of Judah in particular, talks about Mount Sinai and is a big fan of the etymology of words and place names. (I know 'Yahwist' begins with a Y, but Wellhausen was German, and German uses J instead of Y. OK, Ja?)

E or the Elohist. The second calls God 'Elohim', so is known as E. He's – I suppose I should say 'E's' – quite big on stories and traditions to do with northern Israel. He talks about Mount Horeb, not Sinai.

P or the Priestly source. P is obsessed with everything to do with the priesthood – sacrifice, altars, ritual, a whole lot of tabernacles: he loves all that stuff. For P, God is 'Elohim' or 'El', and it's Mount Sinai, not Horeb. He's also a big fan of dates and genealogies.

D or the Deuteronomist source. He gives us, unsurprisingly, the book of Deuteronomy. He calls God 'Yahweh', focuses on Judah and anything to do with Jerusalem, doesn't provide any really early tales and loves really, really, really long speeches.

There are various accounts of how the editing was done, and scholars have spent a lot of time going into excruciating detail over which bits are the work of P or D or E or J. But this is the most widely held theory.

There are, of course, detractors. Some people argue that it's all a bit too neat to imagine someone sitting down with their scrolls and the scissors and paste and gluing a new version together. Others say that there are many more sources than just four. Some argue that the material came together in a more gradual manner, like a lot of smaller bits joining together until they formed a larger whole. Or that it was a continual model of alteration and addition, with a series of editors modifying and adding as more material came into their possession, allowing them to issue Torah versions 2, 3, 3.5 and then 3.51 with minor security patches.

Others, of course, argue that no editing took place at all. Fundamentalists claim that the books weren't 'edited' in any real sense, but that they already existed in one set of documents which is and always has been 'the books of Moses'.

But even leaving aside the JEDP stuff, these stories show clear signs of later updating and editing. There are signs of later additions, alterations and even anachronisms.

Like the camels.

The case of the anachronistic camels

Camels crop up quite a bit in Genesis. The servant whom Abraham sends to find a wife for his son Isaac takes ten camels with him on the journey (Gen. 24:10). Jacob's gift to Esau includes 'thirty milch camels and their colts' (Gen. 32:15). And when Jacob's unfortunate son Joseph is sold into slavery he is taken away by 'a caravan of Ishmaelites coming from Gilead, with their camels carrying gum, balm, and resin, on their way to carry it down to Egypt' (Gen. 37:25).

The only problem with this is that these stories are set some-time between 1800 and 2000 BC. And camels were not domesticated until at least 700 years later, in the twelfth century BC.[1] The camel does not appear in any Egyptian texts or art from the times of the Pharaohs. So having Abraham use camels is a bit like having Richard the Lionheart ride a motorbike. Either the Patriarchs and the Ishmaelites were way ahead of their time in their transport use, or the writers of this text have added the camels in for a bit of detail.

There are lots of other examples of anachronisms in the text. At one point Abraham goes to live in 'the land of the Philistines' (Gen. 21:34). A few chapters later, his son Isaac goes to 'Gerar, to King Abimelech of the Philistines' (Gen. 26:1). Both of them are a bit early, since the Philistines didn't arrive in Canaan until around 1200 BC. So we have Richard the Lionheart on a motorbike, going to meet the President of the USA.

Genesis also provides a list of the Kings of Edom, which begins, 'These are the kings who reigned in the land of Edom, before any king reigned over the Israelites' (Gen. 36:31). So it's clearly been inserted by someone who lived after the foundation of the kingdom of Israel.

Nor is it just in Genesis. In Exodus, for example, Moses talks a lot about what appears to be the Israelite monarchy, and a lot of Deuteronomy anticipates situations that only came about during the time of the exile.

These are obvious anachronisms, but there are other insertions which hint at different agendas, other than adding a bit of detail.

Take the Priestly source. As we've said, he's a big fan of all the sacrificial, ritual stuff. He's the one who collects together all those laws in Leviticus (which is really the priests' handbook). He gives us all the measurements of the Tabernacle and the detailed descriptions of the Ark of the Covenant and the different rituals. He probably did some editing on the first Genesis account, as it has God observing the Sabbath (Gen. 2:1–3), and Cain and Abel make sacrifices (Gen. 4:3–4). So he wants to emphasise that certain aspects of the priestly stuff go way back.

Sometimes, though, he overplays his hand a little.

The biblical account records that the Law was given to Moses. And the Law included the idea of clean and unclean foods. (You can find the major lists in Leviticus 11 and Deuteronomy 14.) But if you read the story of Noah, you find the following instruction:

> Take with you seven pairs of all clean animals, the male and its mate; and a pair of the animals that are not clean, the male and its mate. (Genesis 7:2)

And when Noah's ark comes to rest he builds an altar and 'took of every clean animal and of every clean bird, and offered burnt-offerings on the altar' (Gen. 8:20).

Now it is possible, of course, that Noah, as a righteous man, knew the difference between clean and unclean animals. But it seems more likely that someone (and, let's face it, a priest is the most obvious suspect) is keen to emphasise the links between the fundamental religious institutions of the Jews and their very earliest stories.

We've already seen that the names Yahweh and Elohim point to stories from different traditions. But there are other clues about this. First there is the issue of duplicate stories, where similar stories appear in slightly different forms. There are two covenants with Abraham (Gen. 15 and 17), and three accounts of a strange episode where wives are disguised as sisters (Gen. 12:10–20; 20:1–18; 26:6–14).

Sometimes these different traditions clash. The story of Joseph, for example, can't decide whether it is Reuben or Judah who tries to save Joseph. When Joseph is attacked by his brothers, his brother Reuben pleads for his life (Gen. 37:21–22). But in verse 26 it is Judah who pleads for Joseph's life. But then in verses 29–30 it is Reuben who returns to rescue him, only to find Joseph gone.

Read it yourself: The story of how the deeply irritating Joseph was sold into slavery is told in Genesis 37. I wouldn't listen to the musical version, as it's not *entirely* faithful to the text.

We have the same problem with the people who purchased Joseph. In verse 25 the traders who buy him are Ishmaelites, but three verses later they are Midianites:

> When some Midianite traders passed by, they drew Joseph up, lifting him out of the pit, and sold him to the Ishmaelites for twenty pieces of silver. And they took Joseph to Egypt.
>
> (Genesis 37:28)

Either we have two traditions at work here, or the storyteller has got very confused.

Now we should say that although there are anachronisms, and although there are different accounts, it doesn't necessarily follow that all the stories were invented later. Editing and amending is not the same as inventing. These stories preserve very ancient accounts of the origin of the Israelites. Indeed, the fact that there are two creation stories, or the whole doublet/triplet thing, shows that the later editors were concerned to preserve all the traditions, even if it made life difficult for them. The editors did not smooth out the wrinkles. They could have created one single narrative, but they chose not to.

But, clearly, someone *has* woven these traditions together. Clearly the Torah is a coat of many colours, and crafted from different cloths.

And we have a good idea of when – and where – all that tapestry work happened.

Survival stories

Let's go back to the story of Ezra reading the Law to the people. When Babylon fell to Cyrus, King of Persia, he allowed the exiles to return from Babylon to Judea. The first group returned in around 538 BC. But the work was hard and the other occupants of the land made life difficult, so nothing much happened. The returning Jews married some of the locals, took up some of their customs and learned how to survive.

Other groups drifted back over the subsequent decades.* One of these groups contained a scribe called Ezra. He probably arrived some eighty years later, in 458 BC, and he was appalled. The city was in a terrible state. The once great Temple was nothing more than a tiny local shrine. And the Jews who had settled there were close to disappearing, to being assimilated into the tribes who lived all around them. Their Jewish identity, which they had fought so hard to preserve in Babylon, was in danger of being lost.

But Ezra had a powerful weapon in his luggage. He had the Torah – the Law; the codified, authorised version of the first five books of the Bible. We know from the account in Nehemiah that it was more than just one book, because the whole thing took several days to read. And, crucially, the reading contained some new information – things that the listeners had never heard before.

On the second day, the crowd – largely comprised, remember, of those who had returned in previous decades – were surprised to hear about the Feast of Booths or Tabernacles. This was new

---

* Like the group led by Nehemiah, which returned around 445–443 BC.

to them. (It had not been celebrated, apparently, since the time of Joshua (Neh. 8:17).)* Why didn't those in Jerusalem know of this festival? Surely if it had been widely known they would have brought it back with them? The implication is that this festival was part of a different tradition of worship, which Ezra had incorporated into the wider work. Or it could have been a festival that had arisen among the émigrés in Babylon.

This is another indication that the Babylonian exile is the most likely period for the editing and recording of the Torah. In the exile, as we've seen, it was vital to the Jews to preserve their identity. And key to that was to collect and preserve all their stories, the stories that contained their history and told of their special relationship with Yahweh, their God. And it was people like Ezra – 'a scribe skilled in the law of Moses that the LORD the God of Israel had given' (Ezra 7:6) – who would have done some of the work.

It's impossible to understate the importance of tradition and myth to the survival of any ethnic group or nation. By myth here, I do not mean fairy story. Myths are origin tales. Myths are stories about who we are as humans or as ethnic groups. They tell us eternal truths about ourselves and our qualities. Myths are ways of connecting the earthly with the divine, the real with the mysterious, the present with the deep past. This is what the stories in Genesis and other parts of the Bible do.

Stories are a survival mechanism. They provide a sanctuary in times of trouble and a light in the darkness. The stories that the Jews preserved in Babylon gave their history meaning and shape. It was their stories of the presence and protection of God that promised these refugees a future.

But the stories promised more than mere survival. They promised victory.

---

* The festival appears in Leviticus (Lev. 23:39–43). It may be the celebration mentioned in Judges 21:19 and 1 Samuel 1:3.

The case of the Babylonian bricks

One of the myths that made its way into the text is not only set in Babylon, but it also mocks the Babylonians and denies their power.

> **Read it yourself:** The Tower of Babel story is in Genesis 11:1–9. This is what's known as an etiological tale – a tale that explains the origins of something, in this case the origins of language and different ethnic groups.

In Genesis 11 we have the story of the Tower of Babel. According to the story, the earth's population has gathered together in Shinar. Shinar apparently corresponds to the region of Sumer and Akkad in the lower Tigris–Euphrates Valley. In other words, Babylon.

They all speak one language and they decide to build a tower, a ziggurat, an ancient, pyramid-like structure, with a series of levels and steps reaching up to the top. In response, God confuses their language and scatters humanity throughout the earth.

Obviously it's not a literal story. Otherwise we would have to believe that God took seriously the idea that humans could build a temple high enough to reach heaven. Nowadays we have the highest buildings in world history and, as far as I know, no one has walked out on the top floor and found themselves face to face with the Archangel Gabriel. The idea behind this story reflects the ancient Hebrew understanding of the cosmos, which believed that there was a firmament up above us, a dome, which kept the waters out (although some water came through the firmament in the shape of rain).*

But, leaving aside questions of historicity and cosmology, one

---

* If you've ever seen the film *The Truman Show*, that fundamentally depicts the Hebrew cosmos.

of the most interesting things about the story is that it's clearly an attack on Babylon and its gods. Because there was a real Tower of Babel, and it stood bang in the middle of Babylon.

The Tower of Babel was a temple to the god Marduk, the greatest of the Babylonian gods. His story is told in an ancient Mesopotamian epic called *Enuma Elish*, which tells of a great cosmic battle between the gods. The goddess Tiamat – who is a huge sea-monster kind of creature – wants to kill all the other gods (who are her descendants). So they ask Marduk to save them. He defeats Tiamat and then uses her carcass to create the cosmos. The upper half of her body becomes the sky or firmament, the lower half of Tiamat's body becomes the land. He then creates lights in the sky and everything else. And he becomes top god and assigns jobs to all the other gods – who are *really* annoyed. They don't want to work for a living. So Marduk placates them by creating humans to be their slaves. He creates the human race out of the blood of Kingu, one of Tiamat's generals:

> Verily, savage man I will create.
> He shall be charged with the service of the gods
>   That they might be at ease!
> ...
> Out of [Kingu's] blood they fashioned mankind...
> He imposed the service and let free the gods.[2]

The grateful gods recognise the supremacy of Marduk and build him a magnificent temple in Babylon, or 'Bab-el' as they call it. Bab-el means 'gateway of the god'.

And that is the Tower of Babel. It really was in Babylon. It was a stepped tower – known as a ziggurat – and it dominated the city.* It had seven storeys and rose to a height of some 300 feet. At the summit was a sanctuary.

---

* Ziggurat' is derived from the Akkadian verb *zaqaru*, meaning, 'to rise up high'.

The outer wall of the temple of Bab-el in Babylon was made of oven-fired bricks. Ordinary buildings had bricks that were just dried in the sun. I mention that not merely because of an incipient historical nerdiness, but mainly because the Genesis story actually describes the same technique: the builders of Bab-el say, 'Come, let us make bricks, and burn them thoroughly.' The story goes on to say, 'And they had brick for stone, and bitumen for mortar.' In Canaan, stone was the best building material and mortar was made out of clay. But in Babylon, stone was in short supply: numerous inscriptions report that Babylonian buildings were constructed 'with bitumen and burnt-brick'.

This is not just a story about the origins of language and ethnicity; it's a story that mocks Babylon and its pretensions to grandeur.* Maybe the original bones of the story – men wanting to be gods – might have predated the exile, but the details show that the Tower of Bab-el is a story shaped and altered in Babylon, by people living in the shadow of the great ziggurat. And Babel is never referred to elsewhere in the Hebrew Bible. Although the prophets frequently mention Babylon as a symbol of evil and corruption, they never mention this story at all. Whenever they talk about destruction of this type, they talk about Sodom and Gomorrah. Why? Because it's a story that comes out of exile, after the time of the prophets.

But it also shows something else that is important: the stories of ancient Israel are not just stories about the origins of the Israelites. They are also attacks on the stories of the other nations.

We've seen how, in Babylon, the temptation would have been for the Jews to simply give in and find a god who would return them to winning ways. But they didn't do that. Instead, they rejected the claims of the other gods completely.

What we also see in Genesis is a rejection of the stories of the cultures around them. Not for the Jews all that stuff in the *Enuma*

---

* It's also based on a pun. Bab-el means 'gateway of the god'. But it's very close to *balal* which means 'confusion'.

Elish, where families of gods do battle in some kind of cosmic soap opera. Marduk has to create the heavens and earth by cutting his great-great-grandmother in half. But Yahweh just speaks and things happen. To a Babylonian, therefore, these stories would have been baffling and even offensive. Where's the great cosmic conflict?

But God doesn't need a cosmic punch-up.

Nor does he create people to be slaves, out of the blood of his defeated enemies. Humans are created in his image (Gen. 1:27). This is utterly unlike other ancient ideas about the origins of humans. Yahweh is not like the other gods. He cares for humans, provides for them.

At the heart of the Genesis story is the idea that humans are immensely valuable. So valuable that God even gives them free will. Humans are not slaves or playthings of the gods. They bear the image of God: they have moral choices.

And the world is good. It does not emerge from primordial evil, or from violence and fighting.

The biblical texts emerge from the culture around them. But, badly behaved as ever, they refuse to play nicely and conform to that culture. The Bible is a counter-cultural narrative. It does not just say things about the kingdom of God; it also critiques the kingdoms of this world. Genesis doesn't bother explaining where God has come from. God just is. He has no background life story. He is not subservient to nature. He is one supreme being. Frankly, he makes Marduk look a bit of an amateur.

And that's the point.

Thinking again about who wrote the Bible

When it comes to the Pentateuch, we can see the hands of different authors and editors. But the same is largely true of the rest of the Bible as well. Pretty much all the biblical texts have been worked on in similar ways. They all reflect the images and cultures of their time. They have all been edited, even if it's just down to someone putting the text in order, or writing it down. I believe that, rather than seeing this as a weakness, we should recognise it as one more example of the collaborative activity of God in the world. The Bible is not just the witness or the vision of one man: it is a tapestry woven together by many different craftsmen. And most of the time we don't even know who they were.

Who, for example, compiled the book of Amos? It wasn't Amos, obviously, since it begins with a brief biography of the prophet, written in the third person and giving the date of his prophecies. But whoever it was, he made sure that the prophet's words were recorded – so today we can be stirred and stung by Amos' vision.

Who were all the Isaiahs? Most scholars agree that the book of Isaiah is the work of not one, but several different prophets. Isaiah 1 was born about 765 BC and had a long career, prophesying through the reign of several monarchs. But the second section of the book (chapters 40–55) is the work of another Isaiah. Isaiah 2 lived two centuries later, around the time of the capture of Jerusalem and the exile. The language of Isaiah 2 is entirely different. And it's likely that there were a load more little Isaiahs whose work has been collected in chapters 56–66. In fact, we know that the first Isaiah – Isaiah 1, Isaiah the Great, Isaiah Classic – had disciples, because he gives them instructions: 'Bind up the testimony, seal the teaching among my disciples' (Isa. 8:16). Whoever they were, they preserve for us poetry of an unparalleled power and majesty.

Who put together the book of Daniel? Whoever he was, he had one of the hardest tasks in the collection of the Old Testament: welding together several chunks of material in wildly different styles and two different languages. The first part (Dan. 1–6) is a narrative about the witness of Daniel and his friends in exile in Babylon. The second half (chapters 7–12) is a series of apocalyptic visions. Not only that, but the book is written in two languages: there's a big section of five chapters or so in Aramaic

(2:4–7:28) and the rest is in Hebrew. The book was probably written between 167 and 164 BC, but beyond that we don't know much about its formation. But whoever was involved, he gives us stories of perseverance and integrity in the midst of a culture that wanted to crush and destroy any other form of worship. And in the second part of the book he offers such a rich source of language and imagery that it was adopted by John of Patmos and even Jesus himself.

How many songwriters wrote the psalms? There's a lot of debate about the psalms. The phrase 'a psalm of David' might mean 'written by David', but it could just as easily mean 'attributed to David' or 'about David' or even 'in the style of David'. Isn't it fantastic, though, that at the heart of the Bible we have such honesty, such raw emotion? However many people compiled this collection, they ensured that the real, lived experiences of human beings were part of the songbook of ancient Israel, and still give us the language to sing about God today.

So we need to get our heads around the idea that the texts in our Bibles are a team effort. And different writers bring their own personalities to their books. There is the dour grimness of Jeremiah; the grandiloquent Isaiah; the bitingly cynical author of Ecclesiastes; the breathless, grammatically challenged excitement of Mark; and the passionate and at times potty-mouthed Paul. It's all in there.

All these people were writing under very different conditions as well. Some of them were free; others were living as captives of foreign powers. Some of them were poor; others came from the aristocracy. Their writings were written in places such as Israel, Persia, Babylon, a small island in the Aegean and a prison cell in Rome.

The books cover a wide range of subjects. Many of them were wondering where it all went wrong. Some were thinking about deep philosophical problems of suffering and evil; at least one of them was thinking about rumpy-pumpy. Some of them were writing instructions for worship, or songs to be used in the liturgy;

others were constructing a history. Most of the New Testament letters were written to solve disputes in the church.

With all that, it's hardly surprising that the books reflect divergent opinions as well. They do not all come from the same viewpoint. There are books that assume that everything makes sense and books that say that nothing makes sense at all. There are alternative histories. There are books that say it's all about faith and books which say it's all about work.

Once again, the problem is not with the Bible itself, but with what people say about it. More, the problem is almost physical, with the way the Bible is presented to us. The book in your bag, or in front of you, or lost somewhere down the back of the bookshelves, is not *one* book. I mean, I know it *looks* like a book – it has a front and back cover, and a spine, and a humungous number of pages inside and it's all printed in the same font, and it all sounds as though it was written in the same style, but that's just so much window dressing. We get fooled by the fact that we have given it a title in the singular – the Bible – when it should be in the plural – the books. The Bible is not one book, but many books. Just. Stuck. Together.

We need to break it apart and celebrate the differences.

Because if we insist on seeing the books as one unified work then we will always have problems with the fractures, the edit points, the duplications and the differing details. But if we just let the text speak for itself, then a different picture emerges: one of collaboration and careful preservation, one of multiple authors and witnesses, each doing their bit to tell the great story of God and humanity.

3 Binding up the Bible

SCENE. INTERIOR. DAYTIME. A ROOM IN ROME.

There is a man sitting at a desk, holding a pen. It is St Paul and he is thinking about who to write to next. There is a knock at the door.

PAUL: Go away! I'm writing my Epistle to the Mancunians.

The knocking continues. Paul gets up grumpily, goes to the door and opens it. A beautiful man is standing there, emitting a strange glow.

PAUL: Do you mind? I'm under house arrest here and I'm trying to get through my epistles.

STRANGELY GLOWING MESSENGER: Yea, verily, I have a package for thee.

PAUL: *(Slightly awed)* What is it?

STRANGELY GLOWING MESSENGER: It is THE BIBLE.

At the mention of this word, a heavenly choir can be heard singing and several small birds fly around, tweeting.

PAUL: The Bible! Oh, joy!

STRANGELY GLOWING MESSENGER: Signest thou here.

PAUL signs and the messenger disappears in a puff of incense. Paul opens the jiffy bag and takes out a large, black, leather-bound volume.

PAUL: *(Reading)* The Holy Bible.

He quickly leafs through it.

PAUL: Wow! They've got loads of my stuff in here.

He pauses.

PAUL: Thessalonians? Why have they put that in? The letter to the Rastafarians was a lot better . . .

The loose canon

Christians aren't really taught much about how the Bible was actually put together. It's an interesting, if convoluted, history, but the key thing to understand is that there was no point when a voice came from heaven and saith, 'Here's what I want in the Bible: Genesis, Exodus, Leviticus, Numbers . . . but miss out the Jannes and Jambres nonsense . . .'. In fact, what constituted Scripture was the subject of intense argument, discussion and debate over a long period of time.

The official contents list of the Bible is known as the 'canon'. The word comes from the Greek word *kanon*, which means 'reed' (we borrow it for the word 'cane'). These long, straight reeds were used as measuring rods. So when we talk of canonicity, or the canon of Scripture, we mean those books that 'measure up' to a certain standard, a certain set of rules. Usage of the term for Scriptures – in the sense of meaning a precise list of sacred writings – seems to have started in the late fourth century AD.

Deciding which books measured up in this way actually took a lot of people a long time, and what we'll see is that, like the writing of the Bible, it was a collaborative process. It was also a lengthy process: the contents of the Jewish Scriptures were not finally settled until about AD 90; the contents of the New Testament not until around AD 400.

When it comes to talking about the formation of the Bible, we run into problems of terminology. For example, Christians call the sacred writings of Judaism the 'Old Testament'. ('Testament' in this context, means 'promise': for Christians the Old Testament refers to the promises given by God to the Jews, and the New Testament to the promise given through Jesus.) However, to the Jews, whose sacred Scriptures these are, there is nothing 'Old' about them at all, thank you very much. Jews call their Scriptures the *Tanakh*, an acronym taken from the three main sections: *Torah* ('Law' or 'Instruction'), *Nevi'im* ('Prophets') and *Kethuvim* ('Writings'). Torah, Nevi'im, and Kethuvim – hence *Tanakh*.

One term that scholars often use is 'Hebrew Scriptures', but then what do you do with the New Testament? Because although that is the 'Christian Scriptures', so is the Old Testament. I suppose you could rebrand them completely and call them Part One and Part Two. But that would just confuse people. Most of all me. So I'm going to stick to Old Testament/Hebrew Scriptures and New Testament.

And here's how we got them.

The Hebrew Scriptures

Nothing starts as Scripture. Something only becomes scriptural when it is accepted as such by believers. For the Jews, the first set of writings to become 'Scripture' was the Torah, and this was only widely accepted after the time of the Jewish exile in Babylon in 587–538 BC.

We don't know how much of it was widely known before that – certainly the stories from the books of Samuel and Kings show a society that does not often follow the law. It tends to go AWOL. At one point, a copy of 'the book of the law' is discovered in the Temple, much to the surprise of King Josiah, who immediately institutes reforms and laments that 'our ancestors did not obey the words of this book' (2 Kgs 22:13). The text says that Passover had not been celebrated 'since the days of the judges who judged Israel, even during all the days of the kings of Israel and of the kings of Judah' (2 Kgs 23:22).

> **Read it yourself:** The story of the discovery (which most scholars believe is the book of Deuteronomy) and Josiah's reforms is in 2 Kings 22–23.

Torah is often translated as 'Law', but a better translation might be 'instruction' or 'teaching'. The Torah is the bedrock of Judaism, containing not only their religious, social and criminal law, but also the stories of their origins and their divine right to the land of Canaan. When biblical writers or characters talk about 'the Law' they are referring to the Torah. The section is also known as the Pentateuch or the books of Moses.

The second section of the Hebrew Scripture, the *Nevi'im* – the Prophets – was gathered together during and after the exile. We know this because it includes books that conclude with the exile (e.g. Kings and Samuel), as well as prophets who worked after the exile was over (e.g. Ezekiel, Haggai and Zechariah).

The *Nevi'im* is subdivided into the Former Prophets and the Latter Prophets. The Former Prophets includes books such as Joshua, Judges and Samuel. The Latter Prophets contains the three major prophets – Isaiah, Jeremiah and Ezekiel – and the twelve minor prophets. (In the Hebrew Bible the twelve minor prophets are counted as one book, for the simple reason that you can get all their writings on one scroll.) The contents of the *Nevi'im* was probably decided by 190 BC because in a book called *The Wisdom of Jesus Ben Sirach*, written around this time, there is a list that praises Isaiah, Ezekiel, Jeremiah and 'the Twelve prophets' – which is the contents of the Latter Prophets. However, some Jews never accepted the *Nevi'im* as Scripture in the same sense as the Torah.

The final set of books admitted into the Hebrew Scriptures was the *Kethuvim*, which simply means 'Writings'. This contains a load of stuff that didn't fit into the other two sections, including wisdom literature and poetry, history and even historical fiction. It's certainly a diverse collection and includes histories (Chronicles, Ezra and Nehemiah), stories (Ruth, Esther and Job), poetry (Psalms, Lamentations, Song of Songs), and Wisdom books (Ecclesiastes and Proverbs). Finally there's Daniel – part narrative history, part apocalyptic prophecy. Although books like the Psalms were widely accepted, other books in this section, such as Song of Songs, Ecclesiastes, Job and Esther, were disputed. So the list was not finalised until around AD 90.

As to how this was all decided, the traditional accounts of the formation of the Hebrew Scriptures depict a process of debate and discussion, all of which took place against a background of loss and failure. (As we shall see, there is nothing like exile for bringing you a sense of what is important in life.) In this case, the trauma took place in the mid-first century AD. In AD 66 the Jews revolted against their Roman overlords. It took the Romans four years to get their act together, but in 70 they finally crushed the revolt, and in the process destroyed the Temple in Jerusalem. It was never to be rebuilt.

It was a devastating loss. And during the siege, according to Jewish tradition, a group of rabbis and scholars fled Jerusalem and settled in Jamnia or Jabneh, a town some twelve miles south of Jaffa, where they set themselves the task of trying to salvage Judaism from the wreckage. Part of that meant defining what actually constituted their Scriptures. Previously, although everyone accepted Torah as authoritative, there was disagreement about the status of the other sections, and even about which books should be included. The Sadducees, for example, refused to accept anything as Scripture *except* the Torah. (That's why they did not believe in the resurrection of the dead, because it's not in those books. Jesus often appears to deliberately wind up the Sadducees by asking them, 'What do your scriptures say?' and then quoting a bit from books that they didn't accept as being scriptural.)

The rabbis who gathered at Jamnia were not Sadducees, but Pharisees. But even they had problems with certain books. Some of them didn't like Job, for example, not only because the central character wasn't Jewish, but also because it seemed to deny any kind of afterlife. 'If mortals die, will they live again?' says Job at one point (Job 14:14).

Ezekiel was also problematic. Not only did it have some extremely rude language, but it also included material that ran counter to Torah, such as the material in chapters 45–46 which contain laws about sacrifices that directly contradict the laws in Numbers 28–29.* Debate about this book went on well into the first century AD. One rabbinic tale tells how the first-century Jewish scholar Hananiah ben Hezekiah shut himself away in his study with the purpose of reconciling Ezekiel to the Torah. He took some three hundred vessels of oil for his lamps, and used them all up before he concluded that it was OK. But it wasn't only the contradictions: the visionary mysticism of Ezekiel was also seen as hazardous to spiritual health. Public discussion and reading of the first chapter was prohibited, because it claimed to show secrets of God's throne room, and no mortal should see that. In the fourth century AD, the Christian scholar Jerome reported that some rabbis prohibited the reading of the beginning and end of the book by anyone under the age of thirty.

Then there were books like Proverbs, Ecclesiastes, Song of Solomon and Esther. Proverbs is a collection of sayings, some of which actually contradict one another; Esther doesn't once mention God; the Song of Songs is a book of poetry that deals with rumpy, and, indeed, pumpy; and Ecclesiastes is so cynical and dark that it could have been written by a particularly depressed art student.

The debate took many years, and was not properly decided until around the last decade of the first century AD. The list that emerged was the list of Scriptures we find in our Old Testaments today. (Even then, not all groups of Jews stuck to the list. In AD 170 Melito, the Christian Bishop of Sardis, drew up a list of the Old Testament books, based on information from Jews in Syria. His list didn't contain Esther. Either he missed it out by accident, or people still had issues with it.)

---

* We'll see more issues with Ezekiel vs Torah in Chapter 8.

The Christian Scriptures

When it came to deciding the contents of the New Testament, the process was equally protracted.

Certainly within a few years of Jesus' death, stories of his life and teaching were being shared among the believers. Paul talks about the way in which significant accounts were carefully 'handed on' from one believer to another (1 Cor. 15:3), and he also quotes from early Christian hymns and sayings. We don't know what the earliest written accounts of Jesus' life were like, but there was probably an account of his Passion, and a collection of his sayings in circulation as well. There were also letters written by Paul and others which began to circulate from church to church. These accounts were written in *koiné* or common Greek – the kind of Greek spoken by the merchants and tradesmen of the Graeco–Roman world. An ordinary language for ordinary people, but telling of extraordinary things.

Gradually, these turned into Scripture. First were the Gospels: by AD 150, Justin Martyr was arguing for the primacy of the 'memoirs of the apostles' and, a little while later, Irenaeus of Lyons (writing c. 170–180) argued that only Matthew, Mark, Luke and John were 'true and reliable'.[1]

Later, letters written by various major Christian figures were added to the canon. These letters, written to various churches around the Mediterranean, were written by people like Paul, but there are also letters ascribed to John, James, Jude and Peter, as well as a letter to the Hebrews written by an anonymous author. Technically, these letters are the earliest Christian documents we have. The earliest of Paul's letters date from the late 40s/early 50s AD, whereas the Gospels didn't take their final form until the 60s AD. Finally there is the book of Revelation, a poetic, visionary book. Technically this is also a letter, since it was sent to seven churches in Asia Minor, but in almost every other way, Revelation is in a category of its own.

But, just as among the rabbis at Jamnia, there were discussions in the early church about what constituted Scripture. There were reservations about certain books, particularly Jude, 2 Peter, 2 and 3 John and Revelation. One early Christian called Marcion decided that Christianity was far too Jewish and argued that it should jettison all the Hebrew Scriptures, and even any overly Jewish New Testament writings. He whittled down the Christian Scriptures to an edited version of Luke's Gospel (the only one written by a Gentile), ten of Paul's letters and, naturally, a work called the *Antitheses* which had been written by . . . er . . . Marcion himself. The church in Rome listened carefully to his arguments before chucking him out and ignoring him.

Around AD 170 a Syrian scholar called Tatian took a different approach. He combined the four Gospels into one account, removing any repetitions and smoothing out discrepancies. This was immensely popular and was widely used in Syria for some three hundred years until a bishop came in and decided to use the proper versions.

Despite all this, the Church did not rush into declaring a definitive list, and discussions continued for a long time. Even as late as AD 325 the church historian Eusebius of Caesarea (c. 260–c. 340) listed as disputed works James, Jude, 2 Peter, 2 and 3 John and Revelation. In the spring of AD 367, Bishop Athanasius of Alexandria distributed a letter which listed what he considered to be the canonical books of the Christian Bible, and this was probably the first time that the twenty-seven books of our New Testament were listed as a definitive canon. However, even that didn't decide things. Around 385, Gregory of Nazianzus produced a list of the canonical books in verse – presumably as a memory aid. He had the same Old Testament but his New Testament was missing Revelation. Around a decade later, a list attributed to a man called Amphilochis also rejected Revelation, along with 2 Peter, 2 and 3 John and Jude.

Generally in the first centuries after Christ, what you defined as 'Scripture' depended on where you were standing. In Antioch, only James, 1 Peter and 1 John were accepted as canonical among the non-Pauline epistles. In Caesarea, Origen felt able to refer to the Wisdom of Solomon, one of the apocryphal books, as 'the word of God'.[2] In Constantinople, the greatest preacher of his day, John Chrysostom (AD c. 347–407) preached hundreds of sermons, none of which quoted from 2 Peter, 2 and 3 John, Jude or Revelation. Meanwhile, in the Latin-speaking western half of the empire we have one list containing all twenty-seven books from the Athanasian list, which also adds some extra books (Barnabas, Hermas, the Acts of Paul and the Apocalypse of Peter), while a list from North Africa, written around 360, omits Hebrews, Jude and James but includes Revelation.

The fact is that there never was a point when the Church sat down and decided what constituted the New Testament. It was a fluid and open process which attempted to bring together a list on which everyone could agree. It was probably the production of one-volume Bibles as much as anything else that fixed the contents. And they didn't happen until the late fourth century onwards. Up until then, the Bible was a collection of separate texts, kept in cupboards.

And it wasn't called 'the Bible'. That comes from the Greek *ta biblia*, which means 'the books'. Plural. And the word 'scripture' comes from the Latin *scriptura*: writings. These are later titles given to the collection. In Jesus' day they didn't have a generic term for their Scriptures. The closest the Bible comes to giving itself a title is in the book of Daniel where Daniel looks in 'the scrolls' – the Hebrew word is *ha-sefarim* – to consult the works of Jeremiah (Dan. 9:2).

The first time *ta biblia* was explicitly used to describe the Old and New Testaments is in the works of John Chrysostom (c. AD 347–407).* Clement of Rome, writing in the late first century AD, talks about the *hieras graphas* ('holy writings') and also *ta biblia*

---

* The first recorded use of the word 'Bible' comes from around AD 1300. It's from the Old English, in a poem where the anonymous author uses the phrase, 'As þe [the] bibul sais'.

ta hagia ('the Holy Books'), by which he probably means the Hebrew Scriptures. Justin Martyr (c. 100–c. 165) talks about the 'writings' and also 'the memoirs composed by them [i.e. the apostles], which are called Gospels'. The epistle to Diognetus,* written sometime between AD 150 and 220, talks about 'the faith of the Gospels' (Diognetus 11:6). Jerome (c. 342–420) used the term *bibliothēca* – or library – for the Scriptures, and use of this name continued for several centuries.

But the really important thing about this story is this: it was the Church that decided what went into the Bible. In fact, I might repeat that. In bold. And underlined. It was the **<u>Church</u>** that decided what went into the Bible.

As to *how* they decided what to include, there were various tests. A work had to be by a recognised apostle, or connected to the apostles somehow. (Mark and Luke weren't apostles, but their works were connected to Peter and Paul respectively.) These were the eyewitnesses, so their testimony was paramount. Any work had to accord with the received teaching of the Church: it had to be orthodox. This is important: many books that claimed apostolic lineage were rejected because they did not reflect the teaching.

But a key criteria was simply the experience of the Church. A book that had been valued and used by a wide range of churches, and across generations, was much more likely to be accepted than one that had only gained local currency. Had the book proved itself? Did it have a track record, as it were?

And this was not done in secret; this is not the tale of some ridiculous Dan-Brown-like conspiracy. The contents of the Bible were not decided by a secret cabal of mitred bishops who met in the back room of a pub somewhere in Asia Minor with the deliberate aim of excluding books that didn't fit their theology. It was the experience and response of the wider Church as much

---

* We don't know who Diognetus was. And the author of the Epistle simply calls himself 'Mathetes', which is Greek for 'disciple'.

as anything that decided the debate. The texts that form the Bible were the ones with a track record, the ones that were authenticated by both authorship and experience.

You might say that they were the buildings where God was to be found, the books which had the breath of God within them.

The Bible as we have it was not born by miraculous means. It was not teleported down to Paul. It was not delivered on the back of a unicorn to the house of Peter. God's hand did not appear and write the list on a wall. The Bible was not only put together by humans, it was put together by humans working in a typically messy, churchy kind of way – through compromise and consensus. For this reason the Eastern Orthodox Church has always seen the Bible as *within* the Church, not outside it. It recognises the authority of Scripture. But it also remembers that it was the Church that decided what was Scripture in the first place.

And talking of the Orthodox Church . . .

The Apocrypha

If you open a Catholic or Orthodox Bible you will find some extra books in it. These are known as the Apocrypha, or the Deuterocanonical books.

The reason for this goes back to the translation of the Hebrew Scriptures produced in Alexandria, Egypt, from the third century BC onwards. Alexandria at this time was an énormous, cosmopolitan city, and home to one of the biggest Jewish populations outside Palestine. However, most of these Jewish émigrés spoke Greek, and not Hebrew. So, some three hundred years before the time of Christ, the Hebrew Scriptures were translated into Greek, beginning with the Torah and then followed by the rest of the Scriptures. This version became known as the Septuagint, from the Latin phrase *Interpretatio septuaginta virorum* – 'translation of the seventy interpreters'. The legend goes that it was produced by some seventy Jewish scholars, each of whom worked independently, and who miraculously came up with the identical translation. Amazing. What are the chances, eh?*

The Septuagint includes thirteen books that are not in the Hebrew canon, as well as additional chapters to Esther and Daniel and an extra psalm. We don't know exactly when these books became part of the Septuagint. But we do know that they had been included by the first century AD, because they were known to the writers of the early church.

These books are known as the Apocrypha. They are also known as Deuterocanonical – Secondary Canonical – books.

Naturally, for Greek-speaking Christians of the early church, the Septuagint was the default translation, which is why those extra books remained in the Bibles of the Greek Orthodox Church. But it was also used as the basis of the Latin Old Testament used by the Western Church for more than a thousand years, so they also remain part of Catholic Scriptures. However, they are not in most Protestant Bibles, because when the reformers of the sixteenth and seventeenth centuries came to make fresh translations of the Bible, they went back to the Hebrew version of the text.

So today we don't all use quite the same Bible.

But there's nothing new in this. Back in New Testament times, they used a different version as well. In fact, the writers of the New Testament used a different version from the one we use.

---

* It's often given the abbreviation LXX, the Latin numerals for seventy. The story of the translation is complete tosh, but it reveals an instinctive anxiety about the task of translating. Some ancient Jewish scholars thought translating the Scriptures suspicious, even sinful. So the story serves as a reassurance: 'It's OK, God approves of the translation – look, he even miraculously did it!' It's a way of comforting the traditionalists: this translation comes with the stamp of divine approval.

Why the New Testament writers get their quotes wrong

One of the things that sometimes baffles readers about the Bible is how the writers of the New Testament get their Old Testament quotes wrong.

Look up virtually any bit of the Old Testament that is quoted in the New and you will find some significant differences between the two versions. Here's James, quoting a bit from the Old Testament during a meeting in Jerusalem:

> 'After this I will return,
> and I will rebuild the dwelling of David, which has fallen;
>> from its ruins I will rebuild it,
>> and I will set it up,
> so that all other peoples may seek the Lord –
> even all the Gentiles over whom my name has been called.
>> Thus says the Lord, who has been making these things
>> known from long ago.'   (Acts 15:16–18)

And here's the original version from Amos:

> On that day I will raise up
>   the booth of David that is fallen,
> and repair its breaches,
>   and raise up its ruins,
>   and rebuild it as in the days of old;
> in order that they may possess the remnant of Edom
>   and all the nations who are called by my name,
>   says the LORD who does this.   (Amos 9:11–12)

It's pretty different. Or take this bit from the book of Hebrews, where the writer quotes Psalm 104:4 as follows:

'He makes his angels winds,
　　and his servants flames of fire.'　　　　　　　(Hebrews 1:7)

But the Hebrew text of Psalm 104:4 reads:

You make the winds your messengers,
　　fire and flame your ministers.　　　　　　　(Psalm 104:4)

Why does this happen?

First we have to remember that not many people had access to the Scriptures in Jesus' day, so most people relied on memory. But second, when they did quote the Scriptures, the early Church used the Septuagint – the Greek translation. These quotes from Acts and Hebrews are taken from the Septuagint. And that explains why in Psalm 104 the angels have suddenly become all windy: the Septuagint is in Greek, and the Greek word for both 'angel' and 'messenger' is *angelos*. That's what angels are. The writer of Hebrews chooses to use the text as referring to angels. But that's clearly not what the Hebrew original is about. That's about how God speaks through creation.

What that means is that when the early church quotes the Old Testament, they are actually using a different version to the one we use. And what *that* means, if you want to go all hardline on this, is that the book of Hebrews actually misquotes the Old Testament.

To make matters worse, sometimes they even misquote the Septuagint. In 1 Peter 3, the apostle begins a quote from Psalm 34 like this:

'Those who desire life
　　and desire to see good days,
let them keep their tongues from evil
　　and their lips from speaking deceit.'　　　　　　(1 Peter 3:10)

This is slightly different to the Hebrew version of Psalm 34:12:

> Which of you desires life, and covets many days to enjoy good? . . .

And, interestingly enough, the Septuagint version follows the Hebrew:

> What person is he who wants life, coveting to see good days?
> . . .   (Psalm 33:13–17)*

So Peter has changed the opening of the sentence. It's not a massive difference, certainly, but it is a difference. Why has he done it? Well, either he's changed this deliberately, or he's misremembered it, or he might even be quoting from a different version of the Septuagint.

The use of the Septuagint lies behind one of the most famous translation conflicts – the interpretation of Isaiah 7:14 in Matthew's Gospel. Matthew writes this:

> 'Look, the virgin shall conceive and bear a son,
> and they shall name him Emmanuel.'   (Matthew 1:23)

But look up Isaiah 7:14 in many Bibles and you don't find a virgin. It reads:

> Look, the young woman is with child and shall bear a son, and
> shall name him Immanuel.   (Isaiah 7:14)

The reason is that the Septuagint uses the Greek word *parthenos* ('virgin') to translate the Hebrew word *almah* ('young woman').

---

* In the LXX the Psalms are numbered slightly differently. Among other differences, the LXX combines Psalms 9 and 10 in the Hebrew *Tanakh* into one Psalm – Psalm 9. So Psalm 34 in our Bibles is Psalm 33 in the LXX. Not at all confusing.

Matthew, in recounting the story of the virgin birth of Jesus, naturally saw this event as fulfilment of Isaiah's prophecy because he was using the Septuagint. But Isaiah wasn't talking about anything other than a normal birth, in the context of a war being fought in 734 BC. This doesn't make the virgin birth story untrue, nor does it mean that Matthew is playing fast and loose with the Bible. As we shall see, Matthew was reading the Bible in a way that was perfectly acceptable in the context of his time, which understood that the text might have esoteric, hidden meanings which might be revealed to an inspired reader.[3]

The point of all this is that we tend to think that the Bible we have is the same one that everyone else has – or always had. But people have had different versions along the years.

The case of the edible unicorns

The other thing we must acknowledge from this story is that the Bible only exists in translation.

The Bible was written in four languages: Hebrew, Aramaic, Greek and a few bits of Latin.

The Old Testament was written almost entirely in Hebrew. But it's important to note that by the time the Scriptures were being widely accepted, not many people could actually speak Hebrew. In Jesus' day most Jews spoke Aramaic, so the Hebrew had to be translated for them in the synagogue.

And while many people today have mastered biblical Hebrew, some of the ancient Hebrew is so obscure that it leaves even the best translators baffled. For example, in Exodus there is a passage known as 'the bridegroom of blood'. Here it is:

> On the way, at a place where they spent the night, the LORD met him and tried to kill him. But Zipporah took a flint and cut off her son's foreskin, and touched Moses' feet with it, and said, 'Truly you are a bridegroom of blood to me!' So he let him alone.

It was then she said, 'A bridegroom of blood by circumcision.'

(Exodus 4:24–26)

I have read a lot of commentaries on this passage. A *lot*. And they all have one thing in common: none of them is quite sure what is going on here. *The Jewish Study Bible* says, 'This episode, possibly abridged from a fuller, clearer version, is extraordinarily puzzling because the motive for God's attack is unclear, the pronouns are equivocal, and Zipporah's remarks are enigmatic.'[4] In other words, we don't know who is being attacked, or why, or what really is done about it. And anyone who does claim to have solved this is bluffing.

Sometimes it's not the language but the story itself which leaves even the best scholars scratching their heads, narrowing their eyes and generally agitating their lower intestines in confusion. There are stories like the 'sons of God' story, which is obviously a very ancient myth but which defies explanation.

Read it yourself: It's in Genesis 6:1–4.

Are the sons of God fallen angels? Are they the descendants of Seth? Are they alien beings from the Planet Zarg? The text doesn't say. It just records the story and then steps back to let us get on with it.

There are words that no one understands. In the Psalms, for example, there is the repeated word *selah* which often breaks up sections. Nobody actually knows for sure what this word means. It could mean 'pause'; it could be an instruction to the congregation to kneel or prostrate themselves; it could be some kind of musical instruction, indicating something like 'louder', or marking a place for a musical interlude.[5] (Which means we could read *selah* as 'guitar solo'.)

> **Read it yourself:** You can find it in many psalms. Try
> Psalm 3, which is only 8 lines long but which still
> manages to include it three times.

Some of the flora and fauna listed in the Bible is completely
unknown to us as well. Noah builds his ark out of 'gopher wood',
but nobody knows whether that is a type of tree or a way of
treating wood, like 'squared' or 'smoothed' wood. I think we can
rule out chipboard and MDF, but beyond that it's anyone's guess.
But I don't think this kind of thing should worry us. Indeed, I
think it's rather to be celebrated, not least because this kind of
uncertainty resulted in unicorns appearing in the Bible.

Or, I should say, in one *version* of the Bible. They appear in
The King James Version, and have several mentions.* My
favourite, though, is Isaiah 34:7: 'And the unicorns shall come
down with them, and the bullocks with the bulls; and their land
shall be soaked with blood, and their dust made fat with fatness.'
That whole line is fab, I mean, who doesn't want their dust made
fat with fatness? Even if your shoes do get all bloody in the
process.

There are three reasons why unicorns appear in the KJV:

1. Because nobody knew what the word meant. The Hebrew
   word for this animal is *re'ēm*, which probably means 'wild
   ox', but nobody knows for sure.
2. Because they were following a precedent. The translators
   of the KJV had other translations to draw on, and in this
   case they were using the Geneva Bible which had been
   translated by a group of ultra-Protestant émigrés fifty
   years earlier in 1560. The Geneva version actually has an

---

* Numbers 23:22; 24:8; Deuteronomy 33:17; Job 39:9–10; Psalms 22:21; 29:6;
92:10; Isaiah 34:7.

additional mention of the unicorn – in Deuteronomy 14:4–5, where it is listed along with 'the beef, the sheep, and the goat, The hart, and the roebuck' and a few other animals as 'clean' animals which the Israelites were allowed to eat. So, according to the Geneva Bible, the unicorn is edible!

3. Unicorns were a 'thing' in Jacobean times. The Geneva and KJV translators weren't 'wrong', as such. The translators of the KJV weren't experts on the flora and fauna of the Ancient Near East – indeed, they weren't experts on the flora and fauna of anywhere, really – so when they were choosing an animal to translate *re'ēm*, it seemed obvious to go for 'unicorn' – which in the seventeenth century were definitely a thing. They were simply using the knowledge of their time.

So the first thing to take from this is that translation is not an exact art. It always draws on the culture and ideas of the time.

Sometimes the translators have to fill in the gaps, because the original text is either missing entirely or seriously confused. In 1 Samuel 13:1, for example, the real numbers have gone awol from the text. The New Jerusalem Bible version has:

> Saul was . . . years old when he became king, and reigned over Israel for . . . years.

The NRSV has a different take:

> Saul was . . . years old when he began to reign; and he reigned for . . . and two years over Israel.

The actual Hebrew reads, 'Saul was one year old when he became king and he reigned over Israel for two years.' Which makes no sense at all. Basically, as the note in the New Jerusalem Bible says, 'Saul's age at his accession either was not known or has accidentally fallen out of the text.' But some translations have a problem with the gaps, so they make a guess at it. The ESV, for example, has:

> Saul lived for one year and then became king, and when he had reigned for two years over Israel . . .

(Although it does include the actual Hebrew text in a footnote.)

Even when it comes to the relatively recent Greek text of the New Testament, there can still be problems. In Luke's Gospel there is the famous story of the young Jesus being left behind after a family pilgrimage to Jerusalem.

Read it yourself: Luke 2:39–52. It's an interesting passage because it's the only story in the Gospels of Jesus' childhood.

When his parents eventually locate him he says, 'Did you not know that I must be in my Father's house?' (Luke 2:49). Except that the word 'house' isn't in the Greek. There isn't actually a noun at all. Jesus says, 'Don't you know I must be in the of my father?' There's nothing. Most translations put the word 'house' in there because he's standing in the Temple. Others translate it as the 'business' of the Father. But Luke doesn't tell us what Jesus is actually in. You could put anything in there if you wanted. He could be in the garden. In the shed. Jesus could be in the car, although I admit that is unlikely.

So translators have to make their best guesses, on the grounds of the context. Now these are very minor stories, relatively speaking. But they do serve as a reminder that there are some things in the Bible that we will never understand; there are some bits where the text has gone AWOL, and every translator is making their best guesses.

Your Bible exists in translation. In fact, the Gospels *only* exist in translation. Jesus spoke Aramaic, but the Gospels are in Greek. So when people say we can only understand the Bible in the original languages, that's not entirely true. We can never get back to the Aramaic originals of Jesus' sayings.

As E.A. Speiser says, 'All translations are but arrested pursuits of the given source. In each case the chase halts with the publication of the version. But the target does not remain stationary.'[6]

It's a good reminder that the Bible is always moving, always surprising, and that we will always be chasing the unicorns.

Not everything in your Bible is the Bible

The Church decided what went in the Bible. The Church decided to call it 'the Bible'. And since the very earliest times, the Bible has had a lot of stuff added to it.

Some of this you have to have. Things like, oh, vowels. And punctuation. The original Hebrew text does not contain any vowels. Sometimes this makes working out the exact text tricky, although later generations of Jewish scholars helped by putting in small marks above the text. (But even they weren't certain in every case.) The Greek text contains lots of vowels, but no punctuation, soallthewordsruntogetherlikethis. So when you see speech marks or other punctuation in the New Testament, it's been added by the translators.

Some of this stuff is useful. For example, the original text is not divided into chapters and verses. Chapter division goes back quite a long way – it was initially used in the first 'proper' bound Bibles (known as codices) which were made in the fifth century AD. But there was no uniform system until the thirteenth century, when a man called Stephen Langton devised the numbering system we use today. Verses were not added until the fifteenth century, 1,400 years after the originals were written. Occasionally I come across Christians who have devised elaborate theories around verse numbers, but Jesus didn't speak in verses, and Paul didn't add tiny little numbers to his letters as he went along. They are very useful tools, though.

But some tools can be actually misleading. I'm thinking of the titles we use for certain well-known passages – all of which are later inventions. The Sermon on the Mount (Matt. 5–7) was first called that by Augustine writing in the fourth century. The Lord's Prayer was given that title by Cyprian of Carthage writing around AD 252.* The problem is that these 'tools' can give an entirely false impression of what is going on in the text. The Sermon on the Mount is not a 'sermon' as we would understand it. And there are no real mountains near Capernaum. So, at best, it was a chat up a hill. The Lord's Prayer is not his prayer but ours – it was given to the disciples.

Perhaps the most pervasive of these titles is 'The Great Commission', which is often found in Bibles as a summary heading for the end of Matthew, especially where Jesus says:

'All authority in heaven and on earth has been given to me. Go therefore and make disciples of all nations, baptizing them in the name of the Father and of the Son and of the Holy Spirit, and teaching them to obey everything that I have commanded you. And remember, I am with you always, to the end of the age.'

(Matthew 28:18–20)

But the term 'Great Commission' isn't found anywhere in the Bible. It wasn't even invented until the seventeenth century – maybe around 1650 – while the person who really began to popularise it was the great missionary Hudson Taylor in the late nineteenth century. And it has become the key Bible passage for missionary societies and

---

* He wrote a book called *On the Lord's Prayer* (*De Dominica Oratione*), although, interestingly, the version in his book is not the same as the one we use. And actually there are two versions of the Lord's Prayer in the Gospels. And other versions recorded elsewhere.

evangelists of all flavours. Now, I'm not denying that it's quite an important bit, but is it really *the* great commission? Jesus said that the most important thing was to love God and love our neighbours as ourselves. So why isn't that the great commission?

The problem is that by putting in a title, we make an artificial hierarchy. *This* is the great bit, as opposed to any other bits. But the titles weren't there. They've been added by translators, theologians, editors: the *Church*.

Thinking again about the canon

The Bible tells us about God, it points us to God, but it is not God. But because of the language we use about it, and because of our ignorance about where the Bible actually came from, we end up treating it as if the Bible is really God with an ISBN. It's called bibliolatry – and it's the process by which the Bible itself becomes an object of worship.

In case you're not sure, here are three obvious signs that the Bible is not God:

1. It was created by humans.
2. It's not perfect.
3. It's made of paper.

The way that some Christians talk about it, you'd be forgiven for thinking that the Bible is the third person in the Trinity.* The problem with treating the Bible in this way is that we have to make sure it behaves itself in a God-like way. We cannot have a God who disagrees with himself, so we have to argue that the Bible is without contradiction. And if the Bible is God, then it

---

* Actually, it might be the first person for some: the Southern Baptist Statement of Faith begins with '1. The Scriptures', with God only coming in at number 2.

has to be perfect, right? So we have to state that the Scriptures are 'without error'. And God will never fail us, so the Scriptures have to be infallible as well.

But we can only do this by ignoring the evidence within the Bible itself, and the history of how it was made. And when we do that, when we turn the Bible into a kind of magic book like something out of *Harry Potter*, then we lose all hope of being honest about the text, of voicing our doubts and questions. The process of writing, collecting and deciding on Scripture has, from the start, been a very human process, but its humanity does not detract from its uniqueness. For me, the role of human beings in the creation of this God-breathed book is the most wonderful thing. It shows the way that God has always worked – bringing the hearts and craft of human beings to life. The fact that humans wrote it and decided on the contents does not mean that God was uninvolved; on the contrary, God's involvement in the Bible is exactly the same as the way he works throughout history. He works through human beings. He works in the meetings and the prayers and the discussions. He works in the inspiration of the prophets and the ideas of Paul and even the meticulous research of Luke.

There is nothing wrong with reverence, nothing wrong with acknowledging the primacy of Scripture in the life of the Church, but there's a point at which reverence for the message tips over into worship of the medium.

And, actually, I don't think the Bible wants my reverence; what it wants is my attention.

So, the canon of Scripture was decided by the Church. And different Church traditions also have different canons – different books which they deem to be Scripture. And the truth is that, even as individuals, we all have our own canons. We all have books or passages of the Bible that mean more to us than others. And let's be real here: some bits of the Bible are more important than others. The Gospels, for example, are crucial for the faith of Christians. You can't be Christlike if you don't know what Christ was like.

So we should feel free to narrow it down and dive deeper. Spend months with one book. Or one chapter. Or even one verse. Take a deep dive. The Bible is not a book of soundbites. We have to *think* about this stuff.

And you could also get rid of some of the stuff that has been added. One way to read the text afresh is to print out a passage without any title or chapter or verse numbers. Just the text; just what's there.

You could even emulate the very early church and get rid of the text altogether. Bible memorising is less popular than it used to be but I think it's a great thing to do. Learning the passage allows us to take the text with us wherever we go, to think about it, dwell with it, listen to it over and over again. Chew it over. St Bernard talks about really digesting Scripture, keeping the word of God 'in the same way as it is best to keep your bodily food . . . So let it be taken into the stomach of your mind and pass into the things you care for and the things you do.'[7]

4 A land of story

Jamie Coots was the pastor of the rather over-named Full Gospel Tabernacle in Jesus Name in Middlesboro, Kentucky. The church was founded by his grandfather, and Jamie succeeded his own father as pastor. What makes the Full Gospel Tabernacle in Jesus Name different from other churches is that they handle snakes. Real snakes. Real, *live* snakes. They believe that verses found at the end of Mark's Gospel are really a command:

> And these signs will accompany those who believe: by using my name they will cast out demons; they will speak in new tongues; they will pick up snakes in their hands, and if they drink any deadly thing, it will not hurt them; they will lay their hands on the sick, and they will recover. (Mark 16:17–18)

Snake-handling is not something the historic Church has ever done – at least, not willingly. It seems only to date from the early twentieth century.*

'We literally believe they want us to take up snakes,' Coots said. 'We've been serpent handling for the past twenty or twenty-one years.'[1] Coots even starred in a reality TV show called *Snake Salvation*.

---

* And it is illegal: a 1942 Kentucky state law bans the use of poisonous snakes in religious services. Coots himself was charged with illegal wildlife possession after being caught transporting three rattlesnakes and two copper-heads through Knoxville, Tennessee.

He's dead now, tragically. Killed by a snakebite during a service in 2014.*

There is such a thing as taking the Bible too literally.

Why Jesus was not a baguette

Biblical literalism – the insistence that we take the Bible literally – is a relatively recent phenomenon. There's nothing about it in the Bible itself, and none of the historic creeds insists on it. What's more, some of the churches that most strongly insist on a literal interpretation of Scripture are those who most vehemently reject the idea that the bread and wine of the Eucharist become, literally, the body and blood of Jesus Christ.

Anyway, the truth is that nobody – absolutely nobody – believes the Bible is 100 per cent literally true. Not the Pope. Not the Archbishop of Canterbury. Not your pastor. Not Fundie McFundface, the Chairman of the Fundamentally Fundamentalists. Consider these three verses:

> The next day he [John the Baptist] saw Jesus coming towards him and declared, 'Here is the Lamb of God who takes away the sin of the world!'   (John 1:29)

> Ah, you are beautiful, my love;
>   ah, you are beautiful;
>   your eyes are doves.   (Song of Solomon 1:15)

> I am the gate. Whoever enters by me will be saved, and will come in and go out and find pasture.   (John 10:9)

Now, if you argue for complete biblical literalism, you would have

---

* His son, Cody 'Little Cody' Coots has taken over, apparently. And is still handling snakes.

to believe that when Jesus walked towards John he had transformed into a small, woolly quadruped. Or that when he was
addressing the crowds in Jerusalem, he had suddenly changed
into a small, wooden, *talking* gate. Or that instead of actual eyes,
the object of the poet's passion in the Song of Solomon had two
large birds stuffed into her face.

Nobody believes this; they are metaphors.

And there are a bazillion more examples I could cite, because
the Bible is a great big steaming mass of metaphor.* It's full of
images, allusions, comparisons and a whole host of other literary
jiggery-pokery. It features whitewashed tombs, men with swords
sticking out of their mouths, talking trees – all of these are
metaphors. It speaks metaphorically about God: the Bible talks
about God's hand, his fingers, even his backside; it says that God
is a mountain, a fortress, a shield.

And everybody *gets* this. We know instinctively that when Jesus
describes himself as the bread of life he is not literally a baguette.
Or when he says that he is the light of the world he is not a light
bulb. When we say, 'God is my fortress,' we are saying that he
offers protection and shelter, that the arrows of the enemy will
bounce off the walls, that he keeps us safe against attack. We are
not saying that he has battlements, a portcullis and a drawbridge.

As humans we are fluent in metaphor; we know what it looks
like.

Well, *mostly* we do. The problem comes when the metaphor
is extended into other forms such as poetry and stories.
Sometimes we recognise instinctively that the poet is speaking
metaphorically, as in the case of the Psalms and the Song of
Solomon; at other times, though, the poetry is less obvious and
people can go astray. The book of Revelation, for example, is
mainly poetic in form – it's in a kind of highly stylised writing
called Jewish apocalyptic – but people will insist on reading it
literally.

---

* It's not literally steaming. I'm speaking metaphorically.

Similarly, there are complications with the stories as well. The Bible contains shedloads of stories.* It contains stories about good Samaritans, lost sheep, wastrel sons and forgiving fathers. Sometimes people get a bit muddled and they think that the parables are giving us actual physical descriptions – especially the bits about hell and judgement. So Jesus' tale of the workers in the vineyard where everyone gets paid the same – well, that's definitely a metaphor, right? But the bit about him judging the sheep and the goats – that's *absolutely* going to happen exactly as he states it.

That's a misreading of the genre. This type of story simply doesn't work that way. Of course the stories may contain real physical details and even actual historical references, but that's not why Jesus is telling them. He's always making a bigger point. We don't watch *Fireman Sam* in order to find out how to run a modern fire service; we don't read the parable of the persistent widow in order to find out how to win a case in court.

All of which is to say that spotting the metaphor can be problematic at times. But it is absolutely vital to the way in which we engage with the Bible.

And the thing about metaphors is that they are versatile. They can carry more than one meaning. It seems to me that a lot of Bible teachers – and, indeed, translators – aren't happy with this kind of versatility. They would rather view the Bible not as literature but as mathematics, a kind of algebra where we can work out exactly what the symbols mean. So 'lion' always means strength (or Jesus), 'lamb' means sacrifice (or Jesus again) and 'mountains' equals powers. Or nations. (And Jesus, of course.)

Metaphors are by nature risky and even ambiguous. But a lot of translators prefer to sweep away the mystery of the text so that WE CAN BE ABSOLUTELY CLEAR AND CERTAIN WHAT THE TEXT MEANS. In the preface to his brilliant translation

---

* It's another metaphor. Calm down.

of Genesis, Robert Alter talks about the battle between biblical
philology and translation.* Biblical philology is mostly concerned,
he argues, with grammar and lexicography, with achieving clarity
as to what a word means. Of course, that is vital. But the problem
is that that tends to try to sweep away the mystery of the text.
Here's Alter:

> Literature in general, and the narrative prose of the Hebrew
> Bible in particular, cultivates certain profound and haunting
> enigmas, delights in leaving its audiences guessing about
> motives and connections, and, above all, loves to set ambigu-
> ities of word choice and image against one another in an endless
> interplay that resists near resolution. In polar contrast, the
> impulse of the philologist is – here a barbarous term nicely
> catches the tenor of the activity – 'to disambiguate' the terms
> of the text.

The result of this 'disambiguation' is, Alter claims, to 'reduce,
simplify, and denature the Bible'. And especially when the translator 'has an underdeveloped sense of literary diction, rhythm,
and the uses of figurative language; and that, alas, is often the
case'. The problem, as Alter sees it, is that translation has become
all about 'explaining the Bible, instead of representing it in another
language'.[2] In other words, you may be an expert in biblical
Hebrew and Greek but that doesn't make you a good writer. And
that is one of the reasons why Bible translations are so boring
and flat. Because they want to explain everything.

Take this example from Genesis. The Hebrew word *zera'* means
'seed', not only seeds you scatter on the ground, but also the

---

* Philology is stamp collecting. Oh no, hang on. That's philately. Philology
deals with the structure, historical development and relationships of a
language or languages. It's basically the study of literary texts as well as oral
and written records, the establishment of their authenticity and their original
form, and the determination of their meaning.

offspring of human beings and that which produces the offspring – i.e. semen. It occurs loads of times in Genesis, including right at the beginning when God orders up 'plants yielding seed, and fruit trees of every kind on earth that bear fruit with the seed in it' (Gen. 1:11). When the first humans are expelled from the garden, God says to the serpent, 'I will put enmity between you and the woman, and between your [seed] and hers' (Gen. 3:15). When God makes a promise to Abraham he says, 'I will make your [seed] like the dust of the earth; so that if one can count the dust of the earth, your [seed] also can be counted' (Gen. 13:16).

The trouble is that most Bible versions don't leave the word as it is, but explain it. So in the NRSV the verse to Abraham becomes:

> I will make your offspring like the dust of the earth; so that if one can count the dust of the earth, your offspring also can be counted.'
> (Genesis 13:16)

Technically this is what the word means, but by taking away the image, you lose the other things the image conveys – the idea of fruitfulness and growth, fertility, the idea that you couldn't distinguish between dry earth and seed. This is also clearly intimately linked to the idea that Abraham's descendants will be a blessing to the whole earth. Of course they will, because what do seeds grow into? Plants, flowers, crops, trees, cacti – any number of things to bless humankind.

We have to allow the metaphors to work on us. We have to allow ambiguity in the text. Instead, too often the images are removed or interpreted for us. The Bible is told to behave itself, to speak a bit more clearly and to stop using such flowery language.

But, rather alarmingly for the clarity fans among us, the Bible rather likes flowery language. It delights in a wide range of different storytelling and literary techniques: things like puns, rhymes, foreshadowing, irony, satire, understatement, exaggeration, alliteration – all kinds of word play and clever writingy stuff.

For example, the Bible loves a good pun. (I suppose as God is our heavenly Father we should expect him to be fond of Dad jokes.) Again, these are difficult to translate, because ancient Hebrew and Greek don't play well with twenty-first-century English. But puns are everywhere. John the Baptist uses a pun when countering his critics. He says, 'Do not presume to say to yourselves, "We have Abraham as our ancestor"; for I tell you, God is able from these stones to raise up children to Abraham' (Matt. 3:9). In Aramaic and Hebrew, the word for 'children' (*benayyā*) is similar to that for 'stones' (*'abnayyā*). Puns aren't easy for translators to translate, although personally I think a lot of the time they don't even make the effort.

Take one of the most famous puns right at the beginning of the Bible. In Genesis, the Hebrew name for the first man – *adam* – is actually a generic term which just means 'the human'. Indeed, throughout the Eden story, the text uses the definite article, talking of 'the adam' – 'the human' – (Hebrew: *ha-adam*). But it derives from the Hebrew *adamah*, meaning 'earth'. So in Genesis 2:7, the text says God formed the *adam* from the *adamah*. It's a pun. Some translations capture it by translating 'adam' as 'earthling'.

What are all these puns doing? They are making the story more memorable. In John's speech it is making a point. And in Genesis it is telling us something truly profound about the connection between humanity and the earth. Puns are ways of making connections.

Connections are important in stories. The literary device of allusion is absolutely vital in reading the Bible. Stories make allusions to previous events within the same story, or to other stories entirely. The story of Ruth, for example, tells the tale of how a Moabite woman keeps faith with her Israelite mother-in-law, marries a righteous man called Boaz and eventually becomes the great-grandmother of David.

> **Read it yourself:** Read the entire book of Ruth. It's only
> four chapters long.

It's the tale of a faithful, God-loving foreigner. Ruth's future
husband Boaz says:

> 'All that you have done for your mother-in-law since the death
> of your husband has been fully told me, and how you left your
> father and mother and your native land and came to a people
> that you did not know before.'   (Ruth 2:11)

Any Jew hearing this story would pick up an echo of a previous
traveller, where Abraham is told by God to 'Go from your country
and your kindred and your father's house to the land that I will
show you' (Gen. 12:1). The same elements are there: the homeland,
the parents and family, the unknown land. Ruth is another
Abraham, a faithful, obedient woman.

The Bible wasn't just thrown together. It's been crafted and
shaped. It's a much more sophisticated literary construct than we
often grasp. And it often has a structure and artistry that we miss
out on.

Sometimes the writers change the tense. A lot of John's Gospel
is written in the present tense, even when he is relating something
that has happened in the past. John 2, for example, tells the story
of the wedding at Cana, and is translated in the past tense – Jesus
said to her, his mother said to him. But the Greek is actually in
the present tense. So it should really read like this:

> When the wine gave out, the mother of Jesus says to him, 'They
> have no wine.' And Jesus says to her, 'Woman, what concern is
> that to you and to me? My hour has not yet come.' His mother
> says to the servants, 'Do whatever he tells you.'   (John 2:3–5)

Doesn't that make a difference? Actually, doesn't that make it better?

At other times, the Bible uses deliberately ornate poetic techniques like the acrostic.

As in the book of Lamentations.

Being a series of poems,

Containing laments on the fall of Jerusalem.

Delivered in the form of acrostics, where

Each line of the poem begins with the successive letter of the alphabet.

Flipping heck, it's hard to keep this up . . .

The acrostic is a very deliberate, contrived poetic form. Its aim is to give a sense of completeness – it covers everything from A–Z, as it were. But it's difficult to translate, which is why translators don't bother. But then, sadly, the ordinary reader who doesn't know Hebrew misses the clever, technical construction of poems like these because they just look like everything else in the Bible.

Sometimes the Bible quotes other types of writing. Like in Philippians 2:5–11 where Paul suddenly switches from his usual prose Greek to a poem about Christ. This was probably an early church hymn or poem, telling the story of who Jesus was and what he did. (You might find in your Bible that the text layout changes to indicate that this is a different style of writing.)

There are many other kinds of literary techniques we could explore. The point is that the people who shaped this text were craftsman – even artists at points. This is why it's also equally wrong to dismiss the Bible as the work of primitive culture. The Bible certainly depicts a less-developed culture in many ways. They didn't have the mobile phone, TVs, microwave ovens, cricket, penicillin or the Pot Noodle – all the great advances of civilisation. But they knew how to write. And they used a wide range of different literary techniques to grab our attention and invite our response.

In other words, they were storytellers.

Why God loves stories

There's a Jewish Hasidic saying which runs, 'God created man because he loves a good story.'

Well, there's a bit more to it than that. But it's true. When he was on earth, you couldn't *stop* Jesus telling stories: 'Jesus told the crowds all these things in parables; without a parable he told them nothing' (Matt. 13:34). That's creators for you: always inventing stuff.

The Bible is, above all, a story. For all its different authors, voices, styles and literary forms, it is one great story of the coming of the kingdom of God. And this one great tale is made up of thousands of smaller stories carried in different forms. Sometimes they are poetry, sometimes prose, sometimes hymns or credal statements, sometimes even case studies among all those laws.

Why does God love stories? Why fill his book with so many?

Stories are part of what it means to be human. We are storytelling animals. Never mind *Homo sapiens*; we are, in Jonathan Gottschall's phrase, *Homo fictus* – fiction people.[3] We cannot not tell each other stories. When we come home we share the stories of our day. We read stories in the news. We lose ourselves in books, films, TV, radio, video games. It's one of the ways in which we bear the image of the Creator. And it's not going to go away any time soon.

Paul Bloom, a psychologist at Yale University, analysed how much of the leisure time of Americans was spent immersed in story:

Our main leisure activity is, by a long shot, participating in experiences that we know are not real. When we are free to do whatever we want we retreat to the imagination – to worlds created by others, as with books, movies, video games, and television (over four hours a day for the average American), or to worlds we ourselves create, as when daydreaming and fantasising. While citizens of other countries might watch less television, studies in England and the rest of Europe find a similar obsession with the unreal.[4]

Stories change us. Gottschall writes, 'We humans are constantly marinating ourselves in fiction, and all the while it is shaping us, changing us.'[5] There is nothing more powerful, more transformational, than a good story.

In 2 Samuel the prophet Nathan pays King David a visit. He knows that the king has committed adultery and then killed the husband of the woman he has got pregnant. But instead of confronting David straight out, he tells him a story.

> **Read it yourself:** 2 Samuel 11–12 tells the story of David's adultery with Bathsheba, his murder of Bathsheba's husband Uriah, and the terrible consequences. It's a remarkably raw and honest account of a great hero's shame.

The story is about a rich man who steals a poor man's only lamb to feed a guest. When David hears the story he is furious and he swears that the man should be punished:

> [David] said to Nathan, 'As the LORD lives, the man who has done this deserves to die; he shall restore the lamb fourfold, because he did this thing, and because he had no pity.'
>
> Nathan said to David, 'You are the man! Thus says the LORD, the God of Israel.' (2 Samuel 12:5–7)

It's a stunning moment. David, the great king, is taken completely off guard. He doesn't try to dismiss the tale. He doesn't try to get out of it. He says, 'I have sinned against the LORD' and repents (2 Sam. 12:13). The story changes his life.

But why did Nathan need to tell this story in the first place? Clearly he knows all the details of the crime, so why didn't he just go in and list all of David's misdemeanours? Well, part of it was to lull the king into a false sense of security. Perhaps David's anger over the rich man's behaviour reveals something that David has been hiding from himself – the level of his own shame and hypocrisy. But surely the main reason is . . .

Stories make us feel. They engage the emotions. They *involve* us. Nathan's story made David angry. He experienced the injustice; he empathised with the poor man.

A lot of neuroscientists are very interested in what purpose storytelling serves. Why do we tell so many stories – so many that we even recite them when we sleep in the form of dreams? What they have discovered is that we don't just listen to or read stories: we live them.

In his book *The Shallows*, Nicholas Carr reports on a study carried out at Washington University's Dynamic Cognition Laboratory into the effects of deep reading:

> Researchers used brain scans to examine what happens inside people's heads as they read fiction. They found that 'readers mentally simulate each new situation encountered in a narrative.' Details about actions and sensations are captured from the text and integrated with personal knowledge from past experiences. The brain regions that are activated often 'mirror those involved when people perform, imagine, or observe similar real-world activities.'

Carr sums it up with this profound observation: 'The reader becomes the book.'[6]

When we engage with literature – really engage and immerse ourselves in it – we subconsciously enter the world of the book. The areas of our brains that light up are the same areas that would light up if we were actually doing the activities. It means that we can feel the same things that the characters in the Bible feel. We can act out their lives, albeit via a load of neurons firing away inside our brains.

This, surely, is one of the reasons God gave us this book and these stories. So that we would feel it.

Cognitive psychology professor and novelist Keith Oatley writes:

> In literature we feel the pain of the downtrodden, the anguish of defeat, or the joy of victory, but in a safe space . . . We can refine our human capacities of emotional understanding. We can hone our ability to feel with other people who, in ordinary life, might seem too foreign – or too threatening – to elicit our sympathies. Perhaps, then, when we return to our real lives, we can better understand why people act the way they do.[7]

I think this has profound implications for how we read and teach the Bible. And the immersive nature of story, symbol and metaphor was something that the early church understood only too well. In Romans, Paul writes:

> Do you not know that all of us who have been baptized into Christ Jesus were baptized into his death? Therefore we have been buried with him by baptism into death, so that, just as Christ was raised from the dead by the glory of the Father, so we too might walk in newness of life.
>
> For if we have been united with him in a death like his, we will certainly be united with him in a resurrection like his.
>
> (Romans 6:3–5)

Those listening to this letter as it was read out in Rome would not have had to work hard to imagine themselves in this picture: Rome had a permanent crucifixion site on the Vatican Hill. Not many, if any, of his listeners would have been to Jerusalem, but they could picture themselves on a cross by a Roman roadside and laid in a Roman tomb. And then emerging into the light of dawn.

In later ritual, the early church acted out this identification with Christ in baptism to an even greater degree. The baptismal candidate would disrobe on one side of the pool and go down into the water. After immersion they would be given a new set of clothes and milk and honey to drink. And they were anointed with oil. The Greek word *christos*, from which we get 'Christ', means 'anointed'. They were acting out his story and embedding it in their lives.

Jesus enjoins us to become like children. (It's a metaphor again.) Children don't hold back from stories – at least not from good stories well told. They fling themselves into them. They shout the words, point at the pictures, ask questions and imagine what they themselves would do. I think the Bible invites us to read like children – the most wholehearted readers of us all.

And talking of reading . . .

Stories make us think. Have you ever wondered why the Bible is in the form of a written text? God could have given us all this stuff in a different way. He could have sent an audio cassette. Or a diagram. Or a PowerPoint. Something that would have made things, I don't know, a bit *clearer*. But no, he gave us a load of different books by different authors in different literary styles. Why?

OK. Admittedly, up until the twentieth century, writing was the only technology that could preserve teaching in this way. But even so, God could have done things differently if he'd wanted. If he'd wanted to make everything perfectly clear, he could have cut out all the stories entirely and just left some simple instructions.

However the process happened, we believe that this book is his book. He intended us to have the Bible in this form. He intended, in other words, to mediate a crucial chunk of his communication with human beings through story, song, poetry and parable.

Turns out God is a big fan of literature.

Which means that God must actually want us to think for ourselves.

All literature – all text, in fact – is an invitation to engagement.

Words on a page are never just telling us things. Even the most straightforward of instructions – a recipe, a manual, a legal text – requires something more than just reading it. It requires us to think about it, to use our imagination. We have to engage with it. And this is especially true when we think about things like stories and poetry. When we read these kinds of things, we are not just absorbing words from a page; we are interacting with another person's mind.

Sometimes it is the mind of someone very different to us, someone with whom we don't have much in common, and we don't want to spend any more time with them. Sometimes we encounter characters who are just like us, voices whose words crystallise thoughts we have been struggling to articulate, or whose lives bear an uncanny parallel to our own. Read Ecclesiastes, for example, and you are thrown into the mind of a writer who is questioning everything. For those who think they have got everything sorted, this comes as a bit of a shock, but for those who are struggling with questions of meaning, how wonderful to find someone in the Bible who is just like them!

Read it yourself: Try Ecclesiastes 1–3. It's basically the nearest the Bible comes to a midlife crisis.

Literature is an invitation to connect. To join in and play. Any author is inviting the reader not just to believe in the world of the story, but also to participate in it. At one level we do this through our imagination. With a story or text, no matter how detailed the description, there are always gaps to be filled in. The reader always has to supply the visual information, to conjure up in our mind the action, scenery and characters. More than that, we are invited to go beyond the text, to *wonder* about the text, to ask questions and find answers. Stories and metaphors invite us to engage with them, to explore the text and to hunt out meaning. They even invite us to dwell with mystery and ambiguity.

It's all about using the two key tools at our disposal: curiosity and imagination. Now this is a problem, because a lot of people – and a disproportionate number of us Christians, in my experience – have problems with both these areas. But especially with imagination. Some of us have no effective imagination at all. It's like talking to Drax in *Guardians of the Galaxy*:

ROCKET: His people are completely literal. Metaphors are gonna go over his head.

DRAX: Nothing goes over my head! My reflexes are too fast, I would catch it.[8]

But without our imagination we are going to get into some serious problems with the Bible. This, indeed, is why people get into such a mess with something like Revelation. It's an almost entirely non-literal text, pretty much a solid block of metaphor. At the beginning of the book, John the Elder is on the island of Patmos and he sees Jesus in front of him:

On turning I saw seven golden lampstands, and in the midst of the lampstands I saw one like the Son of Man, clothed with a long robe and with a golden sash across his chest. His head and his hair were white as white wool, white as snow; his eyes were like a flame of fire, his feet were like burnished bronze, refined as in a furnace, and his voice was like the sound of many waters. In his right hand he held seven stars, and from his mouth came a sharp, two-edged sword, and his face was like the sun shining with full force. (Revelation 1:12–16)

'Weird' hardly begins to sum it up. But you can see that when reading this the imagination is not optional. We *have* to use our imagination. We look through John's eyes. We see the blue

Mediterranean sky, the dry, sun-scorched rocks of Patmos, and there he is – a man with a white Afro, burning eyes, metal feet and with an enormous sword sticking out of his mouth. We can see straight away the non-literal nature of this image, because when the Son of Man starts to speak to John immediately following this description, his words are very clear and precise. If someone actually had a sword in their mouth surely the most they could say would be, 'Mmmph, mmmph, gurgle,' and probably, 'Ouch.' So the imagination has no choice but to be fired up.

Once the imagination has done its work, then it's time for curiosity to kick in. Curiosity has also had a bad rap, not just with Christians but generally. It killed the cat, apparently, although I have no idea why curiosity is so toxic to kitties. Still, it does explain why cats have never given us any real insights into life. Anyway, we're sometimes warned against it in church. Don't ask too many questions. Just, don't. Yet the Bible is full of curious people, in both senses of the word. And, as I hope to show you a bit further on in this book, without curiosity, questions and even doubt, we get nowhere.

And the thing is, John wants us to be curious about this image. That's the whole point of writing in this way. He wants us to ask questions and make connections. What does it mean?

Who is the white-haired, sword-tongued bloke in Revelation? Why has Jesus got white hair? Why is he holding those stars? Why is there a sword in his mouth? By asking the questions we move towards the meaning. We know the image is of Jesus, but it links to pictures of God in the Old Testament (notably in Daniel). The whiteness symbolises purity and holiness. He holds seven stars because that symbolises all of the cosmos, the entire solar system. And he has a sword in his mouth because his words have power and authority. They cut to the chase, as it were.

All that can be 'read' in the text. And it shows how this is a *true* picture of Jesus, even though in many ways it's completely unreal. Not to say bonkers.

Now, you might, as you imagine this scene, pick up on more

allusions and meanings. But that's OK. There are many tools we use to interpret a piece of text, and the most important one is the bit between your ears. So if it makes you think, that's great. The Bible is literature, and literature – *good* literature – always wants us to think.

This is why literature (especially poetry) is at home with ambiguity and mystery. It doesn't need to join all the dots. It doesn't even want to. It allows, asks, *insists* that we do some of that work. In *Mimesis,* his great work on the representation of reality in literature, the literary critic Eric Auerbach writes of the Bible:

> Since so much in the story is dark and incomplete, and since the reader knows that God is a hidden God, his effort to interpret it constantly finds something new to feed upon.[9]

That's what the gaps and the mystery do. They always give you something new to feed upon.

The revolutionary act of reading

There's one more reason why stories are so important: **Stories empower us.**

Because of the gaps, the invitation to engagement, because of the requirement for us to use our imagination, literature empowers the reader. This is the difference between literature and film. Most films tells you what to think the whole time. The scene is laid out before you, you don't have to imagine what characters look like: they are there and they look like Tom Hanks. Or Meryl Streep. Or whoever is playing them. Film does your imaginative work for you. Increasingly, you are told what to feel as well: no moment in a film is without its soundtrack, the music making sure that your heartstrings are being twanged in precisely the right way.

Literature doesn't do that. I'm not saying it doesn't try to provoke an emotional response – heaven knows all we saddo writers try to do that. But it is much more limited in what it can do. Even speaking is better at that. When I speak I can use the tone of my voice to tell you how to feel. I can shout; I can whisper. I can choke up in a hammy theatrical way.

But when you read a book or engage with a story, how you respond is ultimately up to you. People will tell you what's there, or why it matters, or how to read it, but you have the power. You can decide how to respond. You can choose what to think about the passage, whether you agree with it or not, whether to clear space for it in your mind, or whether to toss it away never to be thought of again.

To be a reader is to have power over the text.

In the words of Damon Young, literature encourages us to 'do away with deference':

> Another part of me, burgeoning and a little buzzed, was doing away with deference. I realised these dark marks on paper were mine to ignore or investigate, enrich or evade . . . I became aware of myself as something powerful: a reader.[10]

Let's think about that for a moment. Reading gives you power. Reading elevates you, raises you to a level where you can make decisions about what you are reading. At a very basic level, you can decide whether to continue reading a book after the first few pages, or whether to discard it and try something else. Or, should you complete the book or the story or the poem, you can decide whether it was any good, and if so, which parts were good.

Isn't that an amazing thing? The act of reading does more than that. It actually gives dignity and agency to the reader.* I believe this is one of the reasons why we have the Bible: because it gives to us the dignity, the delight, the incomparable honour of being invited to use our brains and think.

---

* To be honest, I've met a few of my readers, and dignity is not the word I would normally associate with them. Just saying.

No wonder dictators and demagogues view it with such suspicion. No wonder so many church leaders and pastors want us to read our Bibles, but not too much and not too deeply. Reading, true reading, is always an act of resistance. And reading the Bible even more so. Reading the Bible calls us to resist easy solutions and simplistic soundbites. It calls us to resist today's world of instant gratification and endless distraction. It calls us to do the most radical acts available to human beings on this earth: to listen to God and to think for ourselves.

It is God who invites us to do this. He wants it this way. And he is prepared to take the risks that come with that, the risks that people will get it wrong, or not engage at all.

Here's the thing: no one except God can know what is going on in your head when you read. And even God is not going to tell you what to think.

Kurt Vonnegut once defined literature as the only art in which the audience plays the score.[11] And that's the same with the Bible. We're not merely invited to listen to the music, we're also invited to join in with the band. The very fact that the Bible is a text, and, above all, the reason why it is a story, means that we are allowed to engage with the text, interrogate it, ask questions, use our own imaginations to fill in the gaps.

The Bible empowers us and gives us liberty to think about it, question it and respond. It does this because it is literature – and that's what literature does – but also because it's in the very nature of God to offer us this choice. Both within the pages of the Bible and in the pages of our real life, God puts himself in our hands. We can reject him or accept him: it's up to us.

This may strike you as presumptuous.

You may be thinking that this is way beyond our pay grade as followers of God.

But God gave us all this information about himself in the form of literature. Because he wants us to work at it. He wants us to engage.

More, he wants to give us a choice.

Yes, but is it true?

Literature comes in many flavours. How we respond to the text – how we play along with it – depends on what tune is being played. The Bible uses lots of different genres of writing – poetry, prose, letters, law, etc. – and we have to identify what kind of writing we're dealing with, because we don't read them all the same way. We read a poem like Song of Solomon very differently from how we read the Gospels, or the letters of Paul.

So a key question to ask yourself about any biblical text is, 'What kind of writing is this?'

This is where the rubber hits the road, as it were. Because a lot of the arguments about the Bible are really arguments about what kind of writing we're dealing with.

Jesus, for example, used a variety of techniques to communicate his message. He used stories or parables, of course, but he also left us pithy sayings and ironic jokes, and even spoke in Jewish apocalyptic language at points. Sometimes we just have narrative about him. Jesus uses a lot of hyperbole – massive overstatement – in order to make a point. But we have to recognise that when he says, 'If your right eye causes you to sin, tear it out and throw it away' (Matt. 5:29), he is not giving a literal instruction.

It's easy to misread a lot of this stuff, and even the sharpest minds have got confused. The great scholar, translator and theologian, Origen of Alexandria (c. 184–c. 253), is one of the most influential figures in Christian theology and biblical studies. 'Origen stands out as a giant among the early Christian thinkers,' wrote Henry Chadwick,[12] but there were times when his thinking was a bit more confused. When he was young, he read Jesus' apparent commendation of 'eunuchs who have made themselves eunuchs for the sake of the kingdom of heaven' (Matt. 19:12) and duly castrated himself. Later in life, perhaps as a result of this important, not to say painful, life lesson, he took a less-literal approach to the Bible. Of Genesis, for example, he wrote, 'Who is so silly as to believe that God, after the manner of a farmer, planted a paradise eastward of Eden, and set in it a visible and palpable tree of life, of such a sort that anyone who tasted its fruit with his bodily teeth would gain life?'[13]

Origen thought Genesis was true. But he didn't believe it actually happened. Today, when there are huge arguments about the historicity of certain parts of the Bible, we would do well to remember that a great many believers through history have read the Bible stories in different ways. And the key to this, in my opinion, is to recognise the nature and role of stories.

The historicity of the Bible is one of those key cognitive dissonance issues that face so many readers of the Bible today. People ask, 'Did it actually happen?' and, 'Is it really true?'

What I would want to say is that these are not the same question. The first thing to establish is that good stories are always true. But they don't need to have happened.

Let's go back for a moment to Nathan's story-bombing of King David. Actually, when you look at the passage it's a story about a man telling a story. And let's be clear, Nathan made the story up: *the event he relates to David never happened*. When Nathan says to David, 'You are the man!' he doesn't mean that David, let alone any other rich bloke, actually stole some poor bloke's sheep and barbecued it. It's an extended metaphor. Nathan is using a made-up story to make a point and provoke a response. And boy, does it work.

This is an absolutely crucial point about the Bible. The truth of a metaphor – whether it is carried as a saying, a poem or a story – is not dependent upon the fact that it literally happened. Metaphors and stories do not have to be literally true. But all of them *say* something true.

We accept this readily in other areas of our lives. Let's take the story of Chicken Licken.

An acorn falls on the head of a young chick. The chick believes that the sky is falling and decides to tell the king. On his journey to the seat of power, he meets other animals – such as Ducky

Lucky and Turkey Lurkey and Goosey Loosey. All, you will note, edible fowl. Anyway, Chicken Licken tells each of them, 'The sky is falling!' They immediately fall into a similar panic and join him on his journey. The story has various endings, but the most common is that they meet a fox who invites them to his home to tell him more about it. Then eats them all.

Now, let's be quite clear. Chicken Licken is not real. But it is true.

It's a story about mass hysteria and the danger of believing everything that you are told. (I should really write a modern version where Chicken Licken says to all the animals, 'The sky is falling' and then points them to various stories on social media to confirm this.)

All good stories have something to teach us. In the words of the critic Walter Benjamin, 'the storyteller is a man who has counsel for his readers'.[14] I like that old word 'counsel'. Good fictional stories have wisdom in them. They are saying something true. But they are still fiction.

The fact is that not everything in the Bible actually happened. This, it seems to me, is really important in this day and age where there is so much argument about the historicity of the biblical text. People get very exercised about whether or not there was an Adam and an Eve and whether it happened in six days. Leaving aside the fact that Genesis is not a scientific report (and reading it as such actually creates more problems), the first question to ask is, 'What is this story telling me? What "counsel" does it contain? Never mind whether it happened or not – is the idea that God created the world and thought it good actually true?'

I would argue that Genesis 1–3 is absolutely true. I don't, however, think the world was created in the way that it describes. But the story is true.

Perhaps we can see this at work more clearly if we look at two more famous stories of the Bible: those of Jonah and Samson.

The case of the runaway prophet

Jonah is a prophet in Israel. One day he gets a message from God to go and tell the people of Nineveh to repent. Nineveh is the capital of the Assyrian Empire – the fiercest, most brutal empire on earth. So Jonah runs away. He goes in the opposite direction, towards the Mediterranean coast where he boards a ship for Tarshish.*

> **Read it yourself:** You can find Jonah's story in, unsurprisingly, the book of Jonah. It's only four chapters long, so you might as well read the whole thing.

The story is packed with humour – much of it ironic. Jonah is the chosen prophet, but the pagan, foreign sailors fear God more than he does. In the belly of the fish (it's not a whale), Jonah recites a psalm full of traditional piety and focusing almost exclusively on the Temple in Jerusalem. At the end of it, the fish vomits Jonah onto dry land, with the clear implication that the psalm has made him physically sick. When the Ninevites hear Jonah's message they repent almost immediately. And Jonah is disgusted:

> But this was very displeasing to Jonah, and he became angry. He prayed to the LORD and said, 'O LORD! Is not this what I said while I was still in my own country? That is why I fled to Tarshish at the beginning; for I knew that you are a gracious God and merciful, slow to anger, and abounding in steadfast love, and ready to relent from punishing.'　　　　　(Jonah 4:1–2)

Jonah doesn't want the Ninevites to be saved. But God cares about these confused people (not to mention their animals):

* Although this is usually rendered as a place name, the Hebrew word really means 'open sea'.

'And should I not be concerned about Nineveh, that great city, in which there are more than a hundred and twenty thousand people who do not know their right hand from their left, and also many animals?' (Jonah 4:11)

Jonah is a story about a God who is far greater than the lead character – or Israel – ever imagined. It's about how God loves even Israel's sworn enemies, and how sometimes bad theology can make us run in the wrong direction. God, apparently, cares for all the confused, lost, misguided people in the world, 'and also many animals'.

That is the great truth of Jonah. And it's a truth that, to my mind, does not change whether you believe that Jonah is fact or fiction. Jonah is true: whether it's real or not is up to you.

Some people cannot think this way. A friend of mine went to Bible college to train for the ministry. This was a very traditional, evangelical Bible college, not some hotbed of liberal theology. Anyway, his class had not long started their studies of the Old Testament when their tremendously aged and highly respected tutor suggested that Jonah wasn't actually a documentary news report. It was, in fact, a story. The young, keen students were outraged. They had meetings with the principal demanding that the tutor be thrown off the course. They even formed a protest group called Friends of the Fish. By the end of the course, however, not only was the tremendously aged and highly respected tutor still in post, but many of the students were also entirely of his opinion. They were still friends of the fish, just in a different way.

The case of the very weak strongman

Let's look at another example: the story of Samson. Samson is a story about the world's first superman. As long as he obeys the Lord's instructions he has superhuman strength. But every super-hero has a weakness, and Samson's kryptonite is women. Foreign women, specifically. One by one, Samson stops following the instructions and spends more and more time dallying with the Delilahs. Finally he is grabbed by the Philistines. Which is extremely painful, as anyone who has ever had their Philistines grabbed can tell you.

> **Read it yourself:** It's in Judges 13–16. It's a brilliant story of sex, violence, sultry women and hairy men, and how our hero moves from God's superman to the world's first suicide bomber.

On one level we can read this as simply a story, a wild, epic roller coaster of a folk tale, with comedy and tragedy in about equal measure. But it can also be read in many other ways. It's a warning against compromise – Samson has rules which will keep him strong, and one by one he breaks them. Or we could read it as a psychological tale: the recognition that people can be irresistibly drawn to the very thing that will harm them. You could read it as a character study: Samson is the archetypal man-child – an enormous and enormously strong man who never really grows up. Or as the tragedy of someone who never finds true peace. There is a heart-breaking moment in the narrative when Delilah lets 'him fall asleep on her lap' (Judg. 16:19), and it is in that very moment of childlike purity and apparent safety that he is betrayed.

Significantly, we can also read it as a kind of history of Israel. Like Samson, they had instructions they were supposed to obey, but they didn't. Like Samson, they couldn't resist the lure of foreign women – whether in the form of gods like Asherah or in actual physical form (more on that later). Like Samson, they compromised and compromised until they were captured and enslaved. And, like Samson, how vehemently must those in captivity in Babylon have prayed for one last dose of divine strength to bring the whole city crashing down. Read the text and you will find your own meaning and resonance.

The important thing is to read Samson as a story, first and foremost, as a literary creation. That doesn't necessarily mean that it didn't happen, but even a cursory reading of the story will reveal how much it has been shaped and crafted. The literary nature of Samson is pretty obvious. It uses many different literary features: riddles and repetition, last-minute escapes and broad, almost slapstick humour. It features puns (the Bible loves a good pun): at one point, Samson kills thousands of Philistines with the jawbone of a donkey. He crows:

> With the jawbone of a donkey,
>   heaps upon heaps,
> With the jawbone of a donkey
>   I have slain a thousand men.   (Judges 15:16)

Samson is making a pun, between *hamor* 'donkey' and *hamar* 'to heap'. And just to add more wordplay in, the battle takes place at a place called Lehi, which comes from the Hebrew word *lechi*, meaning, 'jawbone' (Judg. 15:14)

Samson, like Jonah, is another of those stories that seems more like legend or folk tale than historical account. Could one man kill so many Philistines with a bit of bone? Why does he allow himself to be tricked by Delilah not once, not twice, but three times?

I'm not against reading it as history – indeed, I think it might have some interesting stuff to tell us about life on the borders of Israel and Philistia during that period. But ultimately, reading it as history will only keep the questions piling up. Far more satisfying, I think, is to read it as story. That allows us to park the debate about the historical details. In one sense, none of that matters here.

Did it really happen? I don't know. Is it true? Oh, absolutely.

Thinking again about the story

Stories are transformational. Stories make us feel and think. Stories empower us. When we think about the Bible as story, that has implications for our part in reading and listening to it. We have to let the Bible be what it is – story, poem, letter, prophecy, whatever. We can try to make something literal when it clearly isn't, but the Bible has a way of undermining those kinds of things.

I'm not saying the debates about historicity and reality aren't important – although I think it rather depends which events we are talking about – what I'm saying is that we can easily let these things get in the way of the truth of the story.

So maybe if that is a problem for you, you could put aside the question of whether it really happened and, as you read the Bible, ask yourself, 'Is this true? What is the story about? What counsel has this storyteller got for me?'

Participate in the story. That's why this story is there. Ask questions. Use your curiosity.

And feel free to use your imagination. The Bible is not simply saying, 'Here is a story,' but 'Here is your story.' Put yourself in the place of characters in the story. Who would you be? How would you react?

One of my favourite ways of doing this is to answer the questions in the text. For example, in Genesis 3, when God looks for the shame-faced, scared Adam and Eve, he asks, 'Where are you?' It's a simple enough question, but how would you answer God if he were to ask the same of you? Where are you hiding at the moment?

Or when the two disciples of John the Baptist start following Jesus, he turns and asks them perhaps the most important question we face as human beings: 'What are you looking for?' (John 1:38). A reader could spend their life answering that one.

Perhaps it's not that kind of text. Maybe it's a narrative passage. Imagine yourself in the action, looking on, or even participating.

And look out for the characters who are on the fringes of the story. Look for the victims, the there-but-barely-mentioned; the servants, the slaves, the women, the children, the ones who are often in the story but never get a look in. Where are they? What is happening to them?

Using our imagination to visualise Scripture or to place ourselves in the story is nothing new. It forms the core of the spiritual exercises of St Ignatius, for example. But the act of imagination can bring to life the most complicated or unpromising text.

At one point in the 1990s, the Colombian Ministry of Culture used to take library books to remote communities. They would find a village elder and leave a bag of books with him. The books were always handed back, except for one village which refused to return a Spanish translation of Homer's *Iliad*. When asked why they wanted to keep hold of it, they replied that Homer was telling their story: 'It told of a war-torn country in which mad gods wilfully decide the fate of humans who never know exactly what the fighting is all about, or when they will be killed.'[15]

When we find a text that is truly, unmistakably *us*, it becomes something precious, something to hold on to.

We can find ourselves in the oddest places in the strange new land of the Bible. I remember once I had to preach on Judges 19. It's a particularly charming story of a Levite and his concubine. They have some kind of tiff and she leaves him and goes back to her father. He goes to retrieve her and eventually she agrees to return with him. Anyway, on the way back they take shelter in the house of a man living among the tribe of Benjamin. That night, some townspeople come to the man's house and demand that he send the Levite out so that they can have sex with him. The homeowner is shocked. He offers his daughter to them instead, but they refuse. In the end the Levite throws his concubine out and they assault her. In the morning, the Levite finds her at the door. He says to her, 'Get up! We have to go.' But she is dead.

It's a terrible story. (And it gets worse after that.) And preaching on it was a challenge, to say the least. But two things unlocked it for me. One was a newspaper article about the systematic use of rape and violence against women in the Democratic Republic of Congo. Militants in that area fight for control of the mines where they find minerals used in the manufacture of mobile phones and other household devices. The other was to ask myself that question, 'Who am I in this story?' Not the victim, that's for sure. No, I realised I was the Levite. Or the householder. The one who was prepared to throw someone outside so that I could stay safe. I was the one who will throw the girl out so that I can have my mobile phone and my laptop. So I invited a friend of mine who had recently been in the Congo to come and tell the stories of the women he had met, and we looked at what we could do as a group of Christians to help.

It was a shock to hear this passage challenge me so clearly. But that is how it works. When we ask the Bible to show us who we are, we find out things that we might rather not know.

'Invention is finding. Forming is discovery,' wrote Martin Buber.*[16] I think we should have confidence to use our imagination, let God draw us deeper into the story and find our place within.

The key thing is to respond to the text. That's another reason why I personally prefer a paper version of the Bible: I am an inveterate underliner, annotator and general note-scribbler in books. I love to mark up the text, to add ticks (for bits I agree with), stars (for bits I really want to remember), question marks (for bits I don't understand) and even rude words (for bits I really don't agree with) in the margins of books. It's a way of really engaging with the text, responding to it. And I do the same with the Bible (only without the rude words). For me, it's all about being a responsive reader. It's a physical, engaged way to respond and interact with the text.

---

* Martin Buber is not to be confused with Michael Bublé. Martin Buber's Christmas album is a very different production.

The Bible is literature, and for us fans of books and the written word that's a brilliant thing. But not everyone is wired that way. One of the problems with dealing with all these words is that we tend to respond only with words. But you don't have to. We can respond to Scripture in painting, photography, calligraphy, textiles. I have a friend who is drawing her way through the Bible. She is filling her sketchbooks with pictures inspired by the text. You could go and make something for someone. You could cook a scriptural meal: try holding your own last supper, for instance. In the Bible itself there are lots of occasions when people respond to God with actions rather than words. The prophets, for example, often resemble performance artists more than preachers. I mean, look at some of the things that Ezekiel did: he laid on his left side for 390 days and on his right side for forty days, he cut his hair off and weighed it, and he laid siege to a brick.

Read it yourself: It's in Ezekiel 4–5. The man was committed to his art. Just saying.

I'm not saying you should do that, but feel free. The point is that we don't always have to use words. We can respond to Scripture in painting, photography, calligraphy, textiles. You could go and make something for someone. You could cook a scriptural meal: try holding your own Last Supper, for instance.

Perhaps you will want to share your responses to Scripture with others. Remember that they are your responses, they don't have to be explained. The Church often has a problem with art because, like story, art doesn't necessarily provide answers. It's much more interested in the questions. It embraces ambiguity and hiddenness. It means different things to different people. In a culture that is slightly obsessed with people coming to the doctrinally correct conclusions, art doesn't do that. At least, good art doesn't. Art leaves the door ajar for individual interpretation.

You can explore the art of others as well. One of the things that has helped me the most in my recent spiritual journey has been the work of artists like Stanley Spencer, Marc Chagall and others. Their responses to Scripture have helped me to enter into the texts in a new way and to see new things.

The Bible wants our attention.

The great historian of reading, Alberto Manguel, says:

> The existence of the text is a silent existence, silent until the moment in which a reader reads it. Only when the eye makes contact with the markings on the tablet does the text come to active life. All writing depends on the generosity of the reader.[17]

God has given us a wonderful, and slightly awe-inspiring, task. He has given us this book of stories, this wonderful treasure-house of metaphor and tale.

And he calls us to collaborate with him, to read and respond, with prayer, with our own thoughts, and in the presence of the Holy Spirit.

And who knows how the text will come to life?

5 The not-so-good book

Imagine you're at a family gathering. Christmas, maybe. Everything is lovely and sparkly and tinselly. Carols are being played in the background, the children are overdosing on profiteroles, your mother is berating you for not phoning more often and various distant cousins are trying to remember how, exactly, they are related to you. And there, sitting quietly in the corner, sipping her sherry, is Auntie Elsie. Ninety-four if she's a day.

She is, it is generally agreed, 'past it'. But you do your duty and start a conversation. And somehow it gets around to her life and times and you say, 'So, Auntie Elsie, what did you do in the war?'

And this sweet little, sherry-sipping old lady, turns to you and says, 'Oh not much dear. I was parachuted behind enemy lines and killed four of those Nazi b****rs with my bare hands.' She then spits on the floor, drains her sherry in one gulp and smashes the glass in the fireplace.

I guess your view of Auntie Elsie would change slightly. I guess you would think there was more to Auntie Elsie than you had previously imagined.

Now I don't have an Auntie Elsie like that (although I would really like one), but that is exactly how people view the Bible. To them, the Bible is an antiquated, genteel book, which sits quietly on the shelf gently gathering dust. It contains some lovely language and some beautiful stories. But there's nothing shocking about it at all.

'But that,' as Auntie Elsie would say, 'is complete and utter b . . .'

Jesus was not a redhead and Samson was not visiting his landlady

We constantly make the mistake of thinking that the people in the Bible are the same as us. Countless sermons and talks give the impression that characters in the Bible are really just like us, only with loincloths and more sheep. We picture people like Jacob, Daniel and Ezekiel as kind of proto-Christians who would happily have gone to church if there had been one around at the time. I've even heard talks that describe David as a 'worship leader'.

In some ways we can't help it. We have been programmed this way.

My first Bible was *The Children's Bible*, published by Paul Hamlyn. It was a wonderfully hefty volume, bound in Mediterranean blue and illustrated with lush paintings. One of the things that most influenced me, looking back, was that all the characters in it were basically white men in wigs. And Jesus was the whitest of them all. In fact, he was not only extremely pale for a first-century Jewish guy, but he had kind of gingery-blonde hair. He looked like a hippy. It looked as though he and the disciples spent a lot of money on hair products.

But Jesus was not like that. For a start, the average height of a Mediterranean peasant was around five feet two inches. So we should imagine a short man, by our standards, definitely dark-skinned and probably brown-eyed, with black hair. The kind of man who, in our world, gets stopped at every airport security check.

And he was Jewish, of course.

We only know two things about Jesus' appearance for sure: he was circumcised (Luke 2:21) and he wore a Jewish prayer shawl (Mark 6:56; Luke 8:44). The Jewishness of Jesus is crucial for so many reasons, but not least because most Western art (including my *Children's Bible*) has tried very hard to play this down. If you look at a lot of Renaissance paintings, for example, Jesus is often much paler and more Western-looking than the people who are abusing him. It was a feature of art from the Middle Ages onwards to depict Judas with caricatured Jewish features, which culminated in Nazi propaganda always depicting Judas as a hideous Jewish stereotype.

The Bible doesn't really go in for physical descriptions much, apart from when people are freakishly large, or curiously small, or when they have some kind of disease or disfigurement. And that's a good thing in some ways. The lack of a physical description of Jesus means that every culture can picture the Son of God as one of them. It makes it easier for us to identify not only with Jesus but also with the other characters in the Bible. Identification is one thing; assimilation is another.

And in some ways the people in the Bible *are* very like us. They have the same passions and desires. They laugh, cry, sweat, eat, have sex, go to the toilet, play music, make art. They face the same basic issues about life, death and everything else in between. They have moral conflicts, ambitions, hatreds and desires. They can be heroic and cowardly. Sometimes you look at a story in the Bible and you can imagine that self-same tale being played out in the houses down the street.

But in other ways their cultures and their times are completely alien. Their behaviour and their beliefs are radically different from ours. Take, for example, this little incident, when Abraham calls his oldest, most faithful servant and makes him take an oath:

> Abraham said to his servant, the oldest of his house, who had charge of all that he had, 'Put your hand under my thigh and I will make you swear by the LORD, the God of heaven and earth, that you will not get a wife for my son from the daughters of the Canaanites, among whom I live, but will go to my country and to my kindred and get a wife for my son Isaac.'
>
> (Genesis 24:2–4)

To which his servant no doubt replied, 'I promise, but can we do it without the thigh thing.' What's happening here? Well, in the words of the *Word Biblical Commentary*, 'By putting his hand under Abraham's thigh, the servant was touching his genitals and thus giving the oath a special solemnity.'[1] Absolutely. Although I have to warn you, if you try this the next time you sign a contract you might get some very strange looks. Not to mention a lawsuit. On another occasion, Abraham makes a covenant with God and the covenant is sealed by smoking pot. Sorry, a smoking pot. Basically, Abraham cuts a load of animals into pieces, and then:

> When the sun had gone down and it was dark, a smoking fire-pot and a flaming torch passed between these pieces.
>
> (Genesis 15:17)

(In between, Abraham falls into 'a deep sleep . . . and a deep and terrifying darkness descended upon him' (Gen. 15:12). You have to admit, it does sound terribly druggie.) Anyway, the cut-up animals and the flaming torch appear to be ancient, deeply symbolic ways of signifying a covenant.

Sometimes you read the Bible and you realise that these people are just plain *weird*, and I'm not just talking about their unorthodox way of signing a contract. They are in a world where it's OK to have lots of wives. (In Solomon's case, wives on what can only be called an industrial scale.) We're in a world where thousands and thousands of animals are sacrificed at altars every day. We're in a world that believes the world is flat and the sky is a dome with water above it. And we're in a world where everything is a lot more basic, more down to earth in every way. More brutal, even.

Back to the *Children's Bible*. Some of those paintings have stayed with me, haunted me. The paintings I *really* remember are the gory ones. The picture of Absalom, David's son, hanging in mid-air, his head caught in the branches of a tree. Samson, blinded and white-eyed, with a hairstyle just long enough to give him the strength to topple the pillars and bring the temple crashing down on his captors. And the unnamed woman on the ramparts of Thebez, dropping a millstone on the head of Abimelech.

Yes, those are the kind of illustrations that a six-year-old boy tends to enjoy.

I can't imagine that these stories would make it into a children's Bible today. But they illustrate the fact that great chunks of the Bible are deeply unsuitable for children. The Bible may be a story. But it's not a fairy story. The Bible contains rape and incest, murder, treachery, loss, grief, theft, deceit, greed, brutality and . . . well, you get the idea. It's not a flannel-graph-friendly book of fairy tales.* If you're going to talk about the Bible with children, it pays to be very, very selective.

When it comes to presenting the Bible to children, people will go to some lengths to obtain a U rating. In one of Samson's adventures he steals the gates of Gaza and takes them to Hebron, an act that is roughly equivalent to a man carrying three grand pianos thirty-seven miles. But what was Samson doing in Gaza? He was visiting a prostitute. It's not the kind of activity you associate with heroes of the faith. In 1883, the American Sunday School Union decided to clean things up a bit. In their retelling of the story, they said, 'Samson fearlessly went to the Philistine stronghold and took up lodgings for the night.'† Yes, Samson was only taking up 'lodgings'. And that lady with the low-cut dress and too much make-up was his 'landlady'. And that money he's giving her is 'the rent'.

---

* My editor, who is, like a depressingly large number of people, much younger than me, has asked me to explain this. Really, even for those of us raised in Sunday School in the sixties and seventies, flannel-graph is beyond explanation. It involved sticking fabric pictures onto a fabric background. It was the nearest thing we had to videos. Kind of a felt PowerPoint. Oh, just Google it, for heaven's sake.

† This comes from the *American Sunday School Union Biographical Dictionary* of 1883.

And that's OK, because we're *always* selective about the stories we tell our children. (Apart, obviously, from my parents, who clearly thought that a great big blue book full of pictures of people murdering each other was perfect bedtime reading.) But too much re-editing can lead to us missing out significant parts of the stories. The story of David and Goliath becomes a kind of 'Jack the Giant Killer' fairy tale.* We present a Disneyfied version, in which the bit at the end where David takes Goliath's sword and chops the fallen Philistine's head off is hastily skipped over.

Or take the story of Noah and his ark. It's presented as a cheerful tale of a man with all his animals – Noah and his floating zoo. It kind of glosses over the fact that the rest of the population are being drowned all around him. As one who has written children's books featuring biblical stories, I've been part of a process of sanitisation, and, as I say, that's perfectly OK. We don't want to traumatise children. But neither do we want to stay in the children's play area all our life.

The case of the missing inn

The Bible demands our attention. And once you really start attending to the text you begin to notice what is and isn't there.

One of the ways in which we try to get the Bible to behave is to make it conform to our version of the story. If a version of the story is presented in a sanitised, fairy-tale way for long enough, then it is very hard not to see it through that lens. It's hard to leave behind all the things we have been told are in the text, to take off the glasses of our own tradition and really look, simply and unsparingly, at what the text actually says.

Few stories have been more thoroughly Disneyfied, more subtly amended, than the Christmas story. The story, as presented in

* Actually, if it were to be presented as a real fairy tale, that would be OK. Some of those are very violent.

umpteen thousand Christmas cards, nativity plays and Christmas carols features Mary and Joseph on a donkey travelling to Bethlehem where a series of hard-hearted innkeepers inform them that there is no room. Eventually they find a place in a stable, where Jesus is born. They lay him in the manger. A little after the birth some shepherds visit him, along with three-kings-from-Orient-are and possibly a Little Drummer Boy. The little Lord Jesus no crying he makes, the cattle are lowing, and the main characters' heads are illuminated by golden halos.

It's a long way from what the Bible actually says.

There's no mention in the text of hard-hearted innkeepers turning Mary and Joseph away. There's not even an inn: the word that is usually translated as 'inn' is the Greek word *kataluma*, which more usually means 'spare room', or even 'upper room'. If Joseph's family home is in Bethlehem, then why would he need to use an inn? There's no stable either. Jesus is laid in a manger, true, but often the manger for the animals would be in the heart of a peasant home. Jesus doesn't get a visit from three kings: the Bible talks of an unidentified number of 'magi' – a kind of a mix of astrologers, priests and scientists. We only assume there were three because of the three gifts. If you don't believe me, go back and read the story again.*

It's so difficult to talk about this kind of stuff without being accused of taking the magic out of Christmas. But the alternative is to perpetuate a thoroughly sanitised and, indeed, depoliticised version of the story. In Luke's Gospel the story is about the Son of God arriving as a peasant. Mary's song (Luke 1:46–55) is one of the most political statements in the Bible: God has sent the rich packing and given all the goodies to the poor. Jesus is not rejected by his community; he is welcomed into the very heart of a peasant home.

---

* Read it in the latest version of the NIV, which says that Mary 'wrapped him in cloths and placed him in a manger, because there was no guest room available for them' (Luke 2:7).

Yet so many versions of the story, whether in art, literature or song, seek to emphasise the 'otherness' of Christ, like all those terrible Renaissance paintings which show him as basically a very tiny old man with a supernaturally glowing bonce. The story of Christmas is not about his otherness, but his very humanity. It's a story of stars, shepherds, shit, straw and salvation: and they are all wrapped up together.

The very ordinariness of the Bible became a real problem for the Church once it became officially recognised by the Roman Empire in the fourth century. As the ideas of Christianity spread into the Greco-Roman world, the subject matter of the Bible became something of a problem. Christians from a more sophisticated, educated background found the earthy subject matter of the Bible too much to deal with. One of their coping strategies was to read the whole thing as an allegory. This helped them cope with books like Song of Solomon, which is much more 'spiritual' if we read it as an allegory of God's love for the Church. As opposed to being much more fun if we read it as a poem about sex.

Even the way the Bible is written has upset those of a sensitive or more-refined nature. Or even those not of a sensitive and refined nature, come to that. The fourth-century scholar Jerome was not exactly a model of refinement, but even he found the writing style of the Bible 'rude and repellent'.[2] That's because the Bible was written in the language of ordinary people. The Greek in the New Testament is what has become known as *koiné*, or common Greek. It has a rough-and-ready style, and was the style of Greek spoken by merchants and workmen.

For instance, Revelation, I am reliably informed, is full of grammatical errors. It was written by someone with Greek as their second language. But I've never seen a translation of Revelation with those errors left in. It would be wonderful if a translation came out one day that actually caught the style of the original, even if that style was full of mistakes.

Not much of this comes through, though. Translators and

translation committees do their own version of the American Sunday School Union. Particularly when it comes to the rude bits.

David and his vessels

The King James Version of the Bible has a number of issues as a translation, but it's the go-to version for anyone who wants to explore the more earthy parts of the Bible. The early seventeenth century was not an age that was prudish about bodily functions. Which is a good thing, because it allows us to see a side of David that is normally hidden.

In 1 Samuel, David is refused hospitality by Nabal, but Nabal's wife Abigail wisely offers supplies to David and his troops. David says to her:

> 'For as surely as the LORD the God of Israel lives, who has restrained me from hurting you, unless you had hurried and come to meet me, truly by morning there would not have been left to Nabal so much as one male.' (1 Samuel 25:34)

Only he doesn't say 'male'. The KJV captures the actual phrase:

> '. . . except thou hadst hasted and come to meet me, surely there had not been left unto Nabal by the morning light any that pisseth against the wall.' (1 Samuel 25:34 KJV)*

Those 'that pisseth against the wall' means 'men'. I suppose it could mean exceptionally athletic women, but it's unlikely. All the modern translations translate it either as 'men' or 'male'. But that's *not* what the Bible says.

David was a soldier and leader, in this instance, of a band of guerrillas, and this is a soldierly threat: it occurs at other points

---

* The Hebrew word is *shātan*, which means 'to urinate'.

in the Bible, all in a military context. Anyone who pisses standing up will be killed. It's like something from a gangster movie – and that is what David was at this time: he was a soldier operating outside the law.*

The clean-up takes all the character out of the passage. It makes David speak more like a bureaucrat than a guerrilla warrior. But because the translators don't want to upset *us*, they emasculate David. They want him to be more polite, to wash his mouth out, to make him fit in. This is the Holy Bible. We can't have any rudeness, can we?

Once again, the problem is more us than the Bible. We think that the man who wrote all those psalms must have been a pretty perfect human being.† I mean, yes, there was the unfortunate lapse with Bathsheba, when he arranged the murder of her husband (2 Sam. 11–12). And the bit where he allows the execution of seven of Saul's children and grandchildren in what looks uncomfortably like an act of human sacrifice (2 Sam. 21:1–14). And the bit where he actually fights alongside the Philistines (1 Sam. 27:1–12). And the bit where he refuses to punish, or even rebuke, his favourite son Amnon for raping his half-sister Tamar (2 Sam. 13).

But apart from that, he was *almost* a Christian.

But here's the thing: the people in the Bible were not polite. Just the opposite at times. In the prophets, abuse, exaggeration and even obscenity are perfectly acceptable modes of discourse.

They use a lot of irony and sarcasm and even bawdy humour. In 1 Kings, for example, Elijah has an epic battle with the prophets of Baal. They spend hours chanting, dancing, even cutting themselves in order to invoke fire from their God. As their efforts prove fruitless, Elijah tells them to call louder. Maybe he's 'preoccupied or he is busy, or he has gone on a journey; perhaps he is asleep

---

* The New Jerusalem Bible makes an effort by translating it as not 'a single manjack' (1 Samuel 25:34). 'Manjack' was probably quite a strong word in 1925. Sadly the NJB was published in 1985. Still, at least they tried.

† On the authorship of the psalms, see above p. 54.

and needs to be woken up!' (1 Kgs 18:27).* Many Jewish scholars believe that the phrase translated 'gone on a journey' actually means 'on the toilet'.

> **Read it yourself:** The encounter is in 1 Kings 18. But read chapters 18 and 19 because then you get not only Elijah versus the Baal-boys, but also his encounter with God in the wilderness and the calling of Elisha. Not to mention some rather thought-provoking stuff about a guy called Jehu which might come in handy later.

The prophets don't moderate their language. People are not just accused of making mistakes, or failing to live up to an ideal, or even simply worshipping false gods; they are also accused of adultery, murder and cannibalism:

And I said:
Listen, you heads of Jacob
    and rulers of the house of Israel!
Should you not know justice? –
    you who hate the good and love the evil,
who tear the skin off my people,
    and the flesh off their bones;
who eat the flesh of my people,
    flay their skin off them,
break their bones in pieces,
    and chop them up like meat in a kettle,
    like flesh in a cauldron.   (Micah 3:1–3)

Robert Carroll talks of the 'rant factor' in the works of the

* This is from the New Jerusalem Bible translation.

prophets, and says, 'A reading of the Hebrew Bible . . . will reveal a world of rhetorical abuse unlike anything else in world literature.'[3] The high points of this – or low points, depending on your point of view – are surely to be found in Ezekiel, in those passages that are always worth looking up during a boring sermon.

> **Read it yourself:** The two rudest bits of Ezekiel are in chapters 16 and 23. But you could dip into the intervening chapters a bit to see more ways in which the prophet represents God's outrage, especially chapter 17, which contains an early parable, or chapter 19, which is a poem of lament over the fate of Judah's kings.

Ezekiel is addressing a political situation, really. The most notorious chapters are Ezekiel 16 and Ezekiel 23. In these, the history of Judah is told in graphic terms:

Thus says the Lord GOD to Jerusalem: Your origin and your birth were in the land of the Canaanites; your father was an Amorite, and your mother a Hittite. As for your birth, on the day you were born your navel cord was not cut, nor were you washed with water to cleanse you, nor rubbed with salt, nor wrapped in cloths. No eye pitied you, to do any of these things for you out of compassion for you; but you were thrown out in the open field, for you were abhorred on the day you were born.

I passed by you, and saw you flailing about in your blood. As you lay in your blood, I said to you, 'Live! and grow up like a plant of the field.' You grew up and became tall and arrived at full womanhood; your breasts were formed, and your hair had grown; yet you were naked and bare.

I passed by you again and looked on you; you were at the age

for love. I spread the edge of my cloak over you, and covered
your nakedness: I pledged myself to you and entered into a
covenant with you, says the Lord GOD, and you became mine.
(Ezekiel 16:3–8)

That's a pretty startling image: the baby Judah lying 'flailing
about in . . . blood' and growing up under the Lord's care
into a beautiful woman. Sadly, she goes a bit downhill after
that.

Your fame spread among the nations on account of your beauty,
for it was perfect because of my splendour that I had bestowed
on you, says the Lord GOD.

But you trusted in your beauty, and played the whore because
of your fame, and lavished your whorings on any passer-by.
(Ezekiel 16:14–15)

In particular, Judah favours Egypt: 'You played the whore with
the Egyptians, your lustful neighbours, multiplying your whoring,
to provoke me to anger,' says Ezekiel (16:26).

The image is echoed in chapter 23, only this time there are
two sisters, representing Samaria and Jerusalem:

The word of the LORD came to me: Mortal, there were two women,
the daughters of one mother; they played the whore in Egypt;
they played the whore in their youth; their breasts were caressed
there, and their virgin bosoms were fondled.   (Ezekiel 23:1–3)

There's a lot of fondling here, first Samaria with the Assyrians,
then Jerusalem with the Babylonians. Finally, Ezekiel lays into
the remnant left in Judea, who have been dallying with the
Egyptians:

Yet she increased her whorings, remembering the days of her

125

> youth, when she played the whore in the land of Egypt and lusted
> after her paramours there, whose members were like those of
> donkeys, and whose emission was like that of stallions.
>
> (Ezekiel 23:19–20)

Wait . . . what?

The problem is not that we don't want to hear Ezekiel speak this way; it's that we actually get offended if God speaks like this. Ezekiel represents God's feelings in graphic terms. (I'm not even going to go into what he says will happen to these women.) It is the prophet channelling the passionate, angry, hurt message of God into passionate, angry, hurt language of his own. And even here you can see how the translators have changed it. Instead of letting the Bible misbehave they've smartened it up and put it in a nice suit. The language of the barrack rooms is replaced by that of a biology textbook, the shock of the words softened by Victorian prudishness, and God is sent to the cosmic naughty step until he calms down a bit.

But that's the point. God is *not* calm about this sort of stuff. This is something that matters. God does not want people to feel polite disapproval, but a more visceral disgust.

What can we take from this? Well, the Bible talks about God in all kinds of ways. It refuses to always use holy language. Too many modern translations want the Bible to be politely spoken. But it isn't. It's outrageous at times, determined to shock us, rejecting any pretence of propriety and decorum. Anything to make us sit up and listen.

How Jesus is not allowed to mention toilets

This kind of thing is not limited to the Old Testament either. In one of his most provocative statements, Jesus says that 'whatever goes into a person from outside cannot defile, since it enters, not the heart but the stomach, and goes out into the sewer' (Mark

7:14–19). The Greek word translated as 'sewer' is *aphedron*, which means 'toilet'. The NRSV at least has the word 'sewer', even though the word doesn't mean that. Many English translations are so shocked that Jesus used the word 'toilet' that they leave it out completely. The NIV has, 'For it doesn't go into their heart but into their stomach, and then out of the body' (Mark 7:19); while the ESV has 'since it enters not his heart but his stomach, and is expelled' (Mark 7:19).

Why are we so shocked that Jesus might have actually known what a toilet was? Do we think he was so pure that he didn't actually go? Do we think that the contents of his intestines were miraculously taken away in some heavenly poo bag by a specially designated angel? In the words of John A.T. Robinson, we think that 'He looked like a man, he talked like a man, he felt like a man, but underneath he was God dressed up'.[4] Jesus was a man, and that means that he had all the bodily functions that we do. But no. We mustn't let the Bible be what it is. So we censor it. Even when it comes out of the mouth of Jesus.

Paul is another great example of invective and outrageous language that tends to get softened. In Paul's letter to the Thessalonians he talks about sexual morality, and he wishes 'that each one of you knows how to control your own body in holiness and honour' (1 Thess. 4:4). Seems clear enough. Except the literal Greek doesn't have the word 'body'. It runs something like, 'To know each one of you his own vessel to take in holiness and honour'. The KJV helpfully translates it as, 'That every one of you should know how to possess his vessel in sanctification and honour' (1 Thess. 4:4, KJV)

Which is fairly meaningless. Some translations think that 'vessel' – the Greek word is *skeuos* – means 'wife'. Others, like the NRSV, go for 'body'. But in some Greek writings, 'vessel' is a euphemism for a man's meat and two veg (to use another euphemism). In which case, Paul could be saying something much more earthy. And probably a lot more relevant to the discussion, actually.

And actually, it's also used this way in the Old Testament. In

1 Samuel 21 a priest tells David that he may eat some holy bread only if 'the young men have kept themselves from women'. David replies that 'the vessels of the young men are holy'. (And the truly great thing about this story is that the priest is the Priest of Nob).

But that's Paul for you. He wasn't afraid to call a vessel a vessel.

He is very outspoken at times, and even very funny. In Galatians he wishes that those who were so keen on circumcision would cut the whole lot off: 'I wish those who unsettle you would castrate themselves!' (Gal. 5:12).

In Philippians he is at his most graphic. There is an underlying tone of disappointment and even bitterness in the letter. Paul has been deserted by others. He is tired, old. And this is reflected in the extreme language he uses. He writes, 'Beware of the dogs, beware of the evil workers, beware of those who mutilate the flesh!' (Phil. 3.2). The three Greek nouns – *kunas*, *kakous ergatas*, *katatomen* – all begin with this explosive 'k' sound, as though Paul is spitting the words out. You could maybe translate it as, 'Beware of the mutts, the morally wrong workers, the mutilators.'

And when he talks of his previous righteousness he uses graphic terms:

> More than that, I regard everything as loss because of the surpassing value of knowing Christ Jesus my Lord. For his sake I have suffered the loss of all things, and I regard them as rubbish, in order that I may gain Christ. (Philippians 3:8)

The word translated as 'rubbish' is *skubalon*, which means excrement, manure, trash, even rotting kitchen scraps of the type you throw on the compost bin. What Paul is saying is that everything else is a pile of crap. And he might be referring to the book of Isaiah, where the prophet says, 'We have all become like one who is unclean, and all our righteous deeds are like a filthy cloth' (Isa. 64:6). The Hebrew word translated 'filthy cloth' really means the cloth that women would wear during their period.

Once again, my point is not just to show that there are some rude bits in the Bible. My point is that this is what happens when God's revelation is mediated through human beings. It is revealed not only in the content of their message, but also in the way they write, the metaphors they use, the way they understand the world around them.

Paul is clear that the gospel he proclaims comes from God: 'for I did not receive it from a human source, nor was I taught it, but I received it through a revelation of Jesus Christ' (Gal. 1:12).

It's a divine message, but it comes through a very human filter.

Why the Psalms are true but not right

We retro-fit characters to suit our assumptions about how they should behave, to fit into our ideas of the kind of people of whom God should approve. But the Bible will not conform to our desires. The Bible remains resolutely unshockable, and absolutely unafraid of the bad things that people do and say.

The Bible shows us people as they are, not as how we'd like them to be. Samson slept with prostitutes, Abraham passed his wife off as his sister, Jacob was a blasphemous liar, Joseph was a spoilt brat, Moses disappointed God so badly that he wasn't allowed to enter the Promised Land, and Solomon, as well as building the Temple, ended up worshipping all kinds of other gods and marrying any woman with a pulse. And it's not just in the Old Testament. Peter flip-flopped between eating with Gentiles and not eating with them. Jesus' mother and brothers thought he was mad. And Paul had the temper of a bull hippo with a toothache.

In other words, they were human. Very, *very* human.

The Bible is not afraid of the bad side of human behaviour and the many terrible things that people do to each other – sometimes even in the name of God.

And the Bible is not afraid of the wrong things that people say, either.

The Bible contains a lot of wrong statements about God, because it includes the words of haters and liars, false prophets, enemies of faith and those who are just downright mistaken. It contains statements of hope and beauty, grace and mercy, but also intolerance, xenophobia and downright hatred. It includes the words of people who have given up on life and think everything is meaningless, and the curses of those who have lost everything. There is a lot in the Bible that expresses real, honest feelings.

Perhaps the strongest place where this kind of thing comes out is in the so-called imprecatory psalms – the points when the poet is so lost, so hurt, so angry that he calls down the most violent curses on the heads of his enemies.

We've already encountered one of those in Psalm 137, where the psalmist says:

> O daughter Babylon, you devastator!
>   Happy shall they be who pay you back
>   what you have done to us!
> Happy shall they be who take your little ones
>   and dash them against the rock!   (Psalm 137:8–9)

But there are many other examples.

Read it yourself: Psalm 139 is a very popular psalm. It's a psalm of comfort and intimacy. Oh, and violence.

Take Psalm 139, which contains some beautiful writing. 'O LORD, you have searched me and known me,' it begins. 'You know when I sit down and when I rise up; you discern my thoughts from far away.' The psalmist goes on to show that God is everywhere:

'Where can I go from your spirit?' he asks. 'Or where can I flee from your presence?'

He goes on to explore the mystery of creation ('For it was you who formed my inward parts; you knit me together in my mother's womb) and how human beings are 'fearfully and wonderfully made'. He meditates on how all his days have been planned, and how vast and innumerable are the thoughts of God.

And then there is a *slight* change of mood:

> O that you would kill the wicked, O God,
>   and that the bloodthirsty would depart from me –
> those who speak of you maliciously,
>   and lift themselves up against you for evil!
> Do I not hate those who hate you, O LORD?
>   And do I not loathe those who rise up against you?
> I hate them with perfect hatred;
>   I count them my enemies.

Then, just as suddenly, we're back to the loveliness.

> Search me, O God, and know my heart;
>   test me and know my thoughts.
> See if there is any wicked way in me,
>   and lead me in the way everlasting.

It's like some kind of horror film, when the lovely, sweet little girl suddenly turns into a werewolf. Frankly, if you encountered a poem like this outside the Bible, you'd probably send the author for counselling. Anger-management classes at the very least.

The thing is that the Psalms are not always right. But they are always true. This is how people are. They do not always want the right things or behave in the correct way. If you want pious platitudes then buy one of those calendars with sweet Bible verses and pictures of kittens.

Thinking again about the impolite Bible

The Bible refuses to behave itself by being nice and polite. It contains stories that children should not see and language we would rather they didn't hear. It contains human beings doing and saying wrong things, sometimes deliberately through malice, sometimes inadvertently through stupidity. It contains people pouring out their hearts. But it's absolutely vital that all this stuff is in there, because the Bible is about life, in all its reality.

In the words of Aelred Squire, 'It is of the utmost importance that the Bible is an uncensored book. There is no blasphemy or impurity that does not find its place there, since we have to see the human situation reflected there in its completeness.'[5]

The Bible is not a children's book. It's a record of human interaction with God. Sometimes that is expressed in worship and praise, sometimes in sadness, anger and despair. We have to have the courage to see these stories as they are, and not how we would want them to be.

So how do we see what is actually in the text, rather than what we have been told? Well, at the risk of repeating myself, paying real, close attention to what the text says is fairly crucial – reading it slowly, thinking about what is actually there. And not being afraid to question, to probe, to imagine. But what we're trying to do here, as far as possible, is to come to the text in an entirely fresh way. In the words of Martin Buber:

> The modern person must read the Jewish Bible as though it were something entirely unfamiliar, as though it had not been set before him ready made, as though he has not been confronted all his life with sham concepts and sham statements that cited the Bible as their authority . . . He reads aloud the words written in front of him; he hears the words he utters and it reaches him. Nothing is pre-judged.[6]

This is easier said than done. There are stories and passages that we know almost too well. But there are some ways in which we can at least shake things up a bit and break out of our preconceived ideas.

One of the best ways is simply to read it out loud. When we read silently we miss things. Our brains do some editing work and we tend to skip ahead. But if we read the text out loud, we can't skip anything.

If you don't want to do this yourself, then you could use an audio version of the Bible.* Or you could read it out with others. (I once took part in a reading of Mark's Gospel with a group of young people. We gathered together early, had bacon butties for breakfast halfway through and were finished in a couple of hours. It's a great way to get the feel of the whole story. And I began by telling them not to worry about the names!)

But we might want to go off-piste, as it were. Visit different parts of this strange new world, instead of the usual tourist spots we frequent. So try opening the Bible to a book that you haven't read before, search out stories with which you are not familiar, find the passages that the pastor never preaches on.

Another helpful approach is to try out different Bible translations. People get very hot under the collar about translations, but it is really down to personal preference. Remember, though, translations are not perfect. Translation is always a matter of making choices. Sometimes those choices are easy, sometimes they are hard, sometimes there simply isn't a good choice, because no one knows what the text means, or because the original text is missing. The best thing to do is to go into a bookshop that has a range of Bibles – a Christian bookshop should have such a range – and have a look. Or you can easily find most versions on the web. So you can try them out for yourself.

When I write books like this one I tend to stick to the NRSV,

* It would be remiss of me not to recommend the excellent Hodder Audio Bible.

as that is the standard academic text. The NIV is also a good standard translation. But if I'm reading for my own devotions I prefer the New Jerusalem Bible, which has, I think, the best literary style of all the mainstream versions. I also like using the *Jewish Study Bible*, which comes from a very different perspective. A lot of people like *The Message* as well. But for a more radical translation, I really recommend the translations of the Hebrew Scriptures done by the Jewish literary specialist Robert Alter (especially his brilliant *The Book of Psalms*). You could also try the two translations by Mary Phil Korsak: *At the Start: Genesis Made New*, and *Glad News from Mark*, both of which will help you to read the text in a way that you will not have read it before.

Another interesting approach is to try a Bible that is organised differently. The already mentioned *Jewish Study Bible* is, of course, organised into the subdivisions of the *Tanakh*, and it's amazing how something as simple as reorganising the books of the Bible changes your perspective. There are also versions of the Bible in which the text is arranged chronologically. The one I've used in the past – although it's out of print – is called *The Bible in Order*, and it promises, 'All the writings which make up the Bible, arranged in their chronological order according to the dates at which they were written or edited into the form in which we know them.'[7] Admittedly it makes a lot of assumptions, and I don't always agree with the editor's conclusions, but it's a great way of changing your perspective.

Finally, this is a case where you might benefit from some help. If we're going to visit some of the less-salubrious parts of Scriptureland, then it helps to have a guide. The fourth-century Bible translator Jerome said, 'You can make no progress in scriptures unless you have a guide to show you the way.'[*][8] A good

---

[*] Typically for Jerome, though, he believed that was because people could not be trusted to interpret the Bible properly for themselves: 'The art of interpreting the scriptures is the only one of which all men everywhere claim to be masters . . . the chatty old woman, the doting old man, and the worldly

Bible guide or commentary will always help you see the text in a new light (and I always recommend getting hold of a Bible atlas, not least because I've written one and I need the sales). But the same thing is true for commentaries as it is for translations: they are not perfect; they are reflecting opinion. They can be a real help in situating the text in its historical setting and in guarding us against wild misinterpretation. But they do not hold all the answers. Commentaries and guides are no substitute for thinking for ourselves. With commentaries, as with the translations, it can be good to go outside of your own traditions. Don't stick to the theologians who will tell you what you already know; spread your wings a bit.*

Again, people get very anxious about this kind of stuff. Not long ago I quoted one particular theologian in a sermon and I received two separate emails warning me that 'you want to be careful with him'. Apart from the fact that I am perfectly capable of thinking for myself, I thought it was strange to treat theology as though it's some kind of fungal infection. But then, a lot of people think of theology like brain surgery: one false move and you're dead. (Or doomed, to be more precise.) It's more like an exercise class, if you ask me. And sometimes it really helps to exercise a different set of muscles.

And talking about the dangers of theology . . .

_____

sophist, one and all take in hand the scriptures, rend them in pieces and teach them before they have learned them.'

* And you can go back into the past as well, if you like. Personally I find the series of books called the *Ancient Christian Devotional* very helpful. They have weekly readings from the lectionary accompanied by excerpts from the church fathers.

6 Talking about God

We are back in Jerusalem. It's the festival of Pentecost, AD 33, and something strange has happened to the rag-bag group of followers of Jesus of Nazareth. Since the death of their would-be Messiah, they've been keeping a low profile, hiding away, staying under the radar. But something – or someone – has changed them. They seem to be filled with a supernatural power. Here they are, on the streets of Jerusalem and in the Temple courts, bold as you like, preaching to the crowds who have gathered for the festival. And, weirdly, everyone who listens – Parthians, Medes, Egyptians, Romans, Arabs, Welsh and many more – all those people from the far-flung parts of the Empire, they hear words in their own language.

Finally, Peter, their leader, addresses the crowd. He starts by quoting a chunk from the prophet Joel. (Well, he paraphrases, starting off with a bit about 'the last days' which is not actually in the text. But he's a fisherman, and he's working from memory, so, you know, cut the guy some slack.) And then he gets down to the core part of his message:

'Jesus of Nazareth, a man attested to you by God with deeds of power, wonders, and signs that God did through him among you, as you yourselves know – this man, handed over to you according to the definite plan and foreknowledge of God, you crucified and killed by the hands of those outside the law. But God raised him up, having freed him from death, because it was impossible for him to be held in its power.'   (Acts 2:22–24)

Now people are starting to pay attention. Peter goes on to quote some excerpts from the Psalms to bolster his claim that Jesus was the Messiah, before concluding, 'Therefore let the entire house of Israel know with certainty that God has made him both Lord and Messiah, this Jesus whom you crucified' (Acts 2:36).

It's a powerful moment. Peter tells the crowd to 'Repent, and be baptized every one of you in the name of Jesus Christ so that your sins may be forgiven; and you will receive the gift of the Holy Spirit' (Acts 2:38). The text says that he went on exhorting them with 'many other arguments'. They must have been good arguments, because, according to Luke, who recorded this story, 'about three thousand persons' were baptised and 'added' that day (Acts 2:41).

It's the beginning of the Church. The outpouring of the Holy Spirit on the disciples starts a fire which nothing has since been able to extinguish.

The Bible is a problem for theology

But what about those 3,000 new converts? What were they actually signing up to? What did they take with them back to Parthia, Medea, Egypt, Rome, Arabia and Wales? I mean, it wasn't as if the apostles had suddenly got some tracts printed. And they certainly couldn't have taken with them a copy of the New Testament, or even one of the Gospels. What's more, a lot of the core ideas of Christianity hadn't even been worked out yet.

Probably all they had to take home with them were some sayings of Jesus, some stories. And maybe the first, very basic credal statement: *Kyrios Iesous* – Jesus is Lord. It was only later that the Church began to flesh out these beliefs. We see statements popping up in Paul's letters that look like early church hymns or statements of faith. But there was nothing fixed at this stage. Because it was all still being worked out.

And that's what the Bible shows us. It shows us people working out what to think about God. The Bible is not a book of theology, even though it contains lots of words about God.* It provides the raw material – *some* of the raw material – from which theology is shaped. The Bible is not an encyclopaedia of doctrine: it's what we use to measure whether doctrinal ideas are correct.

Robert P. Carroll in his book *Wolf in the Sheepfold* makes the observation that the Bible is 'problematic for theology'.[1] The reason is that theology and dogma require systems, logic, orderliness, precise language and clearly defined terms. Whereas the Bible is basically a book that keeps saying, 'Once upon a time . . .' Nobody in the Bible is doing systematic theology. That is why the letters of Paul, for example, can prove so difficult to make sense of at times: because people insist on treating them as though he was writing doctrine, when he was actually trying to sort out problems in localised faith communities.

I'm not knocking theology, or doctrine. We need both of these things. But the thing is, the Bible doesn't behave itself in those ways. There is too much variety, too many stories, too much *life*. People in the Bible don't always do the right things. They don't always say the right things. And they often don't even believe the right things.

Most of all, the Bible shows a wide variety of people learning about God. God is not some kind of abstract theological term in the Bible; he is the main character. And sometimes those writing about him depict him in ways our theology would reject. Here's Carroll again:

The problem of the Bible for theology is in the first instance the presence of contradictions in the Bible. Not discrepancies of

---

* Theology comes from two Greek words: *theos* meaning God, and *logos* meaning word. So it's really having words about God. But according to the OED, the Greek term originally meant 'an account of the gods, or of God (whether legendary or philosophical)'. It's only from the thirteenth century AD onwards that '*theologia*' came to designate a department of academic study.

account or contradictions in narratives about historical events – the Bible has many of these – but contradictions in the representation of God.[2]

That's where we should start, really.

Because the Bible is set in a world that believes in gods. *Lots* of gods.

The case of the bedridden idols

In the book of Samuel, David is portrayed as the great king, the one whom God loves and with whom God makes an everlasting covenant. But if you actually read the story of David, his character is not quite as clear cut as we think. And, surprisingly, for the author of all those psalms, he may have been a bit more 'inter-faith' than we imagine.

> **Read it yourself:** The rise of David to prominence is outlined in 1 Samuel 16–19. Those chapters contain the anointing of David by Samuel, and the depiction of David as both harp-player and warrior, and reveal that David only ended up fighting Goliath because he was delivering some cheese.

In 1 Samuel 18–19 we read how the increasingly paranoid King Saul makes a series of threats to the life of the young warrior-poet and Shepherd of the Year for 1020 BC, David. David's star had been steadily rising. After defeating Goliath, he had enjoyed military success against the Philistines and ended up with the hand of the king's daughter in marriage (and the rest of her thrown in as well). He is a hero, he is brave, he is even besties with Saul's son Jonathan.

So, naturally, Saul hates him.

David takes a while to realise what is going on, but after Saul hurls a spear at him while he is playing the harp, he gets the distinct feeling that the king might not actually like him that much. David runs home, but Saul sends a band of soldiers to surround his house and capture him. But David is helped to escape from the house by his wife, Michal, the king's daughter. She puts an idol in the bed, sticks a goat-hair wig on it and covers it with bedclothes. When the soldiers come she tells them that her husband is not well and is sleeping. So they go away. Eventually her ruse is discovered, but by then David is out through the window and miles away.

It's a great story, and is probably the first account in literature of the 'decoy dummy' trick, a trick that you can find replicated in many stories, from Sherlock Holmes to the film *Albert RN*, where prisoners make a dummy to cover the absence of their escaping colleagues.

But there is an uncomfortable little detail in this story, and it's this: what was a life-size, pagan idol doing in David's house?

A world full of gods

One of the key elements of the Christian and the Jewish and, indeed, the Muslim faiths is that there is only one God. God created the world. God is in charge of history. There are no other gods but him.

The words of prophets like Isaiah and Jeremiah are clear: 'I am the first and I am the last; besides me there is no god,' says one passage in Isaiah, which goes on to deride the gods of the Babylonians as frauds (Isa. 44:6). And Jeremiah dismisses idols as nothing more than dumb lumps of wood or stone; they are 'like scarecrows in a cucumber field . . . they cannot speak; they have to be carried, for they cannot walk' (Jer. 10:5).

But, actually, Israel didn't always think this way. For much of the Old Testament history they believed that there were *loads* of gods, but Israel's was the best.

It might be useful to get some terms in our heads.

Monotheism is the idea that there is only one God.

Monolatry (or henotheism) is the idea that there are lots of gods, but one is supreme.

Polytheism is the idea that there are lots of gods, all of whom are more or less on the same level. Or that God is a parrot. One of the two.

The Ancient Near East was a polytheistic culture; there were many gods on the loose. When Yahweh first reveals himself to Abraham, he is perceived as being just one among many gods. The difference is that he is promising to be Abraham's God – a tribal or clan God.

Clearly, however, not all the clan buy into this: when Jacob runs away from his Uncle Laban, Rachel takes with her Laban's household gods (Gen. 31:19, 34–35). But for Abraham and his descendants, Yahweh is specifically theirs: the God of Abraham, Isaac and Jacob and their family.

Of course, the descendants of Abraham grow in number, so by the time Yahweh reveals himself to Moses, he is now the 'God of the Hebrews' (Exod. 5:3). He is more than a tribal or clan God; now he is God of a recognisable ethnic group. But again, clearly not everyone in that group buys into this. As far as they can see, Yahweh is just a new god on the block who is going to rescue them. (And the minute he doesn't appear to be doing that they construct a new god in the form of a golden calf.)

The first commandment recognises that there are other options: 'You shall have no other gods before me' (Exod. 20:3), says God. He does not add, in parenthesis, 'but, of course, we all *know* that there are no other gods'. He does not say, 'I am the only God in existence.' They couldn't comprehend such a thing.

After the exodus, things change again. The use of the term 'God of the Hebrews' disappears, and God becomes the God of

Israel (Josh. 24:2). Now God is a national God, a territorial God. But still not everyone has signed up. In his retirement speech, Joshua challenges the Israelites to:

'Choose this day whom you will serve, whether the gods your ancestors served in the region beyond the River or the gods of the Amorites in whose land you are living; but as for me and my household, we will serve the LORD.'   (Joshua 24:15)

Joshua is going to serve only Yahweh, but clearly a lot of the Israelites were either drawn to, or already following other gods – in this case the Amorite gods. If they'd all been dutiful Yahweh-worshippers this challenge would not have been necessary.

And so it goes on. What I'm trying to show here is that (a) Israel's concept of who God is changes through time, and (b) much of the Old Testament assumes the reality and presence of other gods.

In the beginning, at least, the Israelites did not believe that there was only one God. They were monolatrous, not monotheistic. They believed that their God – Yahweh – was the best, but that there were other national or tribal deities, and many of them are mentioned in the text. There was Chemosh of Moab, Dagon the god worshipped by the Philistines, Baal and Astarte of the Canaanites, Milcom and Molech of the Ammonites . . . there were lots of local deities available. And the Bible even depicts Yahweh drawing up boundary lines, based on what gods were worshipped where:

When the Most High apportioned the nations,
    when he divided humankind,
he fixed the boundaries of the peoples
    according to the number of the gods.   (Deuteronomy 32:8)

There are many Psalms which acknowledge the existence of other gods:

There is none like you among the gods, O Lord,
   nor are there any works like yours.   (Psalm 86:8)

For the LORD is a great God,
   and a great King above all gods.   (Psalm 95:3)

For I know that the LORD is great;
   our Lord is above all gods.   (Psalm 135:5)

There are even curious passages that show Yahweh presiding over some kind of council of gods. 'God has taken his place in the divine council', begins Psalm 82, 'in the midst of the gods he holds judgement.' The idea of God convening a council of other deities is strange and surprising to us. Later interpretations turned these beings into angels, and even created certain hierarchies (hence angels and archangels), but the earlier accounts reflect the culture of the time, where the 'council of the gods' was a common feature of other mythologies.

Similarly, some poetic passages talk about Yahweh engaging in cosmic battles against other godlike forces:

You divided the sea by your might;
   you broke the heads of the dragons in the waters.
You crushed the heads of Leviathan;
   you gave him as food for the creatures of the wilderness.
                      (Psalm 74:13–14)

You rule the raging of the sea;
   when its waves rise, you still them.
You crushed Rahab like a carcass;
   you scattered your enemies with your mighty arm.
                      (Psalm 89:9–10)

Was it not you who cut Rahab in pieces,
   who pierced the dragon?

> Was it not you who dried up the sea,
>> the waters of the great deep;
> who made the depths of the sea a way
>> for the redeemed to cross over?   (Isaiah 51:9–10)

'Leviathan' and 'Rahab' appear to be some kind of mythological sea serpent or dragon. 'Rahab' literally means 'boisterous one' which makes me think of a rather large toddler.* The name is unique to the Bible; it's not used in any extra-biblical literature. The *Anchor Bible Dictionary* calls Rahab a 'Canaanite chaos monster', which would be a great name for a professional wrestler.³ The point is that Yahweh has won victory over the forces of chaos and darkness.

So the presence of multiple, albeit lesser, gods is taken for granted in most of the Old Testament. Many of the characters of the Old Testament acknowledge the existence of other gods; some of the great 'heroes' of faith even worshipped them. Gideon seems to have set up some kind of idol or object of divination (Judg. 8:27) and, most notoriously of all, Solomon ended up turning away from God completely, and even built places of worship for other gods:

> For when Solomon was old, his wives turned away his heart after other gods; and his heart was not true to the LORD his God, as was the heart of his father David. For Solomon followed Astarte the goddess of the Sidonians, and Milcom the abomination of the Ammonites. So Solomon did what was evil in the sight of the LORD, and did not completely follow the LORD, as his father David had done. Then Solomon built a high place for Chemosh the abomination of Moab, and for Molech the abomination of the

---

* Not to be confused with Rahab the prostitute in Jericho (in Joshua 2 and 6). Although it appears to be the same word in our Bibles, her name is actually from a different root, meaning 'to be wide or broad'. You can write your own jokes here.

> Ammonites, on the mountain east of Jerusalem. He did the same
> for all his foreign wives, who offered incense and sacrificed to
> their gods. (1 Kings 11:4–8)

The text is careful to separate Solomon's behaviour from that of his father David. But, as we have seen, David lived in a house where there were big, man-sized idols.

Various attempts have been made to explain this away. One Victorian commentary states, 'It is impossible to suppose that David could have either used, or countenanced the use of these images. God was too much a spiritual reality to him to allow such material media of worship to be even thought of.'[4] Talk about trying to get the Bible to behave. If David didn't countenance the use of these images why were they even allowed? The fact is this: *there were idols in his house.* Now it's possible they belonged to Michal – it was she who put the idol in the bed, after all, but the text gives no indication that they were hidden away in a cupboard anywhere, or that David was angry at their presence. The fact is that the golden years of Israel were never quite as golden as we think. There were always – even then – other gods and practices to choose from.

Israel might have believed that Yahweh was the supreme God. But it took a long time before they realised that he was the *only* God. Up until then, other gods were available. So a lot of the Old Testament reflects a monolatrous religion – one that assumed that Israel's God was best – rather than a monotheistic religion (which assumes that Israel's God is the only God there is).

How Israel moved from monolatry to monotheism is the subject of a lot of debate, most of which is highly speculative, and none of which I intend to go into here.[5] But gradually, as revealed through the pages of the Bible, Israel comes to understand that all that talk about other gods is actually bad theology: there are no other gods. There is only Yahweh.

It is the prophets who establish this. It's a major theme in particular for the unknown prophet whose work fills chapters

40–55 of the book of Isaiah. He's known by the name of Deutero-Isaiah (or 'my little Deuty' as his mum called him), and he's been described as 'the first Old Testament theologian explicitly to enumerate the doctrine of monotheism'.[6]

Deutero-Isaiah challenges other gods to prove themselves, if they really exist:

> Tell us what is to come hereafter,
>   that we may know that you are gods;
> do good, or do harm,
>   that we may be afraid and terrified.
> You, indeed, are nothing
>   and your work is nothing at all;
>   whoever chooses you is an abomination.   (Isaiah 41:23–24)

Two chapters later we get the great conclusion:

> You are my witnesses, says the LORD,
>   and my servant whom I have chosen,
> so that you may know and believe me
>   and understand that I am he.
> Before me no god was formed,
>   nor shall there be any after me.
> I, I am the LORD,
>   and besides me there is no saviour.   (Isaiah 43:10–11)

The implications of monotheism are huge. First, God is in charge of all nations. From their situation in exile, the Israelites come to understand that God is using other nations for his purposes: he uses the Assyrians and the Babylonians to punish Israel and he will use Cyrus and the Persians as part of his rescue plan.

But it goes beyond that. He doesn't just *use* other nations; he also wants a relationship with them. So Israel's role changes. They are to be a beacon, a light to all the other nations:

> See, you shall call nations that you do not know,
>   and nations that do not know you shall run to you,
> because of the LORD your God, the Holy One of Israel,
>   for he has glorified you.   (Isaiah 55:5)

This theme is taken up by other writers:

> Thus says the Lord GOD: This is Jerusalem; I have set her in the
> centre of the nations, with countries all around her. (Ezekiel 5:5)

> Thus says the LORD of hosts: In those days ten men from nations
> of every language shall take hold of a Jew, grasping his garment
> and saying, 'Let us go with you, for we have heard that God is
> with you.'   (Zechariah 8:23)

> Rise up, O God, judge the earth;
>   for all the nations belong to you!   (Psalm 82:8)

Probably the most powerful – certainly the most memorable –
expression of this is the story of Jonah, which we looked at earlier.
The tale clearly reflects the expansion of Israel's understanding
of God, and indeed the challenges that this new understanding
presented to their theology. The idea that God might actually
love Israel's enemies was something that caused outrage and even
fear.

It continued to do so in Jesus' day, and it still does. A friend
of mine was involved in the first translation of the New Testament
into an African language. When they presented it, one of the
listeners challenged a word used in Matthew 5.

'You've used a wrong word here,' he said. 'You've said that
Jesus says we should love our "enemies". That must be wrong.'
When he was told that that was precisely what Jesus had said,
he simply couldn't believe it.

Whether he took a boat and headed out to the open sea I
don't know, but it's a scary thing to have your theology upended.

Easier, sometimes, to run away and hide than to recognise that God is bigger, more loving and more merciful than you ever imagined.

The case of Ahab's fake news

This constant redefining and reimagining of God in the Bible goes way beyond just how many gods there were. It also extends to the very character of God, to who God is.

From the start there was something unique about the way in which the Israelites talked about Yahweh. Even when they thought there was more than one God, none of the others was like him. Unlike the gods in many other contemporary mythologies, Yahweh doesn't have a back story: there's no account of his birth or life history. He doesn't age, he doesn't grow, he doesn't have a wife, he doesn't live on mountains or in the sea.

But for all that, some of the Bible depicts God as a very human figure: he strolls in the garden with Adam and Eve, comes down for a site visit to the tower of Babel, sits with Abraham and shares a meal. He gets angry; he gets sad. He rests. And he even changes his mind. When the Israelites create the golden calf at the foot of Mount Sinai, God is determined to destroy them.

> The LORD said to Moses, 'I have seen this people, how stiff-necked they are. Now let me alone, so that my wrath may burn hot against them and I may consume them; and of you I will make a great nation.' (Exodus 32:9–10)

But Moses argues him out of it, reminding God of his covenant promise to the Patriarchs. The text simply says:

> And the LORD changed his mind about the disaster that he planned to bring on his people. (Exodus 32:14)

OK. That's an example of God deciding on a different course of action. He was going to smite and now he isn't. But at other points God's change of mind is to do with the fact that things just haven't worked out the way he wanted.

In the story of King Saul, for example, God decides that things have not worked out. God sends a message to the prophet Samuel that the first king of Israel has failed his probationary period and has to go:

> The word of the LORD came to Samuel: 'I regret that I made Saul king, for he has turned back from following me, and has not carried out my commands.' Samuel was angry; and he cried out to the LORD all night. (1 Samuel 15:10–11)

Samuel's anger is interesting. Clearly he doesn't like this turnaround, but nevertheless he goes to find Saul and tells him that, because he rejected the word of the Lord, the Lord has rejected him as king.

Saul immediately repents and begs forgiveness. There's a rather pathetic scene, with Saul clinging to Samuel's robe, trying to say how sorry he is. But Samuel says that the kingdom is going to be given to someone 'who is better than you', and then he gives this rather startling parting shot:

> 'Moreover the Glory of Israel [i.e. God] will not recant or change his mind; for he is not a mortal, that he should change his mind.' (1 Samuel 15:29)

Saul cannot be king any more. And it's no use begging because God doesn't do U turns. He's not like us. God doesn't change his mind.

Except he just has. About 20 verses earlier.

It's not even as if the narrator has tried to hide it. It's right there in the text. God obviously *has* changed his mind. As the story depicts it, God has buyer's remorse: he chose Saul and now he wants to take Saul back to the shop and exchange him for David.

The implications of this on a literal reading are quite enormous. It shows that things have not turned out how God wanted. The way that the text is written, it's almost as if Samuel is trying to issue a PR statement, he's trying to impose his own theology on God.

Maybe that is what is behind Samuel's anger. Maybe he's angry because of how foolish he's going to look. This, after all, was his first time anointing a king, and now the Lord wants him to choose someone else. Or maybe, like Jonah, he's angry because his ideas of who God is are being fractured. There is clearly a conflict between the idea of a God who knows everything and one to whom Saul's behaviour comes as a disappointment.

For me, this story invites me in to wrestle with the same difficulty. So much of our theology is built on the idea that everything is in God's plan, but what if that doesn't mean quite what we think it means? How much does our disobedience and our failure come as a surprise to God? How much does God change his mind? Is he playing the great tune of history from a written score or is he a jazz improviser working within patterns but always adapting creatively? (And, in fact, the prophecy doesn't turn out as simply as it is portrayed. Saul is not dethroned but continues as king for the rest of his life. It is Saul's death at the hands of the Philistines that ends his reign.) Once again, the Bible proves problematic for theology. But the story is great at getting us to think.

Certainly these same issues are ones with which the biblical writers have to grapple. In particular they have to wrestle with the idea that things don't always work out. That people – and prophets – make mistakes. It is crucial to the theology of Israel – especially during and after the exile – that God is seen as being in charge of all nations and all history. That creates some tension as well. Because if God is in charge of everything, if nothing happens without him knowing about it, then he must be responsible, in some way, even for the disasters. At its most extreme, this leads us to a very perplexing and curious story in 1 Kings, where God, on the face of it, issues some deliberate misinformation.

Read it yourself: 1 Kings 22:1–40 tell this strange story. But Ahab's story begins in 1 Kings 16:29, and it's worth reading because then you get all the stuff with Elijah thrown in as well.

The story is found in 1 Kings 22 and concerns a prophet called Micaiah and Ahab, King of Israel. Ahab wants to know if he is to go and hunt the white whale. Sorry, wrong Ahab. No, Ahab wants to attack the Aramaeans. And he wants Jehoshaphat, King of Judah, to join him. Jehoshaphat says, 'OK, but let's consult the prophets first.' So Ahab consults his court prophets who all agree that this is a tip-top idea, largely on the grounds that it came from the king. Jehoshaphat, who, one is beginning to suspect, is not terribly keen on the plan, asks if there are any other prophets available.

'Well, there is one,' says Ahab. 'There's this guy called Micaiah. But he's no good. He never tells me things I want to hear.'

Nevertheless, Jehoshaphat insists that Micaiah is consulted. And at first he seems to agree with the plan. He says, 'Go up and triumph; the LORD will give it into the hand of the king.' Ahab immediately smells a rat. Maybe it's because for the first time Micaiah has agreed with him. Or maybe it's because Micaiah hasn't specified exactly which king is going to win. Anyway, he insists Micaiah tell him the truth. So Micaiah does. And the truth is very, very odd:

Then Micaiah said, 'Therefore hear the word of the LORD: I saw the LORD sitting on his throne, with all the host of heaven standing beside him to the right and to the left of him. And the LORD said, "Who will entice Ahab, so that he may go up and fall at Ramoth-gilead?" Then one said one thing, and another said another, until a spirit came forward and stood before the LORD, saying, "I will entice him." "How?" the LORD asked him. He replied, "I will go

> out and be a lying spirit in the mouth of all his prophets." Then
> the LORD said, "You are to entice him, and you shall succeed; go
> out and do it." So you see, the LORD has put a lying spirit in the
> mouth of all these your prophets; the LORD has decreed disaster
> for you.'   (1 Kings 22:19–23)

Here we have the heavenly court image again, and they are having
a sort of brainstorming session. God wants to set a trap for Ahab,
and he's calling for ideas. And one of the spirits has A Cunning
Plan: 'I know! Why don't I go and lie to all his prophets?'

'Great idea,' says God. 'Go and do it.'

If we take this at face value, then, we have to believe that God
has deliberately sent an untrue message to these prophets. (And
it's not alone in the Bible: both Jeremiah (20:7, 10) and Ezekiel
(14:9) describe Yahweh as deceiving or tricking prophets.) It's a
story that seems to baffle most commentators. It's essentially the
biblical version of those shadowy Russian agencies that spread
fake news on social media. Taken literally, it doesn't work, because
you have to believe that God lies. Or encourages lying.

Instead, I think what is happening is that Micaiah (or the
person writing the story) is trying to explain where false prophecy
comes from. If you have a monotheistic God, then this kind of
stuff has to come from somewhere, so this story is one attempt
– perhaps not a very convincing one – to explain how that happens.
It's using a historical account to talk about a spiritual problem.

So how can we read this story? Maybe we can say that people
can prophesy for all kinds of reasons, not all of them right. Or
that people can be genuinely mistaken. Or that God is working
through history; even in the stupid, dumb things that people do,
God is working and will always be working. Or that being a
prophet in the ninth century BC was a very risky occupation. Or
all of the above.

Or maybe this is what happens when you portray God in very
human ways. You have to do that in order to understand him,
but in doing so you are also bound to get things wrong.

In the end, Ahab takes no notice anyway. Micaiah is put in prison and given only bread and water. King Ahab attacks Aram and is killed. And this story sits there in the middle of our Bibles, saying strange things about God, provoking us with its ambiguity. Which might be the point.

Why the first Christians weren't very Christian

What is the point of this?

Well, it's not to do your brain in with a lot of surprising/scandalous/baffling stuff from the Old Testament. Although that is quite fun. It's just to show that Israelite ideas about who God was and what he was like changed and developed over the centuries. So we often find theology in the Bible that is either wrong or incomplete. Because the people in the Bible are still trying to work things out.

In that sense it is wrong to assume that people in the Bible have exactly the same ideas about God that we do. This is true even when we get to the New Testament. They were not 'Christians' in exactly the same way that we are. Indeed, the word 'Christian' only occurs three times in the New Testament. First in Acts 11:26, and all that says is that 'it was in Antioch that the disciples were first called "Christians."'. Then there is one mention at the end of Acts, where Agrippa accuses Paul of trying to persuade him to become a Christian (Acts 26:28). Finally, in 1 Peter, the writer says that 'if any of you suffers as a Christian, do not consider it a disgrace, but glorify God because you bear this name' (1 Pet. 4:16). Luke doesn't tell us when the name was first used in Antioch, but the Agrippa story takes place around 58 AD. And the letter from Peter is probably later than that.

So in one sense it's wrong to talk about anybody in the New Testament being a Christian as we would understand it. They saw things differently. I hear many sermons that seem to imply that there is not much difference between the first followers of Jesus and ourselves. But Paul was not an Anglican. And John the

Baptist was not a Baptist. The first followers of Jesus were not evangelical Christians (or Catholic, or Orthodox).

What they were, primarily, was Jewish. We should remember that we only know two things about Jesus' appearance for sure: he was circumcised (Luke 2:21) and he wore a Jewish prayer shawl (Mark 6:56; Luke 8:44). The first followers of Jesus still saw themselves as Jewish. They attended synagogue. They studied Torah. Later, when Gentiles joined, they were following 'the Way' or 'the Way of the Lord'.*

It's not just the name, though. As we've seen, they didn't have a lot of the doctrine and ideas about Jesus that we have today. The first followers of Jesus had not worked all that out. They knew he was the Messiah. They began to see that his death meant salvation. Paul's letters are full of someone wrestling with the implications of a more complex theology, but he also expresses some very odd beliefs that we don't share today. Some of these, like the commands for women to cover their heads and for the men to uncover their heads, reflect the culture of the day – most notably the culture in Greco–Roman Corinth. But there are some odder things as well – slightly strange, gristly bits of belief. In 1 Corinthians 15:29 Paul talks about 'those people . . . who receive baptism on behalf of the dead'. No one has ever been able to explain quite what this means. The practice is completely unknown and we can't even tell if it was something that Paul approves of or not. He also writes that women 'will be saved through childbearing, provided they continue in faith and love and holiness, with modesty' (1 Tim. 2:15). There are various interpretations of this, but it's pretty much a mystery, and we mainly deal with it by forgetting that he ever said it.

What we *don't* do, of course, is agree with it at face value. Unless you seriously want to argue that women who do not, or cannot, have children are beyond salvation.

* Acts 9:2; 18:25–26; 19:9, 23; 22:4; 24:14, 22. I think this name is due for a comeback, actually.

The Bible is not an encyclopaedia of doctrine, with everything already worked out. The Bible shows the working-out going on. It is, in fact, the very *history* of the working-out, like seeing a live stream of people gradually understanding more and more about God. And this is a trajectory and not an end-point. This working out didn't stop at the last page of the Bible. Beyond that, the early church had a lot of thinking to do about the nature of God and Jesus and the Holy Spirit.

Take the idea of the Trinity. It's one of the cornerstones of the Christian faith. But nowhere in the Bible is there a clear statement of the doctrine of the Trinity. There are hints, there are implications, but it's never stated outright. As Christians read the Bible and reflected on the nature of Father, Son and Holy Spirit, they moved towards an understanding that the three were actually one being. The first recorded appearance of the doctrine is in the late second century, in a pamphlet written by the grumpy old theologian Tertullian. He is the first person to use the term *trinitas*, 'threeness', from which we get the concept. If we accept the idea of the Trinity – and I do – we then go back and read the Scriptures through a Trinitarian lens. But it's not explicitly spelt out. We read the biblical text in the light of ideas that have been expanded from the text itself.

We could expand this to other things as well. Nowhere in the Bible is there a clear statement of the mechanics of the atonement. All the New Testament writers are clear that, somehow, we are saved through Jesus' death. But then they use a whole range of different metaphors to explain that. Today, many churches assume that there is one model which is the 'correct' model (it's usually the theory of penal substitutionary atonement), but that's not true. It is just one of several theories of the atonement which have been held by Christians across the centuries.

People will insist on trying to turn the Bible into a systematic theology. But the Bible refuses to behave that way. There's nothing systematic about the Bible, largely because it's about humans who, despite valiant efforts throughout the centuries by various philosophers and sages, generally tend to prefer unsystematic thinking. The Bible isn't a unified theology, but it is a unified *story*. Stories don't deal in systematic thought. Stories may be used to challenge and explain, to connect and to work things out, but they do it by inviting us to think, not telling us what to think.

Thinking again about theology and the Bible

Nobody can come to Scripture without a load of baggage. We bring to our reading of Scripture who we are and what our history is. We bring our political views, education, social status, gender and ethnicity. All of these play a role in shaping our interpretation. And, crucially, we also bring our church background. Our church – whatever flavour we've signed up to – gives us our interpretative framework. We all read the Bible within the tradition of interpretation of our particular communities. However you define the Church – whether you are talking about big denominations like the Roman Catholic Church or the Orthodox Church or the Protestants or a small group of people in Kansas who insist on picking up reptiles – this community shapes our beliefs, and we read the Scriptures through that lens.

Nobody reads the Bible entirely objectively, and nobody ever can.

And it's always been the case. Some Christian traditions frequently quote the reformers' idea of *Sola Scriptura* – only Scripture. But while Luther certainly meant that Scripture should be the arbiter of doctrine, he didn't mean we shouldn't pay attention to the teachings of the Church. (In fact, at his hearings he defended himself using the teachings of the church fathers to show how orthodox he actually was.) We believe in being scriptural, but we operate in a long line of teachers and preachers who have told us what 'scriptural' actually means.

The first thing to do in thinking again about this kind of stuff is to recognise our own tradition and theology, to identify our own starting point, our own biases and beliefs. And it's not just our theological biases and history. Our character, interests, social background – everything we are – feed into the way we approach the holy ground of the Bible.

One thing I've often recommended to students starting to look more deeply into the Bible is to write their own mini biography.

I, for example, am Nick Page, a white, fifty-nearly-sixty male. I'm vaguely left wing, come from a middle-class family and grew up in the 1960s and 1970s. I was raised in a Baptist church, transferred to the Anglican Church and nowadays when people ask my denomination, I tell them I'm an Anglo-Baptecostal. An *Orthodox* Anglo-Baptecostal. I read – and write – books, and do a lot of speaking and teaching. I love history and poetry and humour. I am heterosexual, married and extremely English. I'm an introvert who can put on a show if necessary. I have an obsession with stationery – especially fountain pens. I fight daily battles with anxiety and frequently feel like a failure and a fraud. I am prone to anger and pride. And envy. And lust. And . . . well, maybe that's enough for now. The point is that *all* of this shapes my reading of the text.* It shapes which Bible books I respond to and which I react against. Our reading is always contextualised in things such as who we are, where we live, our social status and, crucially, our religious background. And it is always affected by our hopes, fears, perceptions, desires, hurts and blessings.

And the point is not to escape all this – I couldn't do that even if I wanted to – but just to acknowledge it and to recognise that it brings with it certain biases and presuppositions. That will help us understand our own reactions to Scripture and slow down our rush to read the text the way we've always read it. It will also help us to wrestle with the bits of Scripture that we don't like.

Just as we have our own perspectives as readers, the people writing the text also had their own biases and presuppositions,

* Well, not the fountain pens too much. Although maybe it feeds into why I love all that underlining and marking up stuff that I referred to earlier.

and their own, incomplete – or even faulty – theology. The people who wrote the Bible had not worked everything out. It's not like God ladles out 'correct' theology in a great big dollop onto our plates. 'Correct' theology (a) never arrives in one complete package, and (b) is never totally correct. It is always a case of development, whether evolving from a previous understanding, radically revolting against a previous understanding or moving away from it. The Bible shows people trying to work things out. And the working-out is still going on. The working-out of the nature of God continues beyond the pages of the Bible because working out who God is and what he is like is not a task that ever comes to an end. So as we journey through this strange new world, the key question to ask is, 'What does this story tell me about God?'

There will always be ambiguity and uncertainty. There will always be stuff that we don't know, that we can never know for sure. As Origen said, 'In advanced matters of theology, absolute confidence is possible for only two classes of people: saints and idiots.'[7]

But we do have some certainties. As Christians we have an advantage over the writers of the Old Testament. We have Jesus. Christians believe that the Bible is a constant movement towards Christ, as it were. In him we find the fullest expression of God. The ancient Israelites were groping towards a fuller, deeper, truer conception of who God is. Christians look to Jesus.

But even that realisation did not come at once. It took Jesus' followers a little time to work out precisely who he was and how it made a difference. And they only did that by asking questions, by questioning received wisdom, and by wrestling with the ambiguities.

Or, to put it another way, by expressing doubt.

7 The joy of doubt

At the end of Matthew's Gospel, the disciples are directed to go to Galilee. And there they meet the risen Jesus. Here's what Matthew writes:

> Now the eleven disciples went to Galilee, to the mountain to which Jesus had directed them. When they saw him, they worshipped him; but some doubted.   (Matthew 28:16–17)

The interesting thing about the second of these verses is that the word 'some' is not in the Greek. The Greek literally says, 'they worshipped him, but they doubted'. Every Bible translation I know tries to explain this away by adding words, mainly because the idea of having the eleven core disciples doubt Jesus seems too absurd. It's more acceptable to say that 'some' of them doubted, or even to imply that those who doubted were not among the core group.

But this is not what the text says. The text says that they both worshipped Jesus and had, well, at the very least a lot of questions. And we know from other stories that some of the core disciples did have doubts (I'm looking at you, Thomas).

Despite this, it often seems that doubt is frowned upon in the Church. Especially when it comes to the Bible. The Bible, after all, is *sacred*. So put away your doubts and questions and sail into the serene harbour of certainty. Then we all know exactly where we are.

But the problem with knowing exactly where you are is that you never get to go anywhere new.

And anyway, people aren't built like that. I can't just set my brain to mute when I read the Bible, and the Bible, with all its stories and poetry, and challenges and invitations, doesn't want me to stop thinking. The fact is that the Bible really *likes* doubts and questions. It positively revels in them. The Bible is full of people who ask God questions, who challenge him, talk to him, ask him to explain.

So the idea that it's wrong to question Scripture is, ironically, a deeply unbiblical way of thinking.

The God who explains

It starts very early in Israel's story, with Abraham, the ancestor of the Israelites and a key figure in their history.

Abraham is cited in the New Testament as the ultimate man of faith. But what's interesting about him is that there are a lot of times when he *doesn't* have much faith. When he enters Canaan with his nephew Lot, Abraham dithers over where to go (Gen. 13:8–9). He pretends that Sarah is not his wife, because he's scared people might kill him to take her (Gen. 12:10–20, echoed in Gen. 20:1–18). When God promises the aged couple a son, instead of waiting faithfully Abraham is persuaded to sleep with his wife's maidservant, Hagar, resulting in (a) Ishmael, and (b) a *lot* of arguments (Gen. 16:1–16; 21:8–21).

Abraham is a more complex figure than we think. But later traditions want to smooth his behaviour out. The text says that Abraham 'believed the LORD; and the LORD reckoned it to him as righteousness' (Gen. 15:6), but later extra-biblical Jewish traditions struggled with the occasions Abraham *didn't* just believe. So they added a gloss to this verse: '. . . because he did not raise any objections or speak rebelliously to Him'.[1] I don't know who thought they could get away with that, not least because Abraham raises an objection only two verses later. God repeats his desire to give Abraham the land, and the old man questions it: 'O LORD God, how am I to know that I shall possess it?' (Gen. 15:8).

Read it yourself: The 'Abraham cycle' is not an ancient form of transport, but a group of stories in the Torah about Abraham. (There's also a Jacob cycle, and a Joseph cycle. They could have a race.) It starts with Abraham being called by God at the end of chapter 11 and goes through to the beginning of chapter 25. It's a big chunk but it contains some key stories, including the covenants with Abraham, the destruction of Sodom and Gomorrah and the story of the birth of Abraham's children, Ishmael and Isaac.

Abraham was a man who asks lots of questions. And we see this in one of the most famous stories: the tale of Sodom and Gomorrah.

One day – one hot afternoon, the story tells us – three men come to visit Abraham. Abraham invites them in and cooks them a meal. One of the visitors is the angel of the Lord, and he tells Abraham that Sarah will have a baby in a year's time. Sarah, who is listening outside the tent, laughs to herself. She says: 'After I have grown old, and my husband is old, shall I have pleasure?' (Gen. 18:12), and the text doesn't say whether she's talking about the pleasure of childbirth or the pleasure of sex. Either way, for Sarah, those days are long gone.

Sarah's laugh, though, does not go unnoticed. 'Why did Sarah laugh?' asks the Lord. 'Nothing is impossible for Yahweh.' At which point Sarah sticks her head through the tent flap and says, 'I didn't laugh!' and the Lord replies, 'Oh yes you did!' Usually Sarah's laughter is described as cynical or sceptical and God is presented as sternly telling her off, but there's nothing in the text that says we have to read it that way. It seems to me that they are all enjoying the moment. It's a wonderfully comic scene so I don't know why people are so quick to assume that God doesn't enjoy the joke as well. And God has already told Abraham that the name of the boy is to be Isaac (Gen. 17:19), which means 'God laughs' or 'God smiles'.*

Doubt and questions do not always have to be dark: there is laughter and joy in God's surprises as well.

After this, though, things get slightly more serious. The man – and by now both Abraham and Sarah have worked out who he is – tells Abraham that he is about to completely obliterate Sodom and Gomorrah. There then follows a remarkable scene where Abraham essentially barters with God for the life of the people there. What if God finds fifty upright people in Sodom? What if he finds forty-five? Or forty, or twenty? Or even ten? Will he still destroy the city?

What is the point of this bargaining? God must already know exactly how many upright people there are in the city, otherwise he wouldn't be sending his wrecking crew down there in the first place. I think the bargaining is for Abraham's sake. Abraham needs answers: he needs to be sure that the God he is following is just, that he can be depended upon to do the right thing. And the amazing thing is that God is prepared to hang around and be questioned, to explain, even to justify his actions. He is not like the other gods of the time, whose stories show them doing things, well, just because they could. Yahweh is different. Our God is a God who is willing to explain.

God does not see the need to stand on his own dignity. He doesn't say to Abraham, 'Do you know who I am?' He doesn't feel threatened or challenged or angered by the questions, because the qualities in God which Abraham is seeking to establish – qualities of justice and mercy – are not externals which God puts on. They are not some kind of uniform. God is not a being who

---

* The name is 'typical of early second-millennium Amorite names, consisting of a verb in the imperfect and a divine name (cf Ishmael or Israel). Thus it is usually surmised that the full name of Isaac was Isaac-el, just as the full name of Jacob was probably Jacob-el.' See G.J. Wenham, *Genesis 16–50* (Waco: Word Books, 1994), p. 26.

sort of takes an interest in justice; he *is* just. He's not a being who loves; he *is* love.

God is not insecure.

The idea that we are not to question – or that God is like some Stalinist dictator who would burst into a rage if we were to laugh with surprise, or question any of his orders – is clearly not borne out by the Bible. Abraham wants to be sure that God is just. And God is happy to reassure him. As Robert Davidson writes, 'There is no suggestion that faith expresses itself in silent acquiescence; rather faith compels Abraham to interrogate in a situation where there seems to be a contradiction between a doctrine of God (i.e. that he does what is just) and the facts of human experience.'[2]

The contradiction between doctrine and real experience: that's what doubt is all about.

A few chapters on from Abraham's story, we have the Jacob cycle of tales. In this we see how a thoroughly disreputable trickster, one who is prepared to lie and cheat in order to gain an advantage, ends up alone and frightened, in the middle of the night.

> **Read it yourself:** Jacob gets on his cycle at Genesis 25:19, and the main events of his life take us through to chapter 33.

Jacob is choking on the smoke from all the burning bridges in his life. Behind him is his Uncle Laban (whom he has tricked); ahead of him is his hot-headed, red-haired brother Esau (whom he also tricked). He's got nothing. So he sends his wives and children and servants and flocks on ahead of him in an attempt to appease his angry brother. But he can't be sure that is going to work. And so he finds himself utterly alone. And then, this happens:

> Jacob was left alone; and a man wrestled with him until daybreak. When the man saw that he did not prevail against Jacob, he struck him on the hip socket; and Jacob's hip was put out of joint as he wrestled with him. Then he said, 'Let me go, for the day is breaking.' But Jacob said, 'I will not let you go, unless you bless me.' So he said to him, 'What is your name?' And he said, 'Jacob.' Then the man said, 'You shall no longer be called Jacob, but Israel, for you have striven with God and with humans, and have prevailed.' (Genesis 32:24–28)

According to this story, to wrestle with God and with other humans is at the very heart of what it is to be Israel.

Religious doubt is not alien to the Bible.

In fact, the Bible sort of invents it.

How the Israelites invented religious doubt

I want to pop back to the discussion of monotheism for a moment.

As we saw, monotheism was a major development in Israelite thought. It enabled them to see that God was with them in the exile, that he was in control of the whole world, and that everything that happened was part of God's plan. But monotheism brings with it a problem: if there is only one God, then who can you blame for the bad stuff?

In pantheism, solving the problem of evil is easy-peasy. All you do is blame a different god. Say you're an Egyptian and you worship Ra, the sun god. Your camel fails its MOT owing to emissions problems (and believe me, emissions are a big problem with camels). You don't have to ask why Ra has sent this punishment on you; you simply blame one of the many other gods, some of whom are enemies of Ra. It's easy in ancient cultures to explain wars, famines and other evil events: they are simply the outworking of various punch-ups between different gods, in which human beings are merely collateral damage.

But that explanation doesn't work if you only have one God and that God is supposed to be 'love'.

God cannot have a punch-up with himself.

So a lot of the Bible concerns itself with this question: if there is only one God, and he is a God of love and justice, then why do bad things happen to his followers?

This is one of the things that makes the Bible unique. You don't find these kinds of discussions in the religious literature of other ancient civilisations. Of course, there are characters who question why things are happening to them, but there is no expectation that any of their gods should explain themselves or justify their actions. There is no hint of the powerful, almost bewildered sense of injustice that fills books like Job or some of the psalms. As Robert Davidson writes:

> We are therefore left with the Old Testament giving expression to an area of religious experience – protest, questioning and doubt – which does not feature with any prominence in the surrounding cultures and religions. This suggests that there must be something in the Israelite understanding of God which makes such questions not only possible but acceptable as an authentic element in faith.[3]

In this sense, then, the Bible actually invents the concept of religious doubt.

At first, the answer they came up with to the question was simple: if God created everything, then he created suffering and evil as well.

> So that they may know, from the rising of the sun
>   and from the west, that there is no one besides me;
>   I am the LORD, and there is no other.
> I form light and create darkness,
>   I make weal and create woe;
>   I the LORD do all these things.   (Isaiah 45:6–7)

165

> Is a trumpet blown in a city,
>> and the people are not afraid?
> Does disaster befall a city,
>> unless the LORD has done it?   (Amos 3:6)

Evil was simply God's punishment for when people do wrong. But a note of doubt creeps in, because even the prophets notice that there are times when life refuses to follow the script. Jeremiah says:

> You will be in the right, O LORD,
>> when I lay charges against you;
>> but let me put my case to you.
> Why does the way of the guilty prosper?
>> Why do all who are treacherous thrive?   (Jeremiah 12:1)

Jeremiah is confident that God has an answer, but he can't help noticing that the theory of sin leading to punishment doesn't quite relate to real life. Similarly, Isaiah acknowledges that God isn't always present in an obvious way: 'Truly, you are a God who hides himself, O God of Israel, the Saviour' (Isa. 45:15).

At other times the complaint is about the scale of the punishment. In Lamentations, a beautiful and little-read book in the middle of the Bible, the poet looks at the ruins of Jerusalem and wonders if they have really deserved this much punishment:

> Look, O LORD, and consider!
>> To whom have you done this?
> Should women eat their offspring,
>> the children they have borne?
> Should priest and prophet
>> be killed in the sanctuary of the Lord?
>>>>   (Lamentations 2:20)

Israel's historians and prophets had proposed a simple equation: obey God and you will have a good life; turn away from God and you won't. This is what is presented to them on the shores of the Jordan by Joshua, and it is their prevailing theory of history. Isaiah sums it up: "'There is no peace", says the LORD, "for the wicked"' (Isa. 48:22). The word 'peace' here is *shālôm*, which means more than just the absence of noise or warfare; it means wholeness, health, completeness, well-being. Well, that might be what Isaiah thinks – or even what Isaiah thinks God thinks – but other writers recognise that actually the wicked have quite a lot of *shālôm*.

We can see these thought processes working out through the Psalms. Psalm 1 conveys a breezy, joyful confidence and certainty. Those whose 'delight is in the law of the LORD' are like fine, fruitful, evergreen trees planted by streams of water. 'In all that they do, they prosper.'

The wicked, on the other hand are in for it:

> The wicked are not so,
>> but are like chaff that the wind drives away.
> . . . for the LORD watches over the way of the righteous,
>> but the way of the wicked will perish.   (Psalm 1:4–6)

So *that's* all sorted: good people prosper, wicked people perish. Good people will stand like tall trees; evil people will face the great chainsaw of the wrath of God.

But fast forward to Psalm 44 and you find a direct contradiction of this theology. Psalm 44 begins with the psalmist remembering the tales of the past:

> We have heard with our ears, O God,
>> our ancestors have told us,
> what deeds you performed in their days,
>> in the days of old.   (Psalm 44:1)

The psalmist repeats the old formula: how God drove out the nations, how he 'command[ed] victories' for Israel. So far, so orthodox. But at verse 9 he suddenly goes rogue:

> Yet you have rejected us and abased us,
>> and have not gone out with our armies.
> You made us turn back from the foe,
>> and our enemies have taken spoil for themselves.
> You have made us like sheep for slaughter,
>> and have scattered us among the nations.
> You have sold your people for a trifle,
>> demanding no high price for them.   (Psalm 44:9–12)

Something has gone terribly wrong. Israel is now taunted, derided, scorned, 'a laughing-stock among the peoples'. And here's the thing: they haven't done anything wrong:

> Our heart has not turned back,
>> nor have our steps departed from your way,
> yet you have broken us in the haunt of jackals,
>> and covered us with deep darkness.
> If we had forgotten the name of our God,
>> or spread out our hands to a strange god,
> would not God discover this?
>> For he knows the secrets of the heart.   (Psalm 44:18–21)

The psalm ends with a cry to God to wake up, to reveal himself, to come out from where he is hiding. It's a stunning piece of poetry to find in the heart of the Bible. It directly contradicts the confident assertion of other poems in the book of Psalms. Psalm 121 confidently asserts that 'He who keeps Israel will neither slumber nor sleep' (Ps. 121:4); Psalm 44 ends, 'Rouse yourself! Why do you sleep, O Lord? Awake, do not cast us off forever!' (Ps. 44:23).

The argument that only the guilty get punished is found wanting, because when the Israelites look at real life, they can see that not only are the guilty *not* getting punished, but the guiltless are also having a really crap time of it.

Enter Job.

The case of the man who sued God

Job is an epic poem which addresses the question of suffering. The book takes a machete to the conventional wisdom that a righteous life will bring rewards. It's a complete annihilation of the prevailing – entirely biblical – theology of its day.

It is, of course, a story. It tells of Yahweh's servant Job, a completely righteous man to whom a series of terrible disasters happen. It appears to sandwich two sets of material together: two slices of an original story about a just man who faces suffering (chapters 1, 2 and 42) with 39 chapters of philosophical and theological dialogue filling between them.

> **Read it yourself:** It's a big book, I'm not denying it. I'd recommend the opening chapters (1–2) and then maybe dip into a few of the speeches in between to get a gist of the arguments. Job's big speech is in chapters 29–31. And don't miss 38–42, which is Yahweh's response from the heart of the storm.

The book starts with Yahweh singing the praises of his servant Job to the rest of his heavenly council (yes, it's the board meeting again). Job is upright, blameless and a thoroughly good egg. But then Yahweh is challenged by a figure called The Satan, which means 'the accuser'. Note that: it's *The* Satan. It's a job title, not a name. This is not Satan as featured on a thousand medieval wall paintings and heavy metal covers – the being with big horns and a tail. That idea comes later. This figure seems to be one of the council of heaven, and his job is as some kind of prosecuting council.

Anyway, Yahweh is bigging up Job, but The Satan counters, 'Of course Job is upright and righteous – he's got a great life. Take all that away and what happens?'

'Let me test Job,' he says 'and we'll find out the truth.'

Yahweh accepts the challenge. He allows The Satan to put Job to the test. (It seems to me that, right away, we're in a work of fiction. And if you *don't* think this is a work of fiction, then you have some explaining to do as to why God kills people and tips Job's whole life down the toilet simply to win a bet.) Job's children are killed, his cattle and property are destroyed. Job grieves, but he keeps faith:

> 'Naked I came from my mother's womb, and naked shall I return there; the LORD gave, and the LORD has taken away; blessed be the name of the LORD.' (Job 1:21)

First round to God. So The Satan ups the ante. Job's body is covered in sores. He is in physical and spiritual agony. His wife urges him to curse God and die.

But Job refuses.

That would be too easy.

Instead he determines on a tougher course of action: he's going to sue God.

Job is a man who wants his day in court. He wants God to explain why bad things have happened to someone who didn't deserve it. It's not that he thinks he can win his case – who can win a lawsuit against God? But he is, at least, determined to give it a go.

The defence witnesses soon appear: Job is visited by three 'friends' who explain why all this has happened. Job's friends are certain that he must be to blame for his suffering. I mean that's how this system works, right?

> Think now, who that was innocent ever perished?
>   Or where were the upright cut off?
> As I have seen, those who plough iniquity
>   and sow trouble reap the same. (Job 4:7–8)

As for Job's children, well, maybe *they* did something. In a stunningly tactless move, Job's friend Bildad says:

> Does God pervert justice?
>   Or does the Almighty pervert the right?
> If your children sinned against him,
>   he delivered them into the power of their transgression.
>
> (Job 8:3–4)

In what must be one of the worst pastoral care visits ever, they think that the way to comfort Job is to correct him. But Job is adamant: he is innocent. He gives a long speech of lament (chapters 29–31) calling on God to answer his indictment (Job 31:35). Then, as if the poor man hasn't suffered enough, a bloke called Elihu appears and gives four more speeches defending the justice of God.

The finalé is as sudden as it is surprising. After all this talk, Yahweh, the defendant in this cosmic court case, bursts in. He appears 'out of a storm'. And he doesn't answer the charge.

Instead, he poses a series of rhetorical questions.

> 'Where were you when I laid the foundation of the earth?
> . . . Who determined its measurements –
> . . . Have you commanded the morning since your days began,
>   and caused the dawn to know its place,
> . . . Have you entered into the springs of the sea,
>   or walked in the recesses of the deep?
> . . . Will you even put me in the wrong?
>   Will you condemn me that you may be justified?'
>
> (Job 38:4–5, 12, 16; 40:8)

God even seems to invite Job to have a go himself:

> 'Pour out the overflowings of your anger,
>   and look on all who are proud, and abase them . . .
> Then I will also acknowledge to you
>   that your own right hand can give you victory.' (Job 40:11, 14)

Or, 'Come and have a go if you think you're just enough.'

There are two really important things here.

The first is that Yahweh states categorically that Job did not suffer for any evil or sin that he had done. He doesn't answer the question about why it happened, but he does restore Job's fortunes, and Job goes on to live out a long and peaceful life.

The second key thing is that Yahweh does not condemn Job for his questions. Instead, he condemns Job's accusers for their answers:

> After the LORD had spoken these words to Job, the LORD said to Eliphaz the Temanite: 'My wrath is kindled against you and against your two friends; for you have not spoken of me what is right, as my servant Job has.' (Job 42:7)

It is Job who has spoken 'what is right'. In a final act of delicious irony, it is Job who gets to ask God to have mercy on his 'comforters':

> '. . . my servant Job shall pray for you, for I will accept his prayer not to deal with you according to your folly; for you have not spoken of me what is right, as my servant Job has done.' (Job 42:8)

And what is really incredibly shocking about this is that Job's friends were actually giving the 'biblical' view. They were dishing out impeccably orthodox theology, the kind you find in lots of other passages in the Bible. In the historical understanding of the Deuteronomist, for example, there is no doubt where Israel's suffering comes from:

> If you heed these ordinances, by diligently observing them, the LORD your God will maintain with you the covenant loyalty that he swore to your ancestors; he will love you, bless you, and multiply you; he will bless the fruit of your womb and the fruit of your ground, your grain and your wine and your oil, the increase

of your cattle and the issue of your flock, in the land that he swore to your ancestors to give you. You shall be the most blessed of peoples, with neither sterility nor barrenness among you or your livestock. The LORD will turn away from you every illness; all the dread diseases of Egypt that you experienced, he will not inflict on you, but he will lay them on all who hate you.

(Deuteronomy 7:12–15)

Suffering comes from Israel's disobedience, from their idolatry, from breaking the covenant. For them it is a simple equation: those who disobey God get punished. You are being punished; you must have disobeyed God. The book of Job not only categorically rejects this idea, it also shows *God* categorically rejecting the idea. The idea that suffering is never undeserved is, according to Job, just wrong.

The book of Job is not some kind of abstract discussion of the nature of evil. It's a critique of the theology of other parts of the Bible. It's a rude gesture in the direction of the Deuteronomist. It's the Bible in vigorous debate, not to say argument, with itself.

Job is a wonderful book, and there's lots we could say about it. We could say that suffering is a mystery, and that evil and injustice are not some kind of simple sum. We could say that being God is quite complicated, but that he probably has it all under control.

And we could say that sometimes when you are sure you have the correct theology, the best thing to do is simply to shut up.

Oh God, why?

'Why?' The Bible is full of people asking this question. 'Why has this happened?' 'Why have you allowed this?' 'My God, my God, why have you abandoned me?'

These questions are part of our experience, and this side of eternal life with God they will always be there. God himself recognises this. He responds through both the silence and the storm, and through giving us a book with texts like Job and Ecclesiastes and the Psalms in it.

These texts, with their lament and complaint, comfort us with the knowledge that we are not alone. We all know something of that feeling of abandonment and injustice, of the pain we feel when bad things happen in our lives and we don't know why. To have books that reflect that in the heart of the Bible is to validate our own, real, lived human experiences. We will not always understand. We will not always get answers. And others have been there before us.

But the texts are there for more than just showing empathy. They are there because God wants us to move, and doubt always takes us on a journey.

Let's go back to the Psalms. Remember Psalm 1? Good people are like big trees; bad people are like weeds. We saw how that theology was questioned by other psalms. And it is the questions that start to take people to new places.

Take Psalm 49. This writer has realised that, far from being blown away like chaff, some evil people are remarkably happy. People get rich. They do bad things. *And nothing happens to them in this life.* Contrary to the simplistic notions of righteousness equals reward, many wicked people die comfortably in their own beds, surrounded by their wealth.

First he argues that, well, we shouldn't worry too much, we shouldn't be envious, because we're all going to die:

Do not be afraid when some become rich,
    when the wealth of their houses increases.
For when they die they will carry nothing away;
    their wealth will not go down after them.'

(Psalm 49:16–17)

But he realises that this in itself is not much of a comfort. And so he comes up with a radical thought: maybe death isn't the end. Maybe something else happens.

> . . . straight to the grave they descend,
>> and their form shall waste away;
>> Sheol shall be their home.
> But God will ransom my soul from the power of Sheol,
>> for he will receive me.   (Psalm 49:14–15)

Remember: people in the Old Testament were not Christians. One of the big theological differences from the New Testament is that the Old Testament contains hardly anything about the idea of an afterlife. For the writers of the Old Testament, death was simply a fact. As the admittedly rather depressed author of Ecclesiastes says, 'All go to one place; all are from the dust, and all turn to dust again' (Eccles. 3:20).

But this psalm hints at something more, something new in Hebrew thought. The writer has experienced a contradiction between doctrine and experience. So he rejects the orthodox account and comes up with a new idea – that the ultimate fate of the righteous and the unrighteous person might be different. There might, actually, be more to what happens after death than we realise.

Now, it took a long time and a lot of thought before Israel developed the idea of an afterlife and the resurrection of the dead. (And when they did, Jesus came along and blew a lot of those original ideas apart anyway.) But that's not the point. The point is that the poet of Psalm 49 only gets as far as he does because he is willing to question the received theology. He creates a new orthodoxy solely because he refuses to let the old ideas go unchallenged.

The Bible does not banish doubt to the outer reaches. Instead the Bible confronts these kinds of questions and it wrestles with them. We can point to lots of other examples.

The little book of Habakkuk is a dialogue between the prophet and God over what appears to be happening in the world and whether God is really working through evil tyrants. In the book of Lamentations, the writer sits in the rubble of a conquered

Jerusalem and wonders what has happened. Yes, Judah deserved punishment, but did it really deserve this much horror? And God doesn't seem to be listening:

> You have wrapped yourself with anger and pursued us,
>> killing without pity;
> you have wrapped yourself with a cloud
>> so that no prayer can pass through.
> You have made us filth and rubbish
>> among the peoples.   (Lamentations 3:43–45)

Then there are all the prophets who challenge the supremacy of the Temple and the ritual, who claim that all that stuff is not the most important thing. What really matters is how we treat the poor. And there is Jesus himself. Not only do his thoughts and actions challenge the orthodoxy, he encourages his listeners to think as well. He keeps asking them, 'How do you read it?' when they talk to him about Scripture.

Jesus refuses to endorse the easy answers about suffering. Confronted with a blind man, his disciples ask him, 'Rabbi, who sinned, this man or his parents, that he was born blind?' (John 9:2). But Jesus sidesteps the question and heals the man instead. More than that, though, Jesus says that (a) his disciples will be part of the kingdom of God, and (b) they will all suffer.

In the New Testament, the most prominent example of someone who 'doubts' is Thomas. According to John's Gospel, he wasn't present at the first resurrection appearances and so he demands proof.

Read it yourself: It's in John 20:19–31. Interestingly, this was probably the original conclusion to John, judging from verses 30–31. But then other important resurrection accounts were added.

Thomas is often held up as a bad example, of someone who doubted Jesus. It's even given him his popular epithet: 'Doubting Thomas'. But Jesus never criticises him. Instead he actually gives Thomas what he wants: he turns up again and shows Thomas his wounds.

And Thomas' doubts actually take us to a new place. They show us, importantly, that the wounds of Jesus are still in his resurrected body. They show us that the things that happen to us – the terrible, wounding, destructive things of our lives – can be transfigured and redeemed and resurrected in a glorious way. Jesus' wounds are not wiped out. In the words of Rowan Williams:

> The resurrection is not about the wiping out of our history, pain or failure, it is about how pain and failure themselves – humanity marked by history – may yet be transfigured and made beautiful.[4]

See what I mean? Thomas is a flipping hero. His questions have taken us deeper into the mystery and truth of Jesus, places that we might not have gone if it weren't for his 'doubt'.

We should be grateful that the biblical writers were not prepared to shut up and be quiet. They insist on being heard, on stating the awkward facts. They are not rejecting God; they are clinging on like their ancestor Jacob – in the hope that God will bless them in an entirely new way.

Thinking again about the Bible and doubt

Doubt is not a sin. Doubt is a necessity.

Doubt takes you places. Certainty stops you dead in your tracks.

The problem is that doubt and questions are, by their very nature, challenging and difficult. On a personal level we might not want to go near them, for fear that our faith will be destroyed. We think of doubt like pulling at a thread in a jumper: we tug on one loose yarn and pretty soon we are left with nothing but a great big knotted pile of wool. But if modern psychology has taught us anything, we know that repressing the doubts and the questions doesn't make them go away. Underground fire will find its way to the surface somehow.

For many churches and church leaders, though, the idea of acknowledging the existence of doubts and ambiguities is extremely difficult. For one thing, it smacks of failure: surely our job as leaders, teachers, pastors is to banish doubt and uncertainty? I've certainly fallen into this trap: I saw my job as trying to prove points, win arguments and persuade people into my camp. But I've given this up for a number of reasons: first, I'm really rubbish at arguing and debating and all that so it was a bit pointless; second, I don't think that people really ever are persuaded very much by points made from the front, as it were – dialogue and conversation is far more influential; and finally, I realised that honesty and vulnerability connect far more powerfully with people than certainty and a load of clever answers.

Look, I understand the pressures. Church leaders have enough on their hands trying to keep the thing going without having to deal with someone asking about the problem of suffering, or whether Noah was really that old, or exactly what kind of fruit was forbidden in the garden of Eden, or whatever. I understand that. I understand the difficulties and demands of the pastorate.

But we should also acknowledge that churches that deny oxygen to doubt and questions are really protecting not the Bible but the pastor. There are many churches where debate is closed down because it is seen as analogous to questioning the leadership. One notorious American church leader once said about dissenters in his congregation, 'They are sinning through questioning.' This was the accusation placed against Jesus, against Paul, against others in the Bible: 'Who are you to question our interpretation?'

But stopping people questioning, closing down the discussion and debate – that doesn't strengthen faith; it kills it. As David E. Roberts wrote:

For the most part the churches have not yet learned that the best way to pass from defensive rationalisations to secure faith is to let doubts, inconsistencies, confusions and rebellions come out into the open instead of using various forms of spiritual coercion to keep them hidden or to draw them from awareness altogether.[5]

People who peddle the idea that God will be annoyed by questions, or angry if we Doubt His Infallible Word, are usually hiding something. Maybe it's their own insecurities; maybe it's the flaws in their theology. But, more to the point, those who tell you to keep quiet and just believe, or who try to solve difficulties by just shouting – or, more usually, singing – the party line over and over again, are acting in a profoundly unbiblical way.

So the first thing I think we have to do is provide a safe space for doubts and questions to be aired and explored. Many churches have successfully run Alpha courses for people thinking of becoming Christians; for years I have been arguing that we also need Omega courses for those who are thinking of leaving. In my experience people drift away from church not because they have stopped believing, but because there is no place for them to express how their beliefs have changed.

'A great curiosity ought to exist concerning divine things,' wrote the poet and novelist Charles Williams. 'Man was intended to argue with God.'[6] It's high time that we accepted that it is not disrespectful to question the Bible, it is absolutely vital. Because it's only by questioning that we move to new understanding.

Having said that, you don't have to do any of this. You don't have to worry about things that baffle you, unless, that is, you hear them calling to you. If you hear them calling, then I think it's important that you attend to that voice. The Bible does that, after all. The Bible does not hide from doubt. The writers of the Bible are constantly seeking to rewire their theology. They constantly comment on and critique the received wisdom and the orthodox theology. And they do this because it is through questioning that a deeper faith actually arrives. Remember, the Bible does not demand our worship; it demands our attention. We cannot read the Bible properly – in the way it was meant to be read – if we view it as being beyond question.

To question the text, to reinterpret it, even to challenge it, is a thoroughly biblical way of reading the Bible. And it is a way of reading that has deep historical roots. In Jesus' day, discussing the Scriptures was a much more active event: there was question-and-answer; people argued and disagreed. Similarly, the New Testament letters were supposed to be read communally. Paul explicitly instructed some of his letters to be read aloud to others.*

And in this Omega course we do not travel alone. We need to travel with others: sometimes guides who will give us good counsel, but always people who will be good listeners. We are involved in a conversation with the Bible, and we are involved in a conversation with each other. Years ago I was talking with a friend of mine from South America and I asked him what he thought the main differences were between our country and his. I expected him to talk about things like health provision or transport or all those material things, but instead he thought for a moment and said, 'It's the way you talk to one another.'

'In my country,' he said, 'when we talk to one another it is like there is a rope between us. I pull you one way, you pull me another. But we are connected. In this country it is like there is a wall between us. And we are both shouting over the top.'

Good conversations require good listeners. And we need to learn from the (bad) example of Job's friends and put aside our urge to correct. This, I think, is where so many home-group and discipleship group questions fall down: they are not designed to open up the discussion, but to guide the participants to the 'right' conclusions. There are too many Christians who view any kind of conversation about the Bible as a chance to combat heresy,

---

* 'And when this letter has been read among you, have it read also in the church of the Laodiceans; and see that you read also the letter from Laodicea' (Col. 4:16).

challenge unorthodoxy and generally win the arguments for Jesus. There's the leader of the group who has prepared the study and knows exactly what conclusions we have to come to. Or the expert who knows it all and who is really only attending in order that he can inform everyone else.

But in our Omega course, the course itself is not fixed: the most important thing in any discussion is to find questions that unlock deeper truths. And once we have those questions, we have to be prepared to go where they take us. Or, to put it another way, to answer them honestly.

We need to read the Bible together as a group because it will stop us being isolated in our doubt. And it will encourage us that doubt doesn't have to result in disbelief. It will ensure that we aren't just simply *wrong*. One of the strengths of reading the Bible with others is that it's a good way of making sure we don't go off in an entirely bonkers direction (unless you're all bonkers, in which case you're a bit stuffed). We can seek ways together to be Christlike disciples; we can be those who worship, although they doubted.

Often it is through unpacking the Bible with others that we find new meaning, that we hear God speaking to us. The rabbi and scholar of midrash, Burton Visotzky, writes:

> It is only in the reading and rereading which each community does together that the Bible becomes a timeless text – the Word of God. If and when that happens the Bible ceases to be just another book, gathering dust on a shelf. In a community of readers, conversation takes place. The give and take of interpretation creates an extra voice in the room, the sound of Reading the Book.[7]

We are seeking that 'extra voice in the room', the voice of God speaking to us individually and communally. That whisper which is so hard to describe but which we know when we hear it.

The second thing that we urgently need to do as a church is to recognise the role of question and lament.

Some years ago I wrote a book about the words of worship songs with the not-at-all-provocative title of *And Now Let's Move into a Time of Nonsense*. As part of the research for that book I read the lyrics of about a thousand worship songs. (That, my friends, is called sacrificing yourself for your art.) Anyway, during that exercise, and the long period of therapy that followed, one of the things that really struck me was the almost complete absence of lyrics about pain or loss. The songs were all so happy. They were all 'Worship Songs', and the clear inference was that the experience of worship had no space for lament. It was all about victory, joy and assorted feelings of blessedness.

On the whole, the Church in the UK has avoided the excesses of the 'health and wealth' gospel of so many churches around the world. But we have bought into it emotionally. Our worship songs have turned into spiritual antidepressants. And whatever you do, don't spoil the party.

A similar thing happens in our corporate readings. As few churches read their way through the Psalms as they used to do, the psalms of lament are never present in our worship.

I am convinced that our failure to bring lament into our acts of worship is one of the reasons why so many people drift away from the Church. If we lose the ability to lament, to doubt, to question, we stop growing as individuals and as a body. And we have nothing to say to the people in pain all around us. In Berlin, in 1948, the writer Alfred Döblin told his German audience, 'You have to sit in the ruins for a long time and let them affect you, and feel the pain and the judgment.'[8] But we don't want to sit in the ruins. We don't even want to admit that the ruins exist.

Not so with the Bible. The Bible refuses to infantilise its readers, because it recognises that lament and doubt are crucial to maturity and growth. It was only through reflecting on their failures, reflecting on the apparent absence of God from the world around them, that Israel was able to grow closer to God. That kind of grimly happy, false obedience and docility does not lead to a deeper faith; it leads to despair. It is those who are able to lament who become closer to God. 'Blessed are those who mourn, for they will be comforted' (Matt. 5:4).

The Bible refuses to behave itself in such a happy-clappy way. The psalms are not just a load of poems; they were some of the key liturgical resources of Israel – their hymn-book, in a way. Doubt, anger, sadness, fear: all have a part to play at the heart of their worship. The psalms acknowledge the hiddenness of God. They tell stories of loss and destruction. They lay bare the human experience in all its joy and its pain.

I wonder how this would play out for us. How many modern worship songs say anything very much about the idea that God might be hidden? How many sing of questions and abandonment? Wouldn't it be amazing, just once, to go to one of those big meetings and see the bloke on the stage pick up his guitar and say, 'And now we're going to sing a song about our feelings that God is miles away, asleep somewhere.' I'm not sure it would be a great career move as a worship leader, but you never know. God might sweep in out of the PA system and say, 'My servant has sung right.'

8 The authority of Scripture

Sooner or later, when you get into a discussion about the complexities of the Bible, someone will say, with the air of one who is about to deliver the knockout blow, 'I don't know why we have to have all these debates. Stop making everything so complicated. All you have to do is read the Bible and obey it.'

They then sit down with the air of someone who has simultaneously cured the common cold, solved Fermat's last theorem and settled the argument over whether the chicken or the egg came first.

Now, I have some sympathy with this view. It's quite likely that the history of the world would have been different had people simply read some of Jesus' words and then 'obeyed' them. Words like, oh I don't know, 'love your enemies', for example. And part of the argument of this book is exactly that: we should just read it, read it as the text it is and then let those words work on us, and listen to God.

The problem is that most of the Bible doesn't tell us what to do. Most of the Bible is a story. How do you obey something that effectively begins, 'Once upon a time'? Or which contains poetry, like this bit:

I am black and beautiful,
  O daughters of Jerusalem,
like the tents of Kedar,
  like the curtains of Solomon.   (Song of Solomon 1:5)

How am I supposed to 'obey' that? I mean, I suppose I could get an Afro, but that's not going to be easy. How do I 'obey' the authority of the bits where people pour out their complaints to God? Or the history? Or the long genealogies and lists of tribes?

But that's not what Christians mean when they talk of obeying the Bible.

What they really mean is the *rules*.

Law – what is it good for?

The Law forms a significant chunk of the Torah, the first five books of the Bible. Torah means 'instruction'.[1]

Of the Law, the Ten Commandments – said to be written by the finger of God – were the most important section – they were the bit that was placed in the Ark of the Covenant. The rest of the commandments formed what was known as the 'book of the covenant' (Exod. 24:7). The Law covers a lot of different areas: there are laws about dietary requirements, rituals and sacrifices as well as criminal and social laws. There are laws about the treatment of foreigners, laws about who can marry whom, there are building regulations and hygiene laws, laws about what to do if someone damages your donkey, or if you have a wet dream, or whether or not you can eat dolphins (you can't.)* There are laws to tell you who can and who can't go into the holy places – those outlawed include those who are blind, disfigured, hunchbacked, anyone born out of wedlock and even those with damaged testicles.

There is a *lot* of law.

So how are we to relate to these? Well, in some ways we don't relate to them at all.

One reason for that is simply because these laws reflect the life

---

* Because dolphins don't have scales. Leviticus says, 'Everything in the waters that does not have fins and scales is detestable to you' (Lev. 11:12). Other banned foodstuffs include owls, moles and seagulls.

of tent-dwelling nomads who lived in the Bronze Age, and while it is interesting to know how to purify your tent from mildew, today I'd probably just go at it with some Cillit Bang. Other laws reflect an understanding of biology that is just wrong. The ancient Israelites thought that women during their period were impure and should be avoided for seven days. I've lived in a household of women for many years, and while I thoroughly agree that avoiding them during this time might be a good strategic move, it's got nothing to do with impurity. These laws also reflect a massively different society, one which was overwhelmingly, you might say oppressively, patriarchal: the laws that deal with women generally treat them as property, and that is not something that we could possibly sign up to today. I've checked that with my wife.

But the main reason is that Christians believe that we are set free from the Law. There was a big debate in the first few decades of the Church about whether non-Jewish Christians had to obey the Jewish Law. And the decision was that they didn't have to be circumcised or give up bacon sarnies. And anyone can go to church, never mind whether their tent has mildew or if there is damage to their meat and two veg.

But the discussion between Christians over the Law was not the first debate about the Law and how it should relate to the everyday lives of observant followers of God. Throughout history, even in the pages of the Old Testament, followers of God have always asked the question: 'Law. What is it good for?'

The Law was really an expression of the covenant between God and the Israelites, a response to the liberating act of God in freeing his people from slavery. God had rescued and redeemed, so Israel owed him their loyalty. But it always needed interpretation. We can see this in the text itself where, often, statements of the relevant laws were accompanied by case studies showing how that might work out in real life. (I bet there were questions on day one. I bet the moment after the Ten Commandments were pronounced someone surely went up to Moses and said, 'I know we shouldn't covet someone's donkey, but what about their chickens?') And as the Israelites moved further and further away in time from their nomadic roots, the need for experts to interpret the Law grew ever more pressing. One of these, as we've seen, was Ezra, and when he read the Law to the people in Jerusalem, there were other experts on hand to explain it to them:

> So they read from the book, from the law of God, with interpre-
> tation. They gave the sense, so that the people understood the
> reading.   (Nehemiah 8:8)

Part of this is simply a matter of language: after the exile most Jews spoke Aramaic, not Hebrew. So the language needed to be translated for the listeners. But it's also clear from their response that they needed to understand what it meant. At the end of the reading, Ezra even gave a lengthy 'sermon' or summary of their story and helped them to apply what they had heard by promising not to marry 'the people of the land' and by promising to support the Temple and the priests.* So even the Jews in Ezra's time could not 'just do it'. The Law needed contextualising and applying to contemporary life.

Another problem for the experts of the Law was that there were actually inconsistencies within the text, reflecting the different traditions or sources from which the Torah was constructed. For example, in Leviticus it says that no Israelite can be a slave, only foreigners:

> If any who are dependent on you become so impoverished that
> they sell themselves to you, you shall not make them serve as
> slaves. They shall remain with you as hired or bound labourers
> . . . As for the male and female slaves whom you may have, it is
> from the nations around you that you may acquire male and
> female slaves.   (Leviticus 25:39–40, 44)

---

* It's all in Nehemiah 9 and 10. As part of the response, the people had to agree to pay 'one-third of a shekel for the service of the house of our God' (Neh. 10:32). This was basically Ezra's version of a church building appeal.

But compare that to Exodus 21:2–11 and Deuteronomy 15:12–18. Both of those say it's perfectly OK to have Israelites as slaves; under certain circumstances you can even keep them for life. There are even two versions of the Ten Commandments – or the 'Ten Words' as they are called in Jewish tradition.* They're not very different, but the second version includes more elaboration and a different reason for observing the sabbath.

> **Read it yourself:** The Ten Commandments are found in Exodus 20:2–17 and Deuteronomy 5:6–21.

Also, the laws were not always applied consistently. Again, we can show this from within the text. Deuteronomy says:

> Parents shall not be put to death for their children, nor shall children be put to death for their parents; only for their own crimes may persons be put to death.   (Deuteronomy 24:16)

But this actually happens time and time again. In Joshua 7 the entire family of Achan is killed for his misdemeanours. David kills the descendants of Saul. Zimri and Jehu kill the families of the kings they have deposed.† And *never* are they criticised for breaking the Law.

All of this shows that observing the Law has never been as straightforward as 'just doing it'. And as time went on, the distance between the everyday life of Jewish people and their historic Law made observation ever more tricky. By the time we get to Jesus' day, there was an entire Torah-interpreting industry in full swing, with scribes and scholars, rabbis and experts in

---

* This gives us the Greek title for the Ten Commandments: the Decalogue.
† The gory details are in 2 Samuel 21:1–14; 1 Kings 16:8–14; 2 Kings 10:1–17.

the Law, whose job was to try to apply this ancient Law to the lives of urban Jews in the first century AD. A lot of these inter-pretations and rulings were later collected into a body of text known as the oral, or spoken, Law. Eventually, around AD 200, this was codified and written down in Jewish writings known as the *Mishnah*.

These rulings tried to answer questions of interpretation in modern contexts. For example, it was forbidden to work on the sabbath. But what exactly defined work? The tractate on sabbath in the Mishnah answers that by listing thirty-nine kinds of forbidden activity, including sowing seed, carrying an object, tying or untying knots, even writing two letters of the alphabet. You weren't allowed to go on a journey on the sabbath, but what constituted a journey?* The answer: anything over 1,000 cubits was prohibited. Sabbath observance was complicated. Since any cooking on the day was forbidden – that counts as work – the meals would have to be prepared in advance.

Various ways were found to get round Sabbath legislation. It was forbidden, for example, to carry a tool or utensil or food, or anything really, from one home to another. But if the homes were joined in some way – for example, if they shared a common courtyard – they were regarded as a common dwelling and the food could be placed in the middle of the courtyard and shared. And Jews found creative ways to join houses together, including using bits of rope.

Even being a scribe itself was not just a matter of knowing the rules and applying them. There was a certain amount of creative licence involved, and a recognition that the text was difficult and ambiguous. In one of the apocryphal books, the scribe is described as someone who:

* According to an ancient Jewish religious work called *The Book of Jubilees*, all sex was prohibited, although whether this was deemed 'work' it does not say.

> . . . seeks out the wisdom of all the ancients,
>   and is concerned with prophecies;
> he preserves the sayings of the famous
>   and penetrates the subtleties of parables;
> he seeks out the hidden meanings of proverbs
>   and is at home with the obscurities of parables.
>
> (Sirach 39:1–3)

Practically speaking, there must have been many people for whom complete observance of the Law must have been impossible. For anyone living on the breadline, day to day, the chances of being able to put aside enough food to observe the Sabbath must have been impossible. And the Mishnah says that 'impure' women during their period were even forbidden to enter the city of Jerusalem. In a city of 45,000 people, enforcing that kind of thing must have been impossible.

In Jesus' day there wasn't even one agreed way of interpreting the Law. Different forms of Judaism interpreted the Law in different ways. The Pharisees, for example, believed that bathing for ritual purification could be done in still water, in pools or baths. The Sadducees, however, argued that it had to be running water. And both claimed to be interpreting the Law correctly.

Those might be termed textual or interpretive problems – problems of contextualisation and consistency. But as time went on, some more fundamental issues about the laws began to raise their heads. Never mind context or consistency: this was about contradiction.

The case of the contradictory prophets

In the Exodus version of the Ten Commandments it says this about idols:

You shall not bow down to them or worship them; for I the LORD your God am a jealous God, punishing children for the iniquity of parents, to the third and the fourth generation of those who reject me, but showing steadfast love to the thousandth generation of those who love me and keep my commandments.

(Exodus 20:5–6)

The idea is probably around social solidarity – in a tribal, communal society, what one person did affected their kin. This idea made its way outside of the Law proper, and into credal statements about God:

The LORD is slow to anger,
and abounding in steadfast love,
forgiving iniquity and transgression,
but by no means clearing the guilty,
visiting the iniquity of the parents
upon the children
to the third and the fourth generation.   (Numbers 14:18)

Then you get Jeremiah. And Ezekiel. And they say this:

In those days they shall no longer say:
   'The parents have eaten sour grapes,
      and the children's teeth are set on edge.'
But all shall die for their own sins; the teeth of everyone who eats sour grapes shall be set on edge.   (Jeremiah 31:29–30)

The word of the LORD came to me . . . 'Know that all lives are mine; the life of the parent as well as the life of the child is mine: it is only the person who sins that shall die . . . When the son has done what is lawful and right, and has been careful to observe all my statutes, he shall surely live. The person who sins shall die. A child shall not suffer for the iniquity of a parent, nor a parent suffer for the iniquity of a child; the righteousness of the righteous shall be his own, and the wickedness of the wicked shall be his own.

(Ezekiel 18:1, 4, 19–20)

This is not a reinterpretation, it's a rewrite. Jeremiah sees a new kind of covenant law, one that was written on the hearts of people, not on tablets or scrolls:

> The days are surely coming, says the LORD, when I will make a new covenant with the house of Israel and the house of Judah. It will not be like the covenant that I made with their ancestors when I took them by the hand to bring them out of the land of Egypt – a covenant that they broke, though I was their husband, says the LORD.　　　　　　　　　　　　　　(Jeremiah 31:31–32)

The prophets were responding to the fact that, for many people, observing the Law had become an end in itself, a box-ticking exercise that meant that, whatever else they did, people were alright with God. From the eighth century BC onwards, the prophets start to denounce this idea. So in Amos we read:

> I hate, I despise your festivals,
>   and I take no delight in your solemn assemblies.
> Even though you offer me your burnt offerings and grain offerings,
>   I will not accept them;
> and the offerings of well-being of your fatted animals
>   I will not look upon.
> Take away from me the noise of your songs;
>   I will not listen to the melody of your harps.
> But let justice roll down like waters,
>   and righteousness like an ever-flowing stream. (Amos 5:21–24)

Or in the words of Hosea:

> For I desire steadfast love and not sacrifice,
>   the knowledge of God rather than burnt-offerings. (Hosea 6:6)

The prophets had a different, larger view of God. In a sense their God is more, not less, demanding: he wants love and commitment, not the easy ritual of blood sacrifice and going to the Temple.

And he wants to let everyone in. In the Torah the laws are a way of defining the boundaries of the chosen people. It's about membership – who's in, who's out. But for the later prophets everyone was in – at least, potentially. It was all about inclusion.

Deuteronomy 23:1–6 gives a list of some of those who cannot be admitted to 'the assembly of the LORD'. It includes those 'whose testicles are crushed or whose penis is cut off', anyone 'born of an illicit union'. The Ammonites are banned, as are the Moabites – the only foreigners who might be allowed are (strangely) the Egyptians, and the Edomites who were seen as kin because of the ancient connection with Esau.

But Isaiah contradicts this. Isaiah says that both foreigners and eunuchs are welcome:

Do not let the foreigner joined to the LORD say,
 'The LORD will surely separate me from his people';
and do not let the eunuch say,
 'I am just a dry tree.'
For thus says the LORD:
To the eunuchs who keep my sabbaths,
 who choose the things that please me
 and hold fast my covenant,
I will give, in my house and within my walls,
 a monument and a name
 better than sons and daughters;
I will give them an everlasting name
 that shall not be cut off.

And the foreigners who join themselves to the LORD,
 to minister to him, to love the name of the LORD,
 and to be his servants,
all who keep the sabbath, and do not profane it,
 and hold fast my covenant –

> these I will bring to my holy mountain,
>   and make them joyful in my house of prayer;
> their burnt-offerings and their sacrifices
>   will be accepted on my altar;
> for my house shall be called a house of prayer
>   for all peoples.   (Isaiah 56:3–7)

This is a change of course. It's not an amendment or a sub-clause or even a clarification. In the words of Walter Brueggemann, 'This is an ancient text that corrects an even more ancient text.'[2]

The early church went on to put this into practice – literally, in the case of the Ethiopian convert in Acts, who is both a eunuch and a foreigner (Acts 8:26–40). In the book of Acts we see impure Gentiles and hated Samaritans being welcomed into the kingdom of God. We see ancient purity laws begin to fall one by one. The early church broke the rules. And it did this because it was being Christlike.

But I say this . . .

Jesus followed the trajectory set by the prophets, but took it way, way further. He echoed their vigorous condemnation of religious hypocrisy. He even quotes Hosea:

> 'Go and learn what this means, "I desire mercy, not sacrifice." For I have come to call not the righteous but sinners.' (Matthew 9:13)*

Talking to his own followers, he warns them in Amos-like terms that mere allegiance is not enough:

> 'Not everyone who says to me, "Lord, Lord," will enter the kingdom of heaven, but only the one who does the will of my Father in heaven. On that day many will say to me, "Lord, Lord,

---

* Matthew is using the Septuagint translation.

did we not prophesy in your name, and cast out demons in your name, and do many deeds of power in your name?" Then I will declare to them, "I never knew you; go away from me, you evil-doers."'   (Matthew 7:21–23)

But Jesus did not set the Law aside. In a key statement, Jesus described himself as fulfilling the Law. But fulfilling Torah meant more than just obeying it. Sometimes it meant going beyond it to the heart of what it was really about; sometimes it meant a different, much wider application. To Orthodox Jews this was challenging, incendiary behaviour. The best example of this approach is a series of Jesus' sayings which have become known as 'the antitheses'. Basically, Jesus states, 'You have heard it said . . . but I say this . . .'

> **Read it yourself:** The statements can be found in Matthew 5:20–48. You could also look at times when Jesus does deliberately provocative acts on the Sabbath, like in Matthew 12:1–14.

The Torah instructions say that solemn oaths made by Israelites should be made in God's name: Jesus said true followers shouldn't swear on anybody's name, or even make oaths at all – they should just do what they say they are going to do. If you have total integrity and honesty you have gone beyond that old law.

God said to Moses that Israelites should love their neighbours: Jesus said his followers should love their enemies. (And he completely redefined the definition of a neighbour.)

God said to Moses that justice was to be an 'eye for eye, and tooth for tooth'; Jesus said forgive everyone who harms you – don't take revenge at all.

At other times he seemed to deliberately challenge current

understandings of the Law – even to the point of disobedience. God said to Moses that we should honour our father and mother. But when one man wanted to postpone following Jesus to bury his father, Jesus told him to 'Follow me, and let the dead bury their own dead' (Matt. 8:22). He seemed to challenge the very idea of family bonds being the most important thing: 'Whoever comes to me and does not hate father and mother, wife and children, brothers and sisters, yes, and even life itself, cannot be my disciple' (Luke 14:26; see also Mark 10:30). Obviously this is hyperbole, but the idea of 'hating' your family would have been deeply shocking and offensive to Torah-following Jews of Jesus' day.

Jesus challenged the Jewish dietary laws:

> Then he called the crowd again and said to them, 'Listen to me, all of you, and understand: there is nothing outside a person that by going in can defile, but the things that come out are what defile.'
> (Mark 7:14–15)

And their purity regulations:

> But what comes out of the mouth proceeds from the heart, and this is what defiles. For out of the heart come evil intentions, murder, adultery, fornication, theft, false witness, slander. These are what defile a person, but to eat with unwashed hands does not defile.
> (Matthew 15:18–20)

And even the view of sabbath:

> One sabbath he was going through the cornfields; and as they made their way his disciples began to pluck heads of grain. The Pharisees said to him, 'Look, why are they doing what is not lawful on the sabbath?' . . . Then he said to them, 'The sabbath was made for humankind, and not humankind for the sabbath; so the Son of Man is lord even of the sabbath.' (Mark 2:23–24, 27–28)

What Jesus seemed to be saying here is that compassion is more important than the Law. That's borne out by the fact that he launched his most stinging criticism not at the unclean, impure whores and tax collectors who were excluded by the Law, but at those who were using the Law to condemn, to trap and to control. The Old Testament Law sits within the story of the exodus from Egypt. It is a key component of a covenant that was all about liberation and redemption. The Law was there to protect and ensure the liberty of the Israelites to continue as God's people. Jesus hated the idea of this kind of liberating law being turned into a tool of oppression. The Law had to be continually reassessed in the light of how it was affecting people in the surrounding society.

This approach is taken even further by Paul. Paul argues that while Jews might be still under the Law, Gentiles are free. For Paul, the Law was only a temporary fix, a solution for a particular stage of humanity's journey with God. The Law is like an adult looking after young children, or a master overseeing slaves. But Jesus brings not only true freedom, but also the requirement to reach maturity, to think for ourselves.

This was not a universally accepted view, even among the Christians. The book of Acts and letters such as the one to the Galatians show quite clearly the opposition to Paul's reforms within Christianity. Even people like Peter and colleagues like Barnabas disagreed with Paul on whether Gentile Christians and Jewish Christians could share the same table.

But the important thing to remember is that it was only because Jesus challenged the Law that Paul could do so. Jesus went first. Paul took hold of his approach and ran with it.

And in the end, Paul's view prevailed. The Old Testament Law was not seen as binding on Christians. Except . . . er . . . when it is. Because a lot of us still appeal to the Law when it suits our uses.

Tithes – yes, tattoos – no

Tithing. That's still a thing. It's one of the most popular 'Old Testament Laws Which Is Still A Law Actually'. Christians routinely talk about the act of tithing, which is giving 10 per cent of your income to the church. (Or other charities. But mainly the church.) It's based on passages in Deuteronomy (14:22–29; 26:1–15), where a tithe is collected for the support of the Levites. It was immensely popular in medieval times, when it brought in a lot of money to the Church. And you still hear it preached today as though it's an immutable command. Now, obviously there's a principle here: we are commanded by Jesus himself to be gener-ous.* Paul talks about the need for Christians to be 'rich in good works, generous, and ready to share' (1 Tim. 6:18). When sending the disciples out to tell people the good news, Jesus also says that 'the labourer deserves to be paid' (Luke 10:7) – a principle that is also quoted by Paul, who chucks in an Old Testament command about how to treat your ox (1 Tim. 5:18).

Gifts need to be given. People need to be paid. But it's no longer a law. The tithe as it was originally stated no longer holds force. You can't claim that tithing is obligatory for Christians from the Bible.

The Old Testament laws were not written for us. The Old Testament laws do not apply to us. But they contain principles that may well be very helpful for us. What we need to do is wrestle with this stuff. We need to think long and hard about what the text means for us today. We need to become 'experts' in the Law.

For example, the Law has a great deal to say about social justice, about the obligations to exercise hospitality and to support those in need. It was passages in the Torah that led to the Jubilee

---

* See for example, Matthew 5:42; 6:2–3; 10:8; 25:31–46; Luke 6:30, 38; 11:41; 14:12–13. Jesus is also quoted in Acts 20:35: 'It is more blessed to give than to receive' – a saying that is not recorded in any of the Gospels.

campaign for the remission of international debt. The Jubilee remains one of the most astonishing pieces of legislation in all of history.

> **Read it yourself:** It's described in Leviticus 25.
> Unsurprisingly, given the sacrificial nature of the statute,
> there's no evidence that it was ever enacted.

Jubilee is a kind of sabbath of sabbaths. It's the point where the whole of society hits the reset button: debts are written off and land reverts to its original owners. It's an inspiring principle, but even here we have to remember that the same rules apply: just because it's in the Bible doesn't mean that it's binding. We are free from the Law. In this case, what gives it inspirational power is that it thoroughly fits with the message of Jesus. Jesus spoke a lot about forgiving people's debts. It's even in what we call the Lord's Prayer, which in Matthew's version says, 'And forgive us our debts, as we also have forgiven our debtors' (Matt. 6:12).* The idea of forgiving debts is something that Jesus espoused. And so that brings the Old Testament idea of Jubilee back into play, not as a command but as a principle.

What Jesus detested was the weaponising of the Law, its being used as a way of excluding and punishing people. And we still fall foul of that today. We still pick and choose bits of Old Testament Law just to stop people doing stuff. I've encountered women who have been told off for wearing trousers on the basis of Deuteronomy 22:5:

---

* The popular version as prayed in church follows Matthew's version entirely, except for the bit about debt, where it suddenly switches to Luke's version which has 'forgive us our sins'. I'm not sure how that happened, except to say that forgiving sins might be less expensive than letting people off what they owe us.

> A woman shall not wear a man's apparel, nor shall a man put on
> a woman's garment; for whoever does such things is abhorrent
> to the LORD your God.   (Deuteronomy 22:5).

I'd like to see the people who cite this verse try to stop a Scotsman
wearing a kilt for the same reason.

I've seen people argue that tattoos are sinful on the basis of
Leviticus 19:28,* a law that has nothing to do with a visit to a
tattoo parlour: it's probably more to do with magical practices
and local pagan rituals. It's not unbiblical to get 'I ♥ Beyoncé'
tattooed across your forehead; it's just really dumb.

Having said all that, clearly some of the Law is still in effect.
The Ten Commandments form the basis of our legal system
anyway – like the ancient Israelites, we do not allow murder,
theft, bearing false witness and so on. So we obey those. (Except
for the bit about coveting, which we don't really obey, because a
lot of us work in marketing and, you know, a bit of coveting is
great for sales.) And Jesus himself gives at least two commandments that we are to follow:

> 'The first is, "Hear, O Israel: the Lord our God, the Lord is one;
> you shall love the Lord your God with all your heart, and with all
> your soul, and with all your mind, and with all your strength." The
> second is this, "You shall love your neighbour as yourself." There
> is no other commandment greater than these.'   (Mark 12:29–31)

But when it comes to the rest of it, a lot of Christians still employ
the Old Testament Law as a weapon. It's never the whole Law, just
the bits that suit their purposes. You hear quite a lot of the Old
Testament laws about sexuality cited by people whose houses lack
any kind of parapet and who are dressed head to toe in mixed fibres.†

---

* 'You shall not make any gashes in your flesh for the dead or tattoo any
marks upon you: I am the LORD.'

† See Deuteronomy 22:8 and Leviticus 19:19.

When the Church changes its mind

For good or ill, it is mainly Church teaching that interprets the principles and the laws. The Church pronounces which laws are still in force.

And the Church changes its mind. For centuries, the Church forbade the charging of interest. In the Torah, God specifically forbids Jews to lend money and charge interest to each other.

> If you lend money to my people, to the poor among you, you shall not deal with them as a creditor; you shall not exact interest from them. (Exodus 22:25)

> You shall not charge interest on loans to another Israelite, interest on money, interest on provisions, interest on anything that is lent. On loans to a foreigner you may charge interest, but on loans to another Israelite you may not charge interest, so that the LORD your God may bless you in all your undertakings in the land that you are about to enter and possess. (Deuteronomy 23:19–20)

Historically, Christians also took this practice on. In AD 325 the First Council of Nicaea forbade clergy from lending money at interest – even at interest rates as low as 1 per cent per year. Later this prohibition was expanded to the laity, and it was declared that anyone who accepted interest on loans would be banned from receiving the sacraments or even having a Christian burial.

Nowadays, we are perfectly at home with the idea of receiving or paying interest on loans. It's how our financial system works. Insofar as it does.

The Church changed its mind. Issued a correction. Why? Well, the cynic might say because the Church was rich and wanted a slice of those new-fangled banks that rose in the Renaissance. But it was just as much that the world changed. Capitalism came to town in a big way with the rise of the modern banking sector and a different understanding of how money worked. And that led to a changed concept, frankly, of what was right and wrong.

This is the other thing about the Law: we do not think the same things as our ancestors. Our world is different. I live in a modern liberal democracy. (At least I do at the time of writing. These things have a habit of slipping away if we're not careful.) I believe that things like democracy, free speech and equality before the law are good things. I believe men and women are equal. I think that's *true*. And even where the Bible says otherwise – and in some places it does – I still think that men and women are equal. Again, this may have you reaching for the rocks and organising a stoning party, but this is actually how we all operate. We just have different places where we draw the line. For me, I am not going to take at face value laws formulated in times when women were viewed as possessions. It's not that I'm going to ignore the text, but just because these kinds of things are in the Bible doesn't mean they get to set up permanent residence in my life.

Take marriage. People often talk to me about the 'biblical' view of marriage, as if that were an easy thing to identify. But what kind of marriage are we talking about? Are we talking about Jacob, who had children from two wives, and also from their maidservants? Or Solomon with his hundreds of wives? And even in New Testament times, where polygamy was generally frowned upon, their concept of marriage was different from ours. Marriages in the ancient world were arranged. The bride and groom didn't get much of a say in it. Today we think marriage should be between two people who love each other and want to spend their life together. We even have laws *preventing* arranged marriages – the very kind of marriage espoused by the Bible. Our view of marriage is different from the view of the Old Testament. And here's what I think: *our view is right*. I would rather live in a world where people cannot be forced to marry someone they don't love. I think that that is a good thing.

Another example: slavery. The Bible has virtually nothing to say about the evils of slavery. There is only one reference to the slave trade being evil in the whole Bible, and that is in Revelation.* But we *know* that slavery is an evil. So whatever we take from all the stuff about how to treat slaves, we cannot take the idea that slavery is ever acceptable.

The Bible is not your mother

The Bible does not simply tell you what to do. It's not your mother.

We can pray, we can seek the guidance of the Holy Spirit. We can look around us at the example of our fellow disciples. And we can look to the example of Christ. We have a lot of resources to fall back upon, but we still have to make our own decisions.

The Bible is not, in the popular phrase, 'a manual for life'. I've looked and looked, but I can't see anything in Leviticus that tells me how to unblock my dishwasher. Not to mention how to set up a bank account, or service the car. While the Bible talks a lot about obedience, it also encourages us to pursue wisdom. And wisdom is about much more than simply obeying the rules. Even the so-called books of wisdom in the Bible offer a bewildering variety of approaches, from the emotional extremes of the Psalms to the bleak cynicism of Ecclesiastes. Perhaps the most immediately applicable book here is Proverbs, which is, on the face of it, the closest the Bible comes to a life-coaching manual. But then you get this:

> Do not answer fools according to their folly,
>   or you will be a fool yourself.
> Answer fools according to their folly,
>   or they will be wise in their own eyes   (Proverbs 26:4–5)

---

* In a passage describing the fall of Babylon, John has merchants weeping because they can no longer trade in 'slaves – and human lives'. See Revelation 18:13.

Which is it? I mean, these are saying the exact opposite things, aren't they? It's all in the context, it seems. Sometimes you have to answer idiots; other times you have to avoid getting dragged down to their level. But only you can decide which of these 'rules' to obey, and when.

The basis of all this stuff, behind all the 'just do its' and the 'manual for life' nonsense, is the doctrine of the authority of Scripture. People talk about the Authority of Scripture, as if the Bible were a sergeant-major barking out orders and yelling instructions. But as we've seen, we can't just obey the instructions. And nobody ever really has. In fact, the Church has always been quick to say that the Bible is authoritative, but rather slower to define exactly how that authority is worked out. As Walter Brueggemann writes:

> The Jewish and Christian religious communities have character-istically accepted the scriptures as revelatory, but have been mostly unclear and largely uninterested in stating precisely in what ways this literature is authoritative . . . The problem is that the articulation of any formal criteria concerning authority or revelation turns out to be in tension with the actual concrete practice of the communities affirming the authority.[3]

In other words, as soon as you start to apply rigid rules from the Bible, you find that they just don't work in real life.

Even so, I think the Bible is authoritative. Just not in the way you might think.

The authorising version

The Bible is only authoritative because the Church says it is.

That may be a difficult, even uncomfortable, thing to read. But it's true. Think about the formation of the canon of Scripture: it was the Church that selected the texts it considered to be 'author-itative'. (And before the Church, the Jews from Ezra's time onwards.) The human beings involved in that decision were, no doubt, guided by the Holy Spirit, but they were also guided by their own assessment of the authenticity of the documents and their lung capacity, as it were, for the breath of God. That's why Paul's letters got in but other very valued early Christian texts didn't. Now you can say that the Holy Spirit was in these deliberations, that the Holy Spirit guided the decision-making of all those council and church meetings and Christian experiences of Scripture across the centuries. I wouldn't have a problem with that. But what you can't say is that God delivered the Bible in one lump and then said, 'Here you go. These are the rules. Get on with it.'

Having decided its constituent parts, the Church then went on to grant authority to the Bible, to make Scripture the arbiter of doctrine, so that everything we are told, preached and generally harangued with has to be judged by its rootedness and adherence to the wider body of Scripture. (It has to be the *wider* body of Scripture: doctrines based on one verse are always dodgy. Especially if that verse is in one of the more bonkers bits of Revelation.) The strength of the voice of Scripture in deciding doctrine and practice varies from denomination to denomination, but all acknowledge its crucial role.

Here's another fact: there isn't a single Church, of whatever flavour, that *only* follows Scripture in its beliefs and practices. We've already seen that theology grows out of Scripture and is informed by other factors as well. The same is true for church rules and practice. The Bible is not the only voice we listen to in the way we run our churches.

This has been the way since the very earliest days of the Church. Irenaeus, whom we met earlier talking about the primacy of the Gospels, believed that the Church had inherited two things from the apostles: their writings and a living 'tradition' of what it meant to be a Christian. This has to be the case, otherwise how would people have become Christians, how would churches have worshipped or evangelists witnessed before the New Testament was written?

Irenaeus called this body of teaching the 'canon of the truth'.[4] And every denomination or church tradition has its own canon of truth, which sits alongside the Bible. For example, Jesus never ordained anyone in his life, neither did any of his followers, as far as we can tell. But we go about doing that. We do baptism in a bewilderingly different number of ways, hardly any of which look like the way it was done by John the Baptist.

We share the Eucharist in a lot of different ways as well, but I don't know of any church that does it in the way it was done in that upper room, with a load of people reclining on couches. Even the early church itself soon moved away from that. Jesus' explicit command – 'Do this in remembrance of me' (Luke 22:19) – confirms the Eucharist as the crucial, communal liturgical activity of the Church, but how different Christian communities do that has always been a matter of debate. It's not even as if every church eats bread and drinks wine: some churches use grape juice and many substitute what is apparently an edible cardboard wafer for the bread. And none of us does it the way it was done in the early church. They had a proper meal, not a lot of people kneeling while a bloke in a frock gave them a small sip of very bad wine and a tiny fragment of bread.

> **Read it yourself:** There are different accounts of the Last Supper and the institution of the Eucharist. The event is portrayed in three Gospels: Matthew, Mark and Luke (Matt. 26:26–29; Mark 14:22–25; Luke 22:14–23). In 1 Corinthians, Paul describes both the instructions that were handed on and the way that a rather dysfunctional communion meal was happening in the church in Corinth (1 Cor. 11:17–34).

The roots of all these things are in the Bible – their justification is scriptural – but their expression is entirely shaped by tradition and by whatever 'canon of the truth' we sign up to. So one way of looking at the authority of Scripture is to see that although it sets patterns of behaviour, those patterns are adapted to local circumstances.

I'd go further, actually, and argue that different churches or Christian communities place the emphasis on different parts of Scripture. Evangelicals, for example, place a huge emphasis on Romans. The Orthodox Church has always placed a huge importance on the Gospel of John. And we all have a canon within a canon: not all the Bible is equal.

So when it comes to the authority of Scripture, our tradition treats different parts of the Bible more seriously – more 'authoritatively' – than others. If I am a Franciscan monk, then Jesus' injunction to sell everything and give it to the poor becomes a literal command. If I am an Anglican stockbroker driving a Bentley, it becomes more a kind of guideline. If I'm a Mennonite, then Jesus' complete commitment to non-violence is non-negotiable. If I am an army chaplain, then I'm going to have a more nuanced view of it.

Perhaps most importantly, the Bible never talks about the authority of Scripture, as far as I can see. The New Testament talks about the authority of Christ ('All authority in heaven and on earth has been given to me' (Matt. 28:18)). There is one occasion where Paul talks about the Law having authority ('Do I say this on human authority? Does not the law also say the same?' (1 Cor. 9:8–12)), although given that elsewhere he says that the Law no longer has any power, you might argue that he's cherry-picking. But generally, whenever he talks about authority, it is his personal authority that he's talking about (e.g. 2 Cor. 10:8; 1 Thess. 4:1–8). This is an authority vested in personal example, and in his status as an apostle, and in his faithfulness to Jesus.

It's not the authority of Scripture that matters so much as the authority of Christ in our lives.

Thinking again about the authority of Scripture

A story can't issue instructions and poetry doesn't tell us how to act. But they can help us in other ways. They can identify examples to follow, and patterns of behaviour to share. They won't give us a one-size-fits-all solution that fits every circumstance. Scripture is normative rather than prescriptive: it doesn't give us detailed instructions, but it does set out patterns of behaviour.

In this sense, Scripture is something that *authorises* us to do things, or to behave in a certain way. This is the kind of meaning behind the question that was always put by the 'official' authorities to Jesus: 'By whose authority do you behave in this way?' 'Who,' in other words, 'authorises you to do this kind of stuff?' The Bible doesn't micro-manage our lives, but it supports our right to live in a certain manner.

Ultimately, I believe the authority of Scripture means the authority to live like Jesus.

I'm a Christian. I'm not a follower of Paul of Tarsus or Moses or Isaiah. The stories of Jesus are central to our reading of the Bible. He is what Rowan Williams calls 'the luminous centre'.[5] I read the Bible through the lens of Jesus. And we listen to the Bible to find the voice of Jesus within it and seek to become more like him. That is what being a disciple is actually all about. A disciple is one who learns by imitation – in this case by centring our whole life on the presence, teaching and example of Jesus Christ. This is why in your canon within the canon the Gospels have to take pride of place. When John Ortberg became a pastor he asked the late Dallas Willard for advice. Dallas told him two things: first, 'ruthlessly eliminate rush', and second, to spend the next twenty years reading the Gospels. If you take nothing else out of this book, I reckon that's good advice for all of us.

So reading the Bible is about listening to God in Jesus – which is what Christians ought to be doing in all circumstances anyway.

The Bible scholar James Barr writes:

Christian faith is not faith in the Bible, not primarily. It is faith in Christ as the one through whom one comes to God, and faith that through the Bible we meet him, he communicates with us. The Bible is thus the instrument of faith and the expression of faith, rather than the object of faith.[6]

We test our ideas and reading of Scripture against the life, teaching and example of Jesus. He is our control, as it were, so whatever we bring out of the Bible has to conform to his law of love. That, I think, is a better way to picture the authority of Scripture. The Bible exercises its authority in giving us patterns of behaviour that can inform our lives. The Bible authorises me, for example, to stand against injustice and oppression, to stand up for the rights of those who are marginalised and excluded. It authorises me to forgive others, to stand up for freedom of belief, to protect the rights of human beings made in the image of God. It's not going to tell me exactly how to do that. I have to work that out through prayer, through the presence of the Holy Spirit and simply through using my brain.

If the Bible has authority in my life, then it will not be as a set of rules and regulations telling me exactly what to do in any circumstance, but as a story that authorises me to act in a Christlike way. Ultimately, when it comes to rules to guide our lives, Christians look to Jesus. And he said that there were two absolutely core principles: to love God with all our heart and soul and mind, and to love our neighbours as we love ourselves. Maybe if we are looking for rules to follow, those aren't bad places to start.

Of course, that raises an issue. Because a lot of the Bible isn't very loving; it isn't very peaceful and kind.

I've put it off long enough. We're going to have to go there.

It's time to look at the violent bits.

9 It ain't necessarily so

There is a lot of killing in the Bible.

There are all those animal sacrifices for one thing. (When you read the instructions for animal sacrifice in the Bible you realise that basically they are instructions for a barbecue. The Temple was a cross between an abattoir and a burger bar.)

Then there's the violence. The bloodshed. The first murder takes place just a few chapters into Genesis when Cain kills his brother Abel for motives that are never entirely clear. That's bad enough, but a few chapters further in God decides to drown everyone – *almost* everyone – in a flood.

Throughout Genesis and on into the rest of the Pentateuch there are wars and violence, and rape and pillage. Then you get to Joshua, with its genocidal tendencies, and the book of Judges, which starts with a captured king having his thumbs and big toes cut off and ends with a mass abduction and rape of girls who thought they were going out for a dance. Judges is the gospel according to Quentin Tarantino.

A lot of these incidents are just down to the anarchic state of society: 'In those days there was no king in Israel; all the people did what was right in their own eyes' (Judg. 21:25). So the violence, while horrible, is at least believable as a product of the time. The early Iron Age was not an enlightened era of politeness and refinement: it was brutal, violent, horrific and entirely lacking in decent plumbing.

But this general violence is not really where the problem lies. Humans do horrific things to each other, we know that. The problems come when God commands the violence, when God, apparently, gets really specific about who is to be killed.

The Canaanite Genocide

This is the thing I get asked about more than any other Bible problem: how can we reconcile a God of love with the violent God of the Old Testament?

There are various 'crunch points' when this problem really comes to a head, but the main one is the conquest of Canaan. When God rescued the Israelites from slavery in Egypt he promised them that they could have 'all the land of Canaan, for a perpetual holding' (Gen. 17:8). There was, however, a snag: the land of Canaan was already populated with . . . er . . . Canaanites. Not to mention tribes like the Hivites, Hittites, Perizzites, Jebusites, Chi-lites, Bakelites, Marmites and the Amorites.*

So God issues instructions: the Israelites are to attack the towns of these people and destroy everyone:

> You must not let anything that breathes remain alive. You shall annihilate them – the Hittites and the Amorites, the Canaanites and the Perizzites, the Hivites and the Jebusites – just as the LORD your God has commanded, so that they may not teach you to do all the abhorrent things that they do for their gods, and you thus sin against the LORD your God.   (Deuteronomy 20:16–18)

So just to be clear: kill anything that breathes. Men, women, children, dogs, cats, cattle, chickens – *anything* that breathes.

For towns outside Canaan, the Israelites could offer terms of peace: if the residents surrendered they would be allowed to live. I mean, they'd all be enslaved, but at least they'd be breathing.

---

* Not all of these are real tribes. The Amorites are though, despite sounding remarkably like fossils.

If they turned down this compelling offer, then the Israelites were to slaughter all the males in the town and take everyone and everything else as booty.

But the Canaanites don't even get this option. No deals for them. Just complete extermination.

As I said, this is the crunchiest of these crunch points. But it's not the only one. During their first, abortive attempt to get into the Promised Land, the Israelites attacked the Midianites, killed the men and the married women and divided up the virgin girls between them (Num. 31). And much later, in 1 Samuel, Saul is ordered by God – via Samuel – to slaughter another tribe called the Amalekites:

> Thus says the LORD of hosts, 'I will punish the Amalekites for what they did in opposing the Israelites when they came up out of Egypt. Now go and attack Amalek, and utterly destroy all that they have; do not spare them, but kill both man and woman, child and infant, ox and sheep, camel and donkey.'
>
> (1 Samuel 15:2–3)

The odd thing about this – leaving aside for one moment the brutality of the command – is the reason. According to the Bible, Saul reigned from about 1030–1010 BC. Yet here he is being ordered to punish the Amalekites for something they did during the exodus, some two hundred years previously. It's like the UK government deciding to punish the USA for declaring independence. (Although now I think of it, that hasn't turned out that well . . .)

It doesn't take a genius to see the problems with these passages. They portray a God who seems entirely OK with genocide. I know that some people hate the use of that word in this context, but the Oxford English Dictionary defines genocide as 'The deliberate and systematic extermination of an ethnic or national group.'

What is that if not the destruction of the Canaanites or the Amalekites?

The usual arguments

First, I want to look at some of the usual arguments to support the biblical accounts.

1: God is free to order the extermination of the Midianites/ Canaanites/Amalekites, etc. He is God and he doesn't have to live by our rules.

As the reformed pastor John Piper puts it, 'It's right for God to slaughter women and children anytime he pleases. God gives life and he takes life. Everybody who dies, dies because God wills that they die.'[1] In other words, we're going to die anyway. If God decides we should die sooner rather than later, that's up to him.

There's a certain logic to this. But it also misses the point. The problem here is not death, but injustice and suffering. We're not talking here about people dying from old age or even illness; we're talking about execution and extinction through violent murder. And didn't God command us not to murder? So how is it OK for God to order that? Or is it like President Nixon defending Watergate on the grounds that 'when the president does it, that means it is not illegal'. I have to say, I'm not convinced by any argument that makes God behave exactly like President Nixon.

2: They had to act this way. It's how things were back then. It's kill or be killed, dumbo.

This argument at least has some historical context to it. We are talking about a violent, brutal period, one in which women and children were classed as possessions, and where tribes sought to kill other tribes on a regular basis. But, again, we're not really talking about warfare. This is not about one group of men in armour defeating another group of men in armour, but about one group of men in armour killing 'everything that breathes'. And doing it on the explicit command of God. It's not about humans having to make compromises in a barbaric culture; it's about God apparently endorsing and encouraging barbarity.

3. It was the only way to get the Canaanites out of the land.

Oh, please. This is *God* we're talking about here. The Creator of the universe. I think if he wanted to he could have found a way to move the Canaanites out of Canaan without involving swords and bloodshed. Whirlwinds, sandstorms, the offer of alternative accommodation in nearby Moab – you know, something that didn't involve the killing.

4. Yes, there are parts of the Bible where God isn't very nice. But we have to balance against them all the bits where he is a God of love, mercy, unicorns, kittens, etc.

That's like saying, 'I know my son's a serial killer, but he's very nice to animals.' God is perfect: he can't have some good bits and some bad bits. If God is love, he can't have some bits that aren't love. If he is just, he can't sometimes have time off so that he can act unjustly. And we can't act like that, can we? The bad stuff that we do is not counteracted by the good stuff: it's forgiven by the love and grace of God.

5. The Canaanites deserved it. They were like the worst people ever. God had to punish them.

This is a surprisingly common argument. These, apparently were the WORST PEOPLE WHO EVER LIVED. It's like Hitler married the Wicked Witch of the West and they had loads of babies, who then engaged in idol worship, started smoking and never did any recycling. The usual argument here is that the Canaanites were offering child sacrifices. That's possible, certainly. But does that alone make them the worst sinners ever? Worse than the Assyrians? Or the Babylonians? Or the Nazis? Or Stalin's Red Guard? Or the Khmer Rouge? Or the Crusaders? Or ISIS? Or any of the other crackpot, evil dictators, zealots and maniacs who have maimed and killed in the name of their idols?

Writing in 1900, the fundamentalist R.A. Torrey argued that the 'iniquity' of the Canaanites was 'so full, their rebellion against God so strong and so universal, their moral corruption and debasement so utter and so pervasive, even down to babes just born, as to make such treatment absolutely necessary in the interests of humanity.'[2]

Wait, even the babes just born were corrupt? This is utter tosh. No society is utterly depraved in this way. Even in the most brutal, corrupt, evil societies there are truly evil people and truly not-so-evil people who are just trying to keep their heads down and not be killed. And surely the thing to do, if they were engaging in child sacrifice, is to rescue the children. Talking of which . . .

5b: Maybe not all of the Canaanites were evil, but you have to kill the children, otherwise they might breed.

Evil is like that. It's in the blood. In a tract called *Examination of the Alleged Discrepancies of the Bible*, John W. Haley wrote:

> Had the women and children been spared, there would soon have been a fresh crop of adult Amalekites, precisely like their predecessors. Or suppose merely the children had been saved; if left to care for themselves they must have miserably perished of starvation; if adopted and reared in Israelite families they might, *from their hereditary disposition and proclivities to evil* have proved a most undesirable and pernicious element in the nation. It was, doubtless, on the whole, the best thing for the world that the Amalekite race should be exterminated.[3]   [Italics added].

I think we can all see where this kind of argument takes us. If we decide that there were people in the Bible that God wanted cleansed, then it doesn't take much to find new races whom God would prefer not to breed. And, indeed, this is what has happened. Oliver Cromwell cast his opponents as Midianites or Amalekites and used this story to justify his massacre of the entire population of Irish towns such as Wexford and Drogheda. 'Amalekite theology' fuelled the racial extermination of the native population during the Spanish conquests of South America. It justified the destruction of Native American populations in North America. These ideas fuelled massacres of Zulus in South Africa and Herero and Nama peoples in Namibia. During the Rwandan Genocide in 1994, where the Hutu people decided to annihilate their Tutsi rivals, one pastor compared the Tutsis to the Amalekites:

> 'If you don't exterminate the Tutsis, you'll be rejected. If you don't want to be rejected by God, then finish the job of killing the people God has rejected. No child, no wife, no old man should be left alive.' And the people said 'Amen.'[4]

The real problem with all these arguments is that in every case God behaves completely unlike Jesus. Jesus said that we should love our enemies and forgive those who persecute us. He said that, never mind murdering our enemies, it was wrong to even *think* about bad things happening to them. The doctrine of the Trinity says that God, Jesus and the Holy Spirit are one. The Gospel of John says that Jesus shows us what God is like. In the words of Archbishop Michael Ramsey:

> It is all too easy for us to profess an orthodox doctrine and yet fail to keep to the supremacy of Jesus for our own understanding of God. The heart of Christian doctrine is not only that Jesus is divine, but that God is Christlike, and in him there is no un-Christ-likeness at all.[5]

God is Christlike – and that is why, for me, none of these arguments holds true.

But there are some alternative ways of looking at these passages. And they involve the fact that this is a *story*.

The case of the non-dead Canaanites

This is a story. And the first thing to say is that it's written in a particular style. The language attributed to God here is the kind of hyperbole that was common at the time.

In August 1868, a large engraved stone was found in a field in Jordan. It dates from around 840 BC and describes the victory won by the kingdom of Moab over its next-door neighbour, Israel. It is known as the Moabite Stone or the Mesha Stone, after King Mesha, the Moabite leader at the time, and it records a spectacular victory over the kingdom of Israel, at that time ruled by King Ahab. According to the inscription, Mesha claimed that, through this victory 'Israel has perished for ever!'*

Which is a bit odd, since the kingdom of Israel went on for another 120 years.

Other ancient accounts use a similar amount of hyperbole. A ruler never just won, he totally obliterated the opponent. Wiped them out.† This is the kind of way in which kings talked about their opponents. Anything less than 100 per cent success never made the inscriptions, and these passages seem to reflect a similar approach. It's the language of official Bronze Age war reports.

This formulaic way of talking can also be found elsewhere in the account. Although the land is described as being full of people and covering a large territory, only a handful of battles are actually described in any detail. The bulk of the conquest is described in a strange, formulaic manner. Joshua 10:28–43 describes how Joshua and 'all Israel' take six cities: Makkedah, Libnah, Lachish, Eglon, Hebron and Debir. But it doesn't seem to know many details and it reduces each conquest to a set pattern. First, Joshua and all Israel

---

* This was the post-split Israel, the northern of the two kingdoms. Remember? We *talked* about this. The Mesha inscription is incredibly significant in that it provides historical confirmation of the existence of the northern kingdom of Israel, and King Omri of Israel (Ahab's father).

† In the fifteenth century BC, the Egyptian Pharaoh Tuthmoses III boasted that 'the numerous army of Mitanni was overthrown within the hour, annihilated totally, like those (now) not existent'. (In fact, Mitanni's forces lived on not only to fight another day, but to fight for another 200 years.) The Assyrian ruler Sennacherib (701–681 BC) described how he cut down 'the soldiers of Hirimme, dangerous enemies, I cut down with the sword; and not one escaped'.

'pass on' from one town to the next and assault it. The Lord 'gives' the towns to Joshua and the army, and then we have pretty much the same phrase for each of the six cities: Joshua 'struck [the city] with the edge of the sword, and every person in it'.

This account concludes with the statement that 'Joshua defeated the whole land, the hill country and the Negeb and the lowland and the slopes, and all their kings; he left no one remaining, but utterly destroyed all that breathed, as the LORD God of Israel commanded.'

It's a strange, artificial, formulaic account. And we know that it didn't happen precisely in the way it is described. The Bible itself offers an alternative, contradictory account in which it is Caleb and his nephew Othniel who capture Hebron and Debir – and they do so after Joshua's death (Josh. 15:13–19; Judg. 1:1–15).

The biblical account also shows that whatever God commanded, not only did many Canaanite cities remain unconquered, but the Canaanites also carried on living alongside the Israelites.*

> **Read it yourself:** Judges 1:27–36 shows a gradual and indeed incomplete conquest.

God even says that because of the Israelites' failure, there is a change of plan:

> 'But you have not obeyed my command. See what you have done! So now I say, I will not drive them out before you; but they shall become adversaries to you, and their gods shall be a snare to you.' (Judges 2:2–3)

---

* It's the same with the Amalekite story. Even though Saul was supposed to have destroyed all the Amalekites, there were still Amalekites around later on in history. David even made raids on them.

Now that doesn't solve the issue of God commanding their destruction, but I think it certainly demonstrates that this story has a lot of ambiguity and uncertainty. It is not as clear cut as it might appear. And the Bible, at least, acknowledges that the complete destruction didn't happen.*

All this – the hyperbole, the formulaic writing, the presence of different traditions within the Bible itself – should alert us to the possibility that the account of the conquest is not documentary history as we would write it today. And this possibility is further strengthened by information from the field of archaeology. Because the uncomfortable fact is, that there is virtually no archaeological evidence for the conquest of Canaan as described in these accounts from Joshua. Now archaeology is not an exact science, and I understand that some people might not want to privilege archaeology over the Bible, but I think we need to pay attention to these claims. Because the overwhelming consensus among archaeologists is that if the invasion did happen, it didn't happen in the way that it is described.

Big events like battles, earthquakes, conflagrations, walls falling down when people blow horns very loudly, etc. tend to leave what is called an 'archaeological footprint'. A flood leaves layers of silt. A burned city leaves a layer of soot and ash. A battle leaves behind discarded weapons and lots of bones.

The Bible accounts gives lists of towns that were destroyed in the conquest. But archaeological research of those sites shows hardly any signs of destruction dating from the thirteenth century BC, the time that the Bible depicts Joshua and his army rampaging their way through the area. Some of the cities described in the battles weren't even occupied at the time. In the Ancient Near

---

* Not only were the Canaanites not destroyed, their descendants are still around today. Research published in the *American Journal of Human Genetics* and using DNA extracted from ancient skulls found that more than 90 per cent of the ancestry of modern-day people from Lebanon was derived from the Canaanites.

East, when a city was captured, it was levelled to the ground and a new one was built on a mound on top. These mounds are called *tels*, and if you dig into a *tel* you can see the periods of destruction like a layer cake. But excavations at the sites of biblical battles, like Jericho and Ai, show that both towns were in ruins at the probable supposed time of the conquest. There were no walls in Jericho to tumble: they'd already fallen down 200 years earlier. Of the twenty or so identifiable sites said to be captured by Joshua and the next generations, only two – Hazor and Bethel – show destruction layers from this period.[6]

All this is the archaeological record. But again, the Bible contains alternative traditions. For one thing, the word 'Ai' means ruins. For another, in Joshua 11:10–11, Joshua is described as leading an attack on Hazor, killing everyone and burning the place to the ground. But in Judges 4:2 we find that Hazor has *not* been destroyed and is apparently a major Canaanite city, ruled by King Jabin of Canaan. There is even evidence within the text of the Bible itself of an alternative history of conquest. Exodus 23:23–33 appears to be a traditional conquest narrative, with God's angel going before the Israelites as they blot out the Amorites, Hittites, Perizzites, Canaanites, Hivites, Campsites, Highlites, etc. But then the text hints at a much more gradual takeover:

> I will not drive them out from before you in one year, or the land would become desolate and the wild animals would multiply against you. Little by little I will drive them out from before you, until you have increased and possess the land.
>
> (Exodus 23:29–30)

This seems to me to reflect a different tradition – a different story – from the smash and awe of Joshua.

So let's see where we are:

1. This is a story, written in a particular style: a style full of hyperbole and over-the-top statements.

2. Whatever God commanded, the Canaanites and the Amalekites were not destroyed.
3. The Bible itself contains alternative traditions and accounts.
4. The archaeological record does not support a massive, violent invasion by millions of Israelites. Instead, it seems more likely that the Israelites just sort of moved in.

All of this seems to me to indicate that this account is not history as we would understand it. And, really, there's no way that it could have been. Our kind of history – the investigative kind with cited sources – hadn't been invented. For that we have to go forward a few centuries.

Historian John Burrow begins his *A History of Histories* like this:

> History – the elaborated, secular, prose narrative . . . of public events, based on inquiry – was born, we can claim with confidence, in Greece between roughly 450 and 430 BC.[7]

It begins with the Greek historians Herodotus and Thucydides. Herodotus was the first person to use the word *historia* to describe his task.* But before then, no one was doing history in that way.

But if this account isn't our kind of history, then what is it? Why would you invent such a thing? Where did this story come from? And how can we cope with a Bible where the history turns out not to be very historical?

Defying gravity

Questions about the historicity of the Bible are pretty common. If we're honest, many of us already have those kinds of secret

---

* A *histor* in ancient Greek was someone who made a judgement based on investigating the facts.

thoughts – if not about these parts of the Bible, then about other bits. And we have mastered the art of a kind of biblical double-think. One part of our brain talks about these bits of the Bible as if they actually happened, while the other half of our brain is going, 'Really? *Really?*'

I'm sure you can think of examples. It might be the numbers – like the ages of the patriarchs. Adam lived till he was 930, Seth lived for 807 years, Methuselah got to 969 and Noah managed to get to 950. Really? Or do the big numbers simply mean something else? In the tales of other, contemporary ancient cultures there are similarly long-lived kings and heroes.* It's a kind of shorthand for the fact that these were very special people. Indeed, throughout the Bible we have to treat the numbers with care. According to the Bible some two million people – men, women and children – left Egypt and wandered in the wilderness. It is hard to see how a group of this size could survive in the wilderness for forty years without leaving a trace. But these weren't societies with sophisticated counting methods.

Then there are the fantastic tales – Balaam and his talking donkey, Samson and his jawbone of mass destruction. Or Joshua 10, as we're already looking at that book. Joshua and the Israelites are doing battle against the Amorites and during the conflict 'The sun stopped in mid-heaven, and did not hurry to set for about a whole day' (Josh. 10:11–14). This phenomenon is not recorded by any other culture anywhere, and, frankly, you'd have thought the neighbouring countries would have noticed it at the very least. More to the point, if the sun stood still, then the earth must have stopped revolving. In which case, I believe, gravity would fail and everyone and everything would be flung off sideways from the surface of the earth at more than 1,600 km/hour.

---

* Even greater actually. According to the Sumerian King List, the first eight Sumerian kings lived for a total of 241,200 years.

This is not to say that there is not some historical core to these stories. With the Joshua story we might be dealing with a real event – a battle during a long day, for example. Personally, I believe there was a Moses figure and a mass escape from slavery, an escape that was seen as liberation with the help of God. After all, if you were creating an origin story for your nation, you would not begin your life as slaves. You would invent something a lot better, like being sneezed out of the nostrils of the gods, or being descended from mystical heroes, or something like that. But the real event has been expanded and filtered through a poetic and theological understanding.

I think part of the problem is classification, actually. In the *Tanakh* – the Jewish Scriptures – not only are these books not put together, but they are spread about in two different sections: the *Nevi'im* and the *Kethuvim*, the Prophets and the Writings. But in Christian Bibles, the Old Testament books of Joshua through to Esther – very different books, written in different styles at different times – are lumped together as 'the historical books'. And because we have a post-Herodotus view of history (although even his marvellous book contains loads of fantastic fables), we now view them as *our* kind of history: the documented, verifiable kind, with dates and recorded statements.

Now I think that there are parts of the Bible which are more like that. And those really are the ones written a lot later when the idea of writing a different kind of history had begun to take shape. Ezra and Nehemiah, writing in the sixth century BC, pay a lot of attention to documentation. There are documented sources cited in Kings and Samuel.* When we get to the New Testament period, we have a mass of archaeological, social, historical and literary material to support the Gospel accounts. It's

---

* For example, the Book of Jashar (2 Samuel 1:18), the Book of the Acts of Solomon (1 Kings 11:41), the Book of the Annals of the Kings of Israel and the Book of the Annals of the Kings of Judah (mentioned in lots of places, e.g. 1 Kings 14:19; 14:29; 15:7; 15:23; 15:31; 16:5; 16:14, etc.).

perfectly reasonable to view the Gospels and Joshua, for example, as being completely different kinds of writings. The Gospels date from some thirty years after the events they describe (and the material that the Gospels use dates from even closer to Jesus' death), not anywhere between five and seven hundred years, as is the case with something like Joshua.

My point is that I am not saying we decide on whether something is historical on the basis of what it is describing. This is nothing to do with the idea of miracles *per se*, and it's nothing to do with God speaking and people hearing his voice. It's about letting the text be what it is. It's about the kind of writing we are dealing with.

The Bible refuses to behave like 'proper' modern history. It will not conform itself to our expectations. The writers and editors of these ancient books are not trying to provide an objective, documentary-style, official history on our terms. They are telling a story – a story about the Israelites, their behaviour and their relationship with Yahweh.

Why 'Canaanite' might not mean 'Canaanite'

The books of Joshua and Judges form part of a work which some scholars call the Deuteronomistic History. This runs from Deuteronomy, through Joshua, Judges, 1 and 2 Samuel and 1 and 2 Kings. It collects together material from written and oral sources from different dates and times. The final event mentioned in 2 Kings is the release of King Jehoiachin from prison (2 Kings 25:27–30) which took place in 562 BC. So it must have reached its final form shortly after that time, during the Babylonian exile (586–536 BC).

This was a time when the Israelites were trying to make sense of their national story. They were trying to work out why they had been exiled. So there is an underlying theme of these books reflecting the conviction that Israel's ownership of the land was directly related to its obedience or disobedience to the covenant with God. And the most frequent form of disobedience was idolatry. Time after time, it is the worship of idols that draws the community away from God. Bad kings are those who set up altars to foreign gods; good kings are those who tear them down.

What might that do to the stories about the Canaanites? Well, for one thing it reveals a God who is powerful and victorious. It reveals a God who is concerned with rooting out every last drop of idolatry from the land. For the exiles in Babylon, these stories would be a call to remember that it was only through God's will that they received the land. And that, above all, Yahweh's people have to remain pure. 'All or nothing' is the message of Joshua. Put away the gods; dedicate yourself totally to Yahweh.

In Joshua, we see a point of departure, a point of change. And it is at this crucial moment that Israel is called to dedicate itself totally to Yahweh and to concentrate solely and totally on God. The exiles believed that they would return one day to Jerusalem. We know that when Ezra returned, one of the key problems he faced was that the original group of returnees had intermarried with other tribes and ethnic groups – something Ezra saw as deeply threatening to the restored state of Israel.

The point is that, for the writers, editors and, indeed, audience of these stories, the past was alive and active, something that spoke powerfully about the present.

It was history, but not as we know it . . .

If we insist on viewing the Bible as our kind of history, then we will always face difficulties. For example, there are three different accounts of the choice of Saul as king and two accounts of Saul's rejection by God. There are two accounts of how David came into Saul's service, of David's escape to the Philistines and of his sparing of Saul's life. There are even conflicting accounts of David's most famous deed – the killing of Goliath. The main story is in 1 Samuel 17, but right at the end of Samuel, you get this verse:

> Then there was another battle with the Philistines at Gob; and
> Elhanan son of Jaare-oregim, the Bethlehemite, killed Goliath the
> Gittite, the shaft of whose spear was like a weaver's beam.
>
> (2 Samuel 21:19)*

So who did kill Goliath? David or the man from Bethlehem (and *Star Wars* character waiting to happen), Elhanan son of Jaare-oregim?

Even when we get to the New Testament, there is material from different traditions. Luke, for example has a completely different set of stories about Jesus' birth than does Matthew. Luke has the shepherds; Matthew has the magi. Luke has Mary's song; Matthew has Herod and the escape to Egypt. Both have genealogies; but both are different. Luke and Matthew also know different stories about Judas.

Read it yourself: The two accounts are in Matthew 27:3–10 and Acts 1:15–19.

In Matthew's version, Judas repents of his betrayal and hangs himself. The priests then use the thirty pieces of silver to buy a field as a burial place for foreigners. And that's why it's called 'the Field of Blood'. In the version in Acts it is Judas who buys the field and, while on some kind of site visit, he falls headlong and 'he burst open in the middle and all his bowels gushed out'. And *that* is why the field is called 'the Field of Blood'. They can't both be true.

How does all this help us with the problem of whether God commanded the killing of the Canaanites? Well, there are examples where the Bible itself argues with its own traditions, and

---

* Writing later, the author of Chronicles corrects this verse. In his account, Elhanan kill Goliath's *brother* (1 Chr. 20:5).

even amends previous statements attributed to God. In the case of the killing of the Canaanites, of course, what we're interested in is whether or not God really issued the command.

So let's look briefly at two passages – two more stories – which address similar statements by God. In the first instance we have one writer claiming that God's will was being done, while another utterly condemns the events and says God has a totally different view of it. In the second instance, a problematic command from God is assigned to a different being entirely.

The case of the crimes of Jezreel

Story number one. In 2 Kings 9 a military commander called Jehu, Son of Nimshi, is appointed by God to . . . well, to kill a load of people actually. His mission – should he choose to accept it – is to slaughter 'the house of your master [i.e. King] Ahab.' Ahab by now is dead, but his son Joram is on the throne. Jehu accepts the mission. He not only kills Joram, King of Israel, but also King Ahaziah of Judah. He goes to Samaria and dispatches Jezebel, the wife of Ahab. Then he orders the slaughter of seventy sons of Ahab. And their friends. 'Jehu killed all who were left of the house of Ahab in Jezreel, all his leaders, close friends, and priests, until he left him no survivor' (2 Kgs 10:11).

Read it yourself: The story of the murderous Jehu and his very fast chariot driving is told in 2 Kings 9–10.

It doesn't even stop there. Jehu meets forty-two kinsmen of King Ahaziah of Judah who had made the mistake of coming to visit Jezebel, and he 'spared none of them' (2 Kgs 10:14). Finally, he sent a fake invitation out to the prophets of Baal, promising them that he would join them in worshipping Baal. The prophets gathered in the temple of Baal, whereupon Jehu ordered eighty soldiers to come in and butcher them all.

So, I think we can use the word, 'thorough' to describe him. And possibly 'homicidal' and 'maniac'. Shockingly, though, it seems as though God is pleased with all this work:

> The LORD said to Jehu, 'Because you have done well in carrying out what I consider right, and in accordance with all that was in my heart have dealt with the house of Ahab, your sons of the fourth generation shall sit on the throne of Israel.' But Jehu was not careful to follow the law of the LORD the God of Israel with all his heart; he did not turn from the sins of Jeroboam, which he caused Israel to commit.   (2 Kings 10:30–31)

This is another of those pretty difficult texts, where God commends someone for wholesale butchery, deceit and destruction. But the funny thing is that, elsewhere, the Bible disagrees entirely.

The book of Hosea dates from the mid-eighth century BC, some three hundred years earlier than the finished version of Kings. It's a book that warns that the Assyrians are going to punish the northern kingdom of Israel, then ruled by Jehu's great-grandson, Jeroboam. As a prophetic act, Hosea is told to name one of his sons 'Jezreel'.

> And the LORD said to [Hosea], 'Name him Jezreel; for in a little while I will punish the house of Jehu for the blood of Jezreel, and I will put an end to the kingdom of the house of Israel. On that day I will break the bow of Israel in the valley of Jezreel.'
>
>   (Hosea 1:4–5)

What happened at Jezreel? Jezreel was where Jehu slaughtered Jezebel. Where he began the bloodbath that followed his coup d'état. Jezreel is the symbol of all Jehu's butchery and mayhem. And God is going to punish his 'house' – his ruling dynasty – for it.

So here we have the Bible giving two competing accounts of what God thought of something. In the history of Kings – written much later than the book of Hosea – what Jehu does is a good thing. But to Hosea, Jesu's actions were one of the causes of Israel's ultimate destruction. Two accounts, two competing interpretations of whether or not God approved of violence.

The case of the evil census

Story number two. In one of the most troubling stories of King David, the Lord incites David to take a census:

> Again the anger of the LORD was kindled against Israel, and he incited David against them, saying, 'Go, count the people of Israel and Judah.'   (2 Samuel 24:1)

David does as he is told and makes a headcount. But then he regrets it (2 Sam. 24:10). He realises he has sinned and he begs God for mercy. But God insists on punishing David and gives him three options: choose either three years of famine, three months on the run being pursued by his foes, or three days of pestilence. David chooses the pestilence, and in three days 70,000 people die.

> **Read it yourself:** The two accounts of the census are in 2 Samuel 24 and 1 Chronicles 21. They describe the census, the plague and the purchase of the threshing floor which would one day be the site of the Temple.

It doesn't take much to see the problems here. David was incited by God to take the census, and yet he is also punished for it. Some 70,000 people are killed for something that God told David to do.

We find it hard to reconcile this. And we're not the only ones. The writer of Chronicles found it hard as well. His solution, though, was to change one detail. He starts his story like this:

> Satan stood up against Israel, and incited David to count the
> people of Israel. (1 Chronicles 21:1)

In this version God didn't tell David to do anything: it was Satan.

It certainly solves the theological issue. But it does so by completely contradicting the earlier account. The writer of Chronicles is basically saying that the earlier tradition is just wrong. In other words, we have *within the Bible* a passage denying that God gave a specific order originally attributed to him.

What's happening here? Why does he do this?

I think it's obvious: the writer of Chronicles is altering his view of an earlier account because he has a new understanding of God.

We saw how the Jews' understanding of God changed and developed over the centuries. And we saw how the concept of monotheism brought into new focus the problem of evil. One of the ways in which Jewish theology addressed the latter problem was the development of the character of Satan. As we saw earlier, in the book of Job, he is The Satan – it's a job title. But gradually Satan moved from being 'tester-in-chief' in the heavenly court to being an adversary of God.* In the period between the end of the Old Testament and the beginning of the New, this idea grows

---

* Satan is only mentioned four times in the Hebrew Bible. He appears twice as a kind of job description (in the book of Job and in the story of Balaam's ass, where the angel of the Lord says to Balaam, 'I have come out as a [satan]' (Num. 22:32–33), meaning 'adversary', or even 'roadblock'. Then he appears twice as an adversary of God – in Chronicles, and in another of the later writings of the Bible, the book of Zechariah (Zech. 3:1–2). Although later Christian tradition identifies him with the serpent in Eden, the text of Genesis nowhere identifies the serpent with Satan.

until he becomes the evil figure we encounter a great deal more in the New Testament.*

There isn't space here to go into the development of that idea. The main point I want to make is that the writer of Chronicles simply did not believe that God would order David to do something evil. He *knew* that God was not like that.

There are many points in the Bible where writers and prophets discern God saying different things. Hosea saw only evil in Jehu; the writer of Kings saw a man carrying out the will of God. Maybe God did issue that instruction, or maybe the Israelites just thought he did. Perhaps it is the case that, as Pete Enns writes, 'God never told the Israelites to kill the Canaanites. The Israelites believed that God told them to kill the Canaanites.'[8] Or maybe Joshua isn't that kind of 'history' at all, but a tale told about the past to explain a very different present.

Whatever the case, I think the little incident in Chronicles gives us something very important in shaping our response to these stories. Because whatever happened, or didn't happen, we *know* that God isn't like that.

And we know that because of Jesus.

Thinking again about Old Testament history

Ultimately, it seems to me that we are faced with a choice. We can either change our view of the Bible or change our view of God as a God of love.

I know that many Christians insist on believing both that God is love and that he also ordered the extermination of innocent men, women and children. Personally, this is not a view I am prepared to share.

---

* This is different again to the 'devil' figure pictured in later Christian mythology and in numerous films and heavy metal album covers with the horns and the forked tail. That doesn't come from the Bible, but from medieval wall paintings.

Anyway, the point of this book is to say that we don't have to struggle with those theological contortions. What we can do is rethink our view of the Bible – and particularly the way the Bible writers represent history. It's not the Bible that is at fault – it's that we are trying to force it into our categories. We have to recognise that what is being presented here is not our kind of documentary history, but a series of stories about identity and purpose and our relationship with God.

And the really important thing is that, whatever viewpoint we hold, we must always rethink our relationship with these stories because of Jesus.

However God acted in the past – or is depicted as having acted in the past – he does not act in the same way today. I don't mean that God is not active in the world. I believe he still acts miraculously at times, and through the Holy Spirit he is active in the lives of millions of believers around the world. But let's face facts: unless you know something I don't, God is not currently taking down evil empires with storms of enormous hailstones, or drowning their tank battalions in the sea. We do not see huge numbers of oppressed, enslaved people being led out into the desert by pillars of smoke and fire. I am not meaning to be facetious about this; I'm just plainly stating something that we know to be true but which many Christians, it seems to me, are reluctant to admit. Even if he did do a load of it in the past, God is no longer in the smiting business today.

This was true even for the writers of Bible times. Later texts – particularly those written in the debris of the destroyed Jerusalem – have a plaintive tone. 'Why don't you act now as you used to?' they ask. The writer of Psalm 74, looking around him in the smoking ruins of Jerusalem pleads with God:

> Remember Mount Zion, where you came to dwell.
> Direct your steps to the perpetual ruins;
>> the enemy has destroyed everything in the sanctuary.
> Your foes have roared within your holy place;

> they set up their emblems there . . .
> We do not see our emblems;
> > there is no longer any prophet,
> > and there is no one among us who knows how long.
> How long, O God, is the foe to scoff?
> > Is the enemy to revile your name for ever?
> Why do you hold back your hand;
> > why do you keep your hand in your bosom?
>
> (Psalm 74:2–4, 9–11)

Time and again the poets and the later prophets have to come to terms with the fact that God no longer storms in and smashes their enemies. He works through people – through kings and leaders and politicians – but, in Isaiah's mysterious words he has become 'a God who hides himself' (Isa. 45:15). And the same is true today. I do not think God is any happier with the dictators, the violence and the corruption than he was 3,000 years ago. But he does not act in the same way.

However people understood God in the past, we understand him in a different way today. We need to read the Bible in the light of what *we* know about God. We know that he is Christlike.

Jesus came to show us what God is like. Many people have an image of God that is straight out of Joshua. They think that God really wants to go all Old Testament on us and smite us, yea into many pieces thereof, but that Jesus continually talks him out of it. But the Father and the Son are not playing some nice cop/ nasty cop routine. Jesus is not God's carer. He is not God's anger-management coach. He is not God's tranquilliser. Jesus *is* God.

Jesus says that he and the Father are the same – 'Whoever has seen me has seen the Father' (John 14:9). So it's not just that Jesus is like God, it's also that God is like Jesus. As Christians, our baseline as to what God is like is the figure of Jesus, and Jesus is the very opposite of a smite-first-ask-questions-later God. In the Gospels, every time Jesus has the opportunity to do any smiting, he refuses. He refuses to rain down fire on the Samaritan village; he refuses to stone a woman caught in adultery. Dying and bleeding on the cross, he refuses to call down armies of angels to save him.

Instead, Jesus talks of endless, limitless forgiveness. He calls on people to love their enemies, to offer the other cheek. If we believe in the Trinity – *really* believe in it, rather than just mouthing the words during the Creed – we have to believe that what we see in Jesus is the character and actions of God. Whatever the Israelites heard from God – or thought they did – we cannot possibly behave in the same way. We follow a Christlike God.

God is Christlike, and in him there is no unChristlikeness at all. I just want to repeat that.

If we want to read the Bible properly, we must read it through the lens of Jesus Christ. And if one part of the Bible says something that conflicts with what Jesus says, well, I'm going to listen to Jesus first.

That doesn't mean I reject these kinds of texts, or refrain from grappling with them. I want to keep on praying and talking and thinking about these passages, and asking God to reveal their application for my life. If I put aside the historicity or otherwise and think of the daily battles that I have to fight to take possession of my own life, I have plenty enough 'Canaanites' to fight in that context. Canaanites can stand for all the things that tempt us away from following God. We can read these stories as an encouragement to purity and integrity and resisting the culture around us . . . rather than an encouragement to genocide.

Or I could see these stories as a message about never going into conflict for personal gain. The demand not to take a single item of booty is common to all these texts of destruction.

Or I could reflect on how difficult it is to hear the command of God, and ask myself whether there haven't been many times in my life when I have mistakenly believed that God hates the same people that I do.

Or I could imagine the victims: their terror, their panic, their grief and loss. Maybe that will inspire me to think about the victims today of all those who kill and maim and bomb, believing that somehow God has commanded them to do it.

Or I could simply contrast this passage with the message of Jesus, and wrestle with the challenge of living a Jesus-shaped life in the midst of a culture that is every bit as addicted to violence as the age of Joshua and Judges.

The same kind of approach is true for so many of these difficult stories in the early parts of the Bible. They are trying to tell us lots of important and true things: that the universe was created by God, that human beings are made in God's likeness, that cheats, failures and drunkards can still be a part of God's plan for history, that God is powerful and ever present, and lots, lots more. But they are not trying to be 'our' kind of history, because the writers of ancient history (and this is the same for ancient history outside the Bible) didn't really think that way. Instead, the Bible simply presents us with these stories and invites us to read.

10 Thinking again about reading the Bible

This morning's reading was Zephaniah 3:14–20. No doubt you can all remember that instantly, but just in case, it's a prophecy about the return of the exiles to Jerusalem from Babylon. It concludes with these lovely verses:

> I will deal with all your oppressors at that time.
> And I will save the lame and gather the outcast,
> and I will change their shame into praise
>   and renown in all the earth.
> At that time I will bring you home,
>   at the time when I gather you;
> for I will make you renowned and praised
>   among all the peoples of the earth,
> when I restore your fortunes
>   before your eyes, says the Lord.'   (Zephaniah 3:19–20)

Lots of things occurred to me as I read it. From the point of view of the historical context, I knew what it meant. The oppressors were the Babylonians and the prophet was predicting a return to Jerusalem. I could also see another reading here – how that bit about the lame and the outcast was a challenge to the old understanding of the Law in which the lame were specifically excluded from the Temple.

And yet all I could think about was what it meant for me to be 'gathered'. Some days I feel so fragmented, so shattered, physically and mentally. For me it was as if God was saying this to me: I will gather up all the pieces of you, all that brokenness and failure, and I will bring it all back together.* I really wanted, in that moment, to understand what it meant to be someone gathered together by God. Maybe I could be whole again. Restored.

Then I read an interpretation from Cyril of Alexandria. He wrote this:

> As far as the deeper meaning of the passage is concerned, it clearly commands Jerusalem to rejoice exceedingly, to be especially glad, to cheer up wholeheartedly as its trespasses are wiped out, evidently through Christ. The spiritual and holy Zion – that is, the church, the holy multitude of the believers – is justified in Christ and only in him.[1]

So Cyril thinks it's all about Christ forgiving sins. The people who listened to Zephaniah would have understood it to be about the Babylonians. I thought God was speaking about my fragmented psyche.

Which reading was correct?

All of them.

Why Jesus, Paul and Matthew would all fail preaching class

I want to close by going back to where we started: to the idea of Bible study, an idea which, for many people, is about as appealing as tonsillitis.

All it is, too often, is the opportunity for humiliation or embarrassment. You know, like those moments in house group or youth group when the leader says, 'Why don't we start by reading the

---

* I'm not sure he's going to make me 'renowned and praised among all the peoples of the earth', but I certainly wouldn't say no to a few more book sales.

passage? We'll go round the circle and each of us will read out three or four verses. How does that sound?'

Everyone nods their head. Some people even look excited. But you know exactly how it sounds: it sounds terrifying. Because you know how this is going to end up. You are going to get the *names*. The verses with the places that no one can pronounce. The people with names like Mephibosheth. Or Abimelech. Or Wamalamabinbang.

It's inevitable. It doesn't even matter if there are no names in the passage. They will miraculously appear in the text the moment it gets to you, because that's what Bible study is all about: revealing your ignorance.

As I said at the beginning, I'm all for responsible biblical interpretation. Understanding the historical context, exploring the grammar and the word-meanings: all that exegesis stuff has its place.

But there's one thing that should keep it in perspective. And that is that Paul didn't read the Bible like that at all. Nor did Matthew. Or Peter.

And most of all, nor did Jesus.

Jesus had what you might call a 'flexible' attitude to his use of Scripture.

At one time he goes to his home town of Nazareth and speaks in the synagogue. He gives a very brief exposition of a text from Isaiah about the Jubilee – the 'year of the Lord's favour' – which he claims refers to himself. There is then a brief discussion, after which the citizens of the town try to stone him. It's pretty much par for the course when it comes to Jesus' teaching. It's grievous bodily preaching.

But what is interesting is Jesus' use of the text. The passage Jesus quotes is from Isaiah 61:1–2 in our Bibles. But if you compare the text as recorded in Luke with the text as it appears in Isaiah, it's apparent that Jesus has taken some *serious* liberties with the Bible.

Read it yourself: The incident is in Luke 4:16–30. The text Jesus quotes is a mix-up of Isaiah 61:1–2, with Isaiah 58:6 thrown in for good measure.

First, Jesus omits a complete line from the original (about binding up the broken-hearted). Then he merges two statements together about releasing prisoners and providing liberty to the captives. He then inserts a reference to blind people which is *not* in the original text, and chucks in a phrase from an entirely different passage: 'to let the oppressed go free', which is actually from Isaiah 58:6. Finally, and most significantly, he cuts off the end of the prophecy by leaving out the bit where Isaiah talks about vengeance.

Try this in your own church and you would be barred from ever leading a Bible study again.

This is not just Jesus going rogue, as it were. Luke's account fits with what we know of synagogue practice. Anyone reading a passage from the Torah had to be accurate – in fact, the reader would be supervised and corrected, with someone looking over his shoulder to make sure he got it right – but Isaiah and the other prophets were not seen as 'Scripture' in the same way, so speakers were allowed to be more creative with those. So while Jesus seems to us to be treating Scripture irresponsibly, he is in fact reading Scripture in a way that was perfectly acceptable at the time. It's not his treatment of Isaiah that gets people angry, but his suggestion that the devout Jews in Nazareth are like those who rejected the prophets, and that it will be the outsiders who really get the blessing.

He takes a similarly creative approach in his teaching elsewhere. As we saw, one of the main aims of biblical exegesis is to faithfully recover the original meaning of the text. Well, apparently Jesus isn't interested in that at all. At one point some Sadducees have come to him with an abstract problem about who can marry whom after the resurrection.

> Jesus answered them, 'You are wrong, because you know neither the scriptures nor the power of God. For in the resurrection they neither marry nor are given in marriage, but are like angels in heaven. And as for the resurrection of the dead, have you not read what was said to you by God, "I am the God of Abraham, the God of Isaac, and the God of Jacob"? He is God not of the dead, but of the living.' And when the crowd heard it, they were astounded at his teaching.   (Matthew 22:29–33)

It's a crowd-pleasing answer. But let's be honest, it's also an answer that contorts the original text into a completely new meaning. The verse that Jesus quotes has absolutely nothing to do with the resurrection in its original context. God is simply saying that he is the God of Moses' ancestors. The present tense refers to God, not to the Patriarchs. Yet people seem to approve of the cleverness of the answer. And nobody shouts out, 'Oi! Rubbish exegesis!'

The thing is that, again, Jesus is not doing anything out of the ordinary. Indeed, we can see that this kind of highly allusive, sod-the-context way of reading the Bible was enthusiastically embraced by other New Testament writers. Matthew, especially, is the master of the out-of-context allusion. He is always throwing in Scripture references, yet looked at critically a lot of them seem odd. For example, when Matthew tells the story of the massacre of the innocents, he links it to a line from Jeremiah about Rachel weeping for her children (Jer. 31:15):

> A voice was heard in Ramah,
>   wailing and loud lamentation,
> Rachel weeping for her children;
>   she refused to be consoled, because they are no more'
>   (Matthew 2:18)

The tenuous connection here is Rachel, whose tomb was thought to be in the region of Bethlehem (Gen. 35:19–20; 1 Sam. 10:2). But apart from that, nothing else about the quotation really makes any sense. Ramah – the place mentioned in the quotation – is literally miles away from Bethlehem, where the massacre took place. Eleven miles away to be precise, and on the other side of Jerusalem. And as if that wasn't enough, the 'children' in the Jeremiah passage are not babes or toddlers, but members of the tribes from Israel who have been killed or scattered by the Assyrians.

Similarly, Matthew describes Jesus' flight to Jerusalem and return to Galilee as a fulfilment of the prophecy in Hosea (Matt. 2:15): 'out of Egypt I called my son.' But here's that prophecy in context:

> When Israel was a child, I loved him,
>   and out of Egypt I called my son.
> The more I called them,
>   the more they went from me;
> they kept sacrificing to the Baals,
>   and offering incense to idols.
>
> Yet it was I who taught Ephraim to walk,
>   I took them up in my arms;
>   but they did not know that I healed them.   (Hosea 11:1–3)

This has got absolutely nothing to do with the Messiah: it's all about Israel, the exodus from Egypt and their subsequent disobedience!

So what is happening here? Well, just as an aside, I think this skewers the argument that Matthew invented a lot of stories about Jesus in order to fit Old Testament prophecies. Frankly, most of the time the prophecies he connects to events in Jesus' life simply don't fit very well. Actually, most of the time they are not even prophecies. What I think Matthew is doing is recording genuine Church traditions about Jesus' life, and as he does that he finds other bits of the Scriptures speak to him. The breath of God is blowing through these Scriptures, bringing them to life for Matthew in an entirely new way. We might find the links tenuous, but to Matthew these passages are *inspired*.

But it's surprising how often in the New Testament the writers treat Scripture in a way that strikes us as positively bizarre. In Galatians 3, for example, Paul deliberately interprets a collective noun as a singular just to fit his argument:

> The promises were spoken to Abraham and to his seed. Scripture does not say 'and to seeds', meaning many people, but 'and to your seed', meaning one person, who is Christ.
>
> (Galatians 3:16, NIV)

I've chosen the NIV here because it uses the word 'seed'. The NRSV goes for full-on over-explaining mode and translates it quite ridiculously:

> Now the promises were made to Abraham and to his offspring; it does not say, 'And to offsprings', as of many; but it says, 'And to your offspring', that is, to one person, who is Christ.

Offsprings? *Offsprings?* That's not even a word.

Anyway, back to the point: anyone who reads the original prophecy in Genesis *knows* that 'seed' is not singular in this context. But Paul doesn't seem to care. And he's not doing anything wrong according to the interpretative practices of the time. Jewish rabbis had a tradition of creative reflection on Scriptures, and some of them do the same things as Paul does, such as basing their arguments on the plural or singular forms of a noun.[2]

Sometimes Paul actually alters Scripture to prove his point. In Romans 11:26–27 he quotes from Isaiah:

> And so all Israel will be saved; as it is written,
>   'Out of Zion will come the Deliverer;
>   he will banish ungodliness from Jacob.'
>   'And this is my covenant with them,
>   when I take away their sins.'   (Romans 11:26–27)

But if you look at the passage in Isaiah, it reads:

> And he will come to Zion as Redeemer,
>> to those in Jacob who turn from transgression, says the LORD.
>>> (Isaiah 59:20)

And it's not any different in the Septuagint. It says that the Redeemer will come *to* Zion. Paul appears to have completely changed the direction of the Deliverer. Is he misremembering? Is he quoting from a different, now lost, version? Or is he being 'creative' with Scripture?

Meanwhile, the writer of Hebrews says this:

> By faith Abraham, when put to the test, offered up Isaac. He who had received the promises was ready to offer up his only son, of whom he had been told, 'It is through Isaac that descendants shall be named after you.' (Hebrews 11:17–18)

Wait a minute. His *only* son? What happened to Ishmael? He's been dropped. Not relevant to the conversation.

For the writers of the New Testament, the stories were not to be analysed but to be creatively reinterpreted. That meant they could be 'read' as being about something else entirely. In 1 Peter, for example, the story of Noah becomes a symbol of baptism:

> . . . when God waited patiently in the days of Noah, during the building of the ark, in which a few, that is, eight people, were saved through water. And baptism, which this prefigured, now saves you. (1 Peter 3:20–22)

I mean, that's stretching it a bit. The use of Old Testament stories as allegory or symbolism is an approach that Paul uses as well. In an extended passage in Galatians he uses Sarah, Abraham's wife, and Hagar, her Egyptian slave woman, to represent the 'slavery' of the Law as opposed to the freedom of the Christian gospel. It would be hard to argue that this is proper exegesis – that this was the original meaning of whoever edited that story into Genesis. I don't think that's what Paul is doing either. He's seeing something new, a meaning in Scripture that no one has seen before, a story beneath the story.

Reading rabbinically

Paul was a rabbi, of course, and this is a very rabbinic way of reading the text. Many of the early rabbis believed that every word, every syllable of Scripture counted. So they couldn't discount the difficulties and contradictions, the problematic stories, the missing details and all the kinds of things that we have been discussing. Instead they sought to find a deeper meaning, a hidden layer. They called this approach 'midrash', which is not a stomach complaint: it means 'searching out'. Midrash as a technique or approach only really gets going after the fall of the Temple in AD 70. Midrash increasingly took on the task of exploring Scripture for different, hidden meanings. Scripture for them became something that had to be explored, carefully investigated, and which revealed hidden meanings.

The early church fathers adopted this kind of approach as well, largely because they were taught how to read the Bible by the rabbis. Writers like Origen and Augustine read the Bible in a highly symbolic way, which today strikes us as faintly ridiculous. In one sermon, for example, Augustine talks about the incident where the risen Jesus eats some grilled fish:

> They offered him what they had: a portion of grilled fish. Grilled fish means martyrdom, faith proved by fire. Why is it only a portion? Paul says, 'If I deliver my body to be burned, but have not love, I gain nothing.' Imagine a complete body of martyrs. Some suffer because of love, while others suffer out of pride.

Remove the pride portion, offer the love portion. That is the food for Christ. Give Christ his portion. Christ loves the martyrs who suffered out of love.[3]

So to Augustine it's clear. Grilled fish means . . . er . . . martyrs.

No. No, it doesn't. At least not to us. And I'm pretty sure not to John, whose Gospel records the story. But to Augustine these kind of readings made perfect sense. For the great church fathers – those who helped to form the core doctrines of the Church – this was the way to read the Scriptures.

Now, I'm not trying to undermine the arguments. Though I might find their reading curious, we cannot say that they are reading the Bible incorrectly. It was these very ways of reading Scripture that allowed the church fathers to discern the core doctrines of the Church.

The point is that there never has been just one correct way of reading the Bible. And that's still true today. There isn't space here – you will be relieved to find – to discuss the other ways in which Scripture has been read across the centuries. In recent decades there has been an explosion of different techniques – form criticism, narrative criticism, liberation theology, feminist readings, reader-response criticism, structuralism, postmodernist readings, postcolonial reading, postmanpat readings . . . You name it, some professor somewhere is making a living teaching it.

You are at liberty to google them all and have a go.

That's the thing: just have a go. Dive in. Put aside your fears of getting it wrong and have faith that you might encounter something right and true. If you find a bit that grips you and moves you, praise the Lord. If you find a boring bit, then still praise the Lord, and move on. Ask questions. Use your imagination. Listen for the voice of God. But for heaven's sake don't worry about whether you're going to get it right. Because there never has been a 'right' way to read the Bible. And every generation finds its own ways of listening for the breath of God.

Throughout this book I've been arguing that we have to accept the Bible on its own terms, to stop trying to force it to be something it's not. But it also works the other way round – for us as readers. I think, in a way, the Bible accepts us on our terms as well. God is not going to ask you to fake a response to these stories. What he wants is our reality, our honesty, our willingness to engage. He wants our attention.

In the end, I don't think God will ban people from his eternal presence because they tithe or they don't tithe, if they believe that grilled fish means martyrs, or if they don't. I'm not even sure God is that bothered about whether you take Jonah literally or not. Or whether you read the King James Version, the NIV or the Hamlyn *Children's Bible* circa 1965.

But I am pretty certain he's going to take a harsh view of anyone who uses Scripture to cause harm to others. That's the kind of thing Jesus is criticising here:

'But woe to you, scribes and Pharisees, hypocrites! For you lock people out of the kingdom of heaven. For you do not go in yourselves, and when others are going in, you stop them. Woe to you, scribes and Pharisees, hypocrites! For you cross sea and land to make a single convert, and you make the new convert twice as much a child of hell as yourselves.' (Matthew 23:13–15)

Or maybe I'm misreading it.

Be the badly behaved Bible

The Bible is a book which misbehaves.

That's the point of all this. The point of unlearning all these myths and misconceptions about the Bible is not so that we can get along without it, but so that we can find a place within it.

It's not about defusing the Bible, neutering it, dismissing it as a fabrication, fiction or fairy story. It's about joining in with that story, letting ourselves be swept up in the tale of the coming of God's kingdom.

Here's the thing, the truly amazing thing. Ultimately we are not just called to read the Bible; we are called to *be* the Bible. Listen to Paul writing to those Corinthians:

> You yourselves are our letter, written on our hearts, to be known and read by all; and you show that you are a letter of Christ, prepared by us, written not with ink but with the Spirit of the living God, not on tablets of stone but on tablets of human hearts.   (2 Corinthians 3:2–3)

Paul claims that we can be a 'letter of Christ'. We can be a kind of Scripture. There's an old saying about mission which runs, 'You may be the only Bible that some people ever read.' Whatever we think about the Bible, the fact is that most people – and, sadly, I think, most Christians – will never really read it. They will hear about it; they might hear it read to them, but they will never lose themselves in the text or immerse themselves in the story. They will never be transformed by it.

Now we can face this in two ways. The first way is to change the way we talk about the Bible so that maybe, just maybe, people will think that reading the Bible might be a good thing to do. That's what this book has been about.

The second way is to *live* the Bible, to shape our lives around the teaching, example and presence of Jesus – its central character. Great literature, they say, requires great readers. To read this literature – the greatest literature of them all – requires that we enter into a relationship with it, a conversation with it.

To use the powerful terms coined by Martin Buber, we should stop looking at the Bible as an 'it', and start looking at it as a 'you'. As long as the Bible is an object, an 'it', we will try to master it, use it, excavate it and exploit it for our purposes. Only when the Bible becomes a 'you' can we have a proper relationship with it. Only then will it speak to us and tell us something new.

And we *need* to hear new things. In an important little nugget in Matthew's Gospel, Jesus describes a new kind of scribe, one instructed in the kingdom of God:

> And he said to them, 'Therefore every scribe who has been trained for the kingdom of heaven is like the master of a household who brings out of his treasure what is new and what is old.'
>
> (Matthew 13:52)

The word translated 'trained' literally means 'having been made a disciple'. So there's a sense of combination here, of how the insights of the scribes of the Law have become something greater – transformed, enlarged, supercharged by Jesus-powered disciple-ship. And we should take this injunction seriously: as disciples of Jesus, our call is not to find in the text the same old things, but to bring out new things.

I think that means we have not only the right, but also the responsibility, to approach the text in a different way. We can allow the stories to speak to us without forcing them to conform to our theology. We can dwell with the text and use our God-given imagination. We can ask questions and listen for answers. And I think we can acknowledge that we, as a reader, have a bigger role to play.

Reading the Bible should be more energising, more challenging, more *fun*, dammit. In the words of Peter Enns, 'God did not design scripture to be a hushed afternoon in an oak-panelled library. Instead, God has invited us to participate in a wrestling match, a forum for us to be stretched and to grow.'[4]

There is plenty in the text to wrestle with. What is the text saying to us right now? How is our heart responding to the words? What do we *feel* about it? Are we angry, comforted, scared? How is God calling me into action as a result of this passage? Is this a passage where I sense the breath of God? All this kind of stuff matters, because this is what story is all about.

Few people read the Bible today. And in some ways that is

nothing new. In one of his sermons, the fourth-century bishop John Chrysostom used the example of the Ethiopian eunuch to challenge – and by 'challenge', I mean 'have a go at' – his flock:

> Consider, I ask you, what a great effort it was not to neglect reading even while on a journey, and especially while seated in a chariot. Let this be heeded by those people who do not even deign to do it at home but rather think reading the Scriptures is a waste of time, claiming as an excuse their living with a wife, conscription in military service, caring for children, attending to domestics and looking after other concerns, they do not think it necessary for them to show any interest in reading the holy Scriptures.[5]

Too many people today think that reading the Bible is a waste of time. And loads of those who think this way are sitting in our pews and looking as though they are listening to the sermons. What will change their minds? Not, I suggest, carrying on talking about Scripture in the same old way. Those days are gone. Instead, those of us who care about the Bible have to help people engage with it in new, dynamic ways. We have to help people to see the Bible not as an archaic text, or a doctrinal encyclopaedia, or as a set of instructions handed down from on high, but as a place where God shows up.

And we have to be aware that, when we view Scripture this way, it will not do what we want. It will surprise us and challenge us and catch us unawares. Because the Bible never behaves itself.

Today, the need to understand what the Bible is, where it came from and how we can read it is more important than ever. The issues that are currently exercising and, indeed, dividing the Church – things such as same-sex relationships, gender equality, the use of money, the use of violence – all have at their root competing ways of reading the Bible. And in each of these incredibly complex areas – and many more – the Bible is weaponised. Opponents throw verses at each other like spears. We shout our war chants: 'The Bible says . . .', 'As Scripture clearly shows . . .', 'This is the word of God . . .'

But the Bible refuses to play those kinds of games.

We want to control the Bible, harness it, tame it so that we can ride it into battle. But the Bible bucks and rears and throws us off. We want to pin the Bible down so that it proves our theology, but the Bible evades capture and plays hide-and-seek. We want to master the text, but the text insists on overwhelming us. We want answers, but the Bible keeps firing questions. We want to define it, and it keeps changing shape. We want it to tell us what to do, and it keeps telling us to think. We put it on a pedestal, and it jumps down and runs away. We want to make the Bible dance to our tune, but the Bible has music of its own.

The Bible is an invitation. The Bible is a call. The breath of God lifts its pages; they rise and fall with his breathing.

So open the book. Inhale the breath of God. Become the story.

As my favourite Dr Who, Matt Smith, said, 'We're all stories, in the end. Just make it a good one, eh?'[6]

Appendix: Significant dates

Here's a list of significant dates associated with stuff I've talked about. It goes without saying that the earlier dates here are all conjectural and that even for the later, more certain, chronology, scholars and theologians argue about the dates. But then again, they argue about everything. Anyway, this is what I think, and it's my book, so there.

BC

c. 1850	Arrival of ABRAHAM in Canaan.
c. 1250–1230	The exodus. MOSES, the Law at Sinai.
c. 1220–1200	JOSHUA invades Palestine.
c. 1200–1025	The JUDGES.
c. 1125	DEBORAH and BARAK defeat Canaanites at Taanach.
c. 1050	Philistine victory at Aphek. Death of Eli.
c. 1040	SAMUEL appears. The Ark is kept at Shiloh.
c. 1030–1010	SAUL's reign.
c. 1010–970	DAVID's reign: Capture of Jerusalem c. 1000. Victories over Philistines, Moabites, Aramaeans, Ammonites, Amalekites, Edomites, Skylites, Parasites, etc.
c. 970–931	SOLOMON's reign: Marries Pharaoh's daughter. Starts building the Temple in the fourth year of his reign.
c. 931	The split of the kingdoms. ISRAEL in the north ruled by JEROBOAM, JUDAH in the SOUTH, ruled by REHOBOAM.

From here on lots of different kings take over the two kingdoms. In Judah, all the kings come from one dynasty – the House of David. In Israel, kings come from different families and dynasties as a result of various plots, coups and general shenanigans.

885–874	OMRI rules Israel. Founds Samaria. Controls the territory of Moab.
874–853	AHAB rules Israel. Marries Jezebel. Elijah and Elisha at work around this time.
850	Mesha rules Moab. Makes the Mesha or Moabite Stone.
841–814	JEHU becomes King of Israel. Slaughters Jezebel and Ahab's descendants – 'The crimes of Jezreel'.
c. 750	AMOS and HOSEA.
740	ISAIAH (the first one) gets the call.
721	Israel defeated and destroyed by the Assyrians.
640–609	JOSIAH King of Judah. Repairs the Temple. 'Book of the Law' discovered in the Temple.
627	Call of JEREMIAH.
589–587	Babylonians besiege Jerusalem.
587	Capture of Jerusalem. Judeans deported to Babylon.

EZEKIEL dates from this time.
EXILE. Jews in Babylon. Torah compiled.

539	Cyrus of Persia defeats Babylonians.
538	First exiles return to Judea.
537	Foundation of the Second Temple, but building stalls.
c. 458	EZRA returns. Mass Torah reading.
c. 445–443	NEHEMIAH returns. HAGGAI and ZECHARIAH from this era.
400–300	Books of Chronicles and Ezra–Nehemiah written.
336–323	Greeks under Alexander the Great conquer the

	Persian Empire and take over most of the known world.
300–100	Apocrypha written.
167–160	Jewish revolt against the Greek rulers. Begins a period of Jewish independence.
5	Birth of JESUS.

AD

33	JESUS executed. Resurrection.
33–35	Christianity spreads out from Jerusalem to Samaria and beyond. PAUL'S conversion.
48–62	PAUL writes lots of letters to different groups of Christians.
54–55	Letters to Corinthians.
57	Letter to Romans.
60–62	Prison letters from Paul, including Ephesians, Colossians, Philemon and Philippians, 2 Timothy.
64	Great fire of Rome. Nero persecutes Christians. Deaths of PETER and PAUL in Rome.
60–70	Gospels compiled and written.
66–70	First Jewish revolt. Temple destroyed in AD 70.
c. 90	Jews in Jamnia finalise the contents of the *Tanakh*.
c. 92	Revelation written.
c. 150	Justin Martyr talks about the primacy of the 'memoirs' of the apostles.
325	Eusebius records his New Testament canon, including some disputed works.
367	Bishop Athanasius of Alexandria lists the books of the New Testament.

Notes

Introduction: Holy Ground

1 G.D. Fee, and D. Stuart, *How to Read the Bible for All Its Worth: A Guide To Understanding The Bible* (Grand Rapids: Zondervan, 1982), p. 23.

2 Attributed to E.B. White paraphrased from *A Subtreasury of American Humor* (Michigan: Coward-McCann, 1941), p. 402.

3 Cited in 'Woolf's Darkness: Embracing the Inexplicable' in *The New Yorker*, 24 April 2014.

4 C. Webb, *The Fire of the Word* (Downers Grove, Il: IVP USA, 2012), pp. 20ff. I owe this metaphor entirely to Chris, whose book *The Fire of the Word* had a profound effect on how I read the Bible. Read the whole thing.

5 See K. Barth and D. Horton, *The Word of God and the Word of Man* (London: Hodder and Stoughton, 1928).

Chapter 1

1 On all this, see E. Kamlah, 'Spirit, Holy Spirit,' *NIDNTT*, 3:689.

2 S. Weil, *Waiting for God* (New York: Harper & Row, 1973), p. 105.

3 Quoted in D.L. Ulin, *The Lost Art of Reading: Why Books Matter in a Distracted Time* (Sasquatch Books, 2010), p. 131.

Chapter 2

1 N.M. Sarna, *Understanding Genesis* (New York: Schocken Books, 1970), pp. 104ff.

2 J. Pritchard, *The Ancient Near East* (Princeton: Princeton University Press, 1958), 1:36-37.

Chapter 3

1 See, for example, *First Apology*, ch. 66. Irenaeus, *Against Heresies*, 11.9.
2 Origen, *Contra Celsus*, 3.72.
3 The early church was not blind to these problems, either. Some scholars protested at the mistranslation. Aquila, Symmachus, Theodotian and Justin Martyr all translated *almah* into *he neanis*, i.e. 'the young woman', in their Old Testament translations. See J.D.W. Watts, *Isaiah 1–33* (Waco: Word Books, 1985), pp. 141–142.
4 A. Berlin, M.Z. Brettler and M. Fishbane, *The Jewish Study Bible* (Oxford, New York: Oxford University Press, 2004), p. 113.
5 See P.C. Craigie, *Psalms 1–50* (Waco: Word Books, 1983), pp. 76–77; J. Limburg, 'Psalms, Book Of', in *The Anchor Bible Dictionary* (New York: Doubleday, 1999), 5:527.
6 E.A. Speiser, *Genesis* (Garden City: Doubleday, 1964), p. LXXIV.
7 Quoted in A. Squire, *Asking the Fathers* (London: SPCK, 1973), p. 127.

Chapter 4

1 'Snake-handling pastor from reality TV dies from snake bite', *Daily Herald*, 16 February 2014.
2 R. Alter, *Genesis* (New York, London: Norton, 1996), p. xi.
3 J. Gottschall, *The Storytelling Animal: How Stories Make Us Human* (Boston: Houghton Mifflin Harcourt, 2012), p. xiv.
4 P. Bloom, 'How Do Americans Spend Their Leisure Time?' quoted in A. Jacobs, *The Pleasures of Reading in an Age of Distraction* (Oxford: Oxford University Press, 2011), p. 122.
5 J. Gottschall, *The Storytelling Animal*, p. 153.
6 N.G. Carr, *The Shallows: How the Internet is Changing the Way we Think, Read and Remember* (London: Atlantic, 2010), p. 74.
7 Quoted in L. Cron, *Wired for Story* (Berkeley: Ten Speed Press, 2012), p. 71.
8 *Guardians of the Galaxy* (2014). Directed by James Gunn.
9 E. Auerbach, *Mimesis: The Representation of Reality in Western Literature* (Princeton: Princeton University Press, 1974), p. 17.

10 D. Young, *The Art of Reading* (Scribe UK, 2017), p. 3.

11 Quoted in D.L. Ulin, *The Lost Art of Reading*, p. 16.

12 H. Chadwick, *The Early Church* (rev. ed.) (London: Penguin, 1993), p. 100.

13 Origen, *On First Principles*, trans. G.W. Butterworth (Notre Dame: Ave Maria Press, 2013), IV.IV.1.

14 Quoted in A. Jacobs, *The Pleasures of Reading in an Age of Distraction*, p. 130.

15 The story is told in A. Manguel, *The Library at Night* (Toronto: Knopf Canada, 2006), p. 230.

16 M. Buber, *I and Thou* (Edinburgh: T. & T. Clark, 1953), p. 61.

17 Quoted in A. Jacobs, *The Pleasures of Reading in an Age of Distraction*, p. 55.

Chapter 5

1 G.J. Wenham, *Genesis 16–50* (Waco: Word Books, 1994), p. 141.

2 B.L. Visotzky, *Reading the Book: Making the Bible a Timeless Text* (New York: Schocken Books, 1996), p. 2.

3 R.P. Carroll, *Wolf in the Sheepfold: The Bible as a Problem for Christianity* (London: SPCK, 1991), p. 104.

4 J.A.T. Robinson, *Honest to God* (London: SCM Press, 1963), p. 66.

5 A. Squire, *Asking the Fathers* (London: SPCK, 2010), p. 123.

6 Quoted in W. Brueggemann, *The Book that Breathes New Life: Scriptural Authority and Biblical Theology* (Minneapolis: Fortress Press, 2005), p. 17.

7 J. Rhymer (ed.), *The Bible in Order*, Jerusalem Bible Version (New York: Doubleday 1975).

8 B.L. Visotzky, *Reading the Book*, p. 2.

Chapter 6

1 R.P. Carroll, *Wolf in the Sheepfold*, p. 42.

2 R.P. Carroll, *Wolf in the Sheepfold*, p. 41.

3 J. Day, 'RAHAB (DRAGON)', in D. Freedman et al., *The Anchor Bible Dictionary*, 5:610.

4 W.G. Blaikie, *The First Book of Samuel: Expositor's Bible* (London: Hodder & Stoughton, 1888), p. 307.

5 For a full discussion of the different opinions, see Chapter 2, 'Understanding Biblical Monotheism' in C.E. Hayes, *Introduction to the Bible* (New Haven: Yale University Press, 2012).

6 A. Phillips, *God B.C.* (Oxford: Oxford University Press, 1977), p. 45.

7 Quoted in C.A. Hall, *Reading Scripture with the Church Fathers* (Downers Grove: InterVarsity Press, 1998), p. 55.

Chapter 7

1 R. Davidson, *The Courage to Doubt: Exploring an Old Testament Theme* (London: SCM Press, 1983), p. 43.

2 R. Davidson, *The Courage to Doubt*, p. 48.

3 R. Davidson, *The Courage to Doubt*, p. 209.

4 R. Williams, *God With Us: The Meaning of the Cross and Resurrection – Then And Now* (London: SPCK, 2017), pp. 102–103.

5 D.E. Roberts, 'Psychotherapy and the Christian View of Man', quoted in R. Davidson, *The Courage to Doubt*, p. 17.

6 C. Williams, *He Came Down From Heaven* (London: Heinemann, 1938), p. 14.

7 B.L. Visotzky, *Reading the Book*, p. 4.

8 A. Manguel, *The City of Words* (London: Continuum, 2009), p. 20.

Chapter 8

1 Derived from Hebrew *tôrâ*, meaning 'instruction'. See *The Anchor Bible Dictionary*, 6:605.

2 W. Brueggemann, *Sabbath as Resistance: Saying No to the Culture of Now* (Louisville: Westminster John Knox Press, 2014), p. 55.

3 W. Brueggemann, *The Book that Breathes New Life: Scriptural Authority and Biblical Theology* (Minneapolis: Fortress Press, 2005), p. 3.

4 J.N.D. Kelly, *Early Christian Doctrines* (London: A. & C. Black, 1985), p. 37. (Actually, the whole of Chapter 2, 'Tradition and

Scripture', is really illuminating and a lot more interesting than a
book on early Christian doctrines has a right to be.)

5 R. Williams, *Being Christian: Baptism, Bible, Eucharist, Prayer*
(London: SPCK, 2014), p. 35.

6 J. Barr, *The Scope and Authority of the Bible* (London: SCM
Press, 2002), p. 55.

Chapter 9

1 Cited in R.H. Evans, *Inspired: Slaying Giants, Walking on Water,
and Loving the Bible Again* (Nashville: Thomas Nelson, 2018), p. 65.

2 This was published in his *Difficulties and Alleged Errors and
Contradictions in the Bible*, quoted in P. Jenkins, *Laying Down
the Sword* (New York: HarperOne, 2011), p. 115.

3 P. Jenkins, *Laying Down the Sword*, pp. 113–114.

4 P. Jenkins, *Laying Down the Sword*, p. 142.

5 M. Ramsey, *God, Christ and the World: A Study in Contemporary
Theology* (London: SCM Press, 1969), p. 37.

6 On the archaeological stuff see, 'The Formation of Israel:
Conquest, Immigration, or Revolt?' in C.E. Hayes, *Introduction to
the Bible* (New Haven: Yale University Press, 2012), p. 189ff.;
'Joshua and the Conquest of Canaan' in M.E. Mills, *Historical
Israel, Biblical Israel: Studying Joshua to 2 Kings* (London; New
York: Cassell, 1999), p. 13ff. For an alternative view of Joshua and
this issue see P. Copan, *Is God a Moral Monster?: Making Sense
of the Old Testament God* (Grand Rapids: Baker Books, 2011).
For a defence of the traditional biblical account, see I.W. Provan,
V.P. Long and T. Longman, *A Biblical History of Israel*
(Louisville: Westminster John Knox Press, 2003).

7 J.W. Burrow, *A History of Histories: Epics, Chronicles, Romances
and Inquiries from Herodotus and Thucydides to the Twentieth
Century* (London: Allen Lane, 2007), p. 1.

8 P. Enns, *The Bible Tells Me So: Why Defending Scripture Has
Made Us Unable to Read It* (San Francisco: HarperOne, 2014),
p. 54.

Chapter 10

1 Cyril of Alexandria, *Commentary on Zephaniah 43*, quoted in C. Crosby, and T.C. Oden, *Ancient Christian Devotional: A Year of Weekly Readings: Lectionary Cycle C* (Downers Grove: InterVarsity Press, 2009), p. 22.

2 R.N. Longenecker, *Galatians* (Dallas: Word Books, 1990), p. 131.

3 Augustine, *Sermon 229.3*.

4 P. Enns, *The Bible Tells Me So*, p.22

5 'Homilies on Genesis 35.3' in C. Crosby and T.C. Oden, *Ancient Christian Devotional* (Vol B, 2011), p. 121.

6 *Dr Who*, season 5, episode 13, 'The Big Bang' (written by Steven Moffat, directed by Toby Haynes).

HODDER &
STOUGHTON

Hodder & Stoughton is the UK's
leading Christian publisher,
with a wide range of books from
the bestselling authors in the UK
and around the world ranging from
Christian lifestyle and theology to
apologetics, testimony and fiction.
We also publish the world's
most popular Bible translation
in modern English, the New
International Version, renowned
for its accuracy and readability.

Hodderfaith.com   Hodderbibles.co.uk
@HodderFaith   /HodderFaith